THE CIA
AT WAR

THE CIA
AT WAR

INSIDE THE SECRET
CAMPAIGN AGAINST TERROR

RONALD KESSLER

ST. MARTIN'S PRESS ❧ NEW YORK

www.stmartins.com

ISBN 0-312-31932-0

First Edition: October 2003

10 9 8 7 6 5 4 3 2 1

For Pam, Greg, and Rachel Kessler
and to the memory of my mother, Minuetta Kessler

PROLOGUE

At 8 A.M. on February 15, 2001, Mike,* a trim-looking CIA analyst, gave President George W. Bush his first daily agency briefing at the White House. The next day, Bush would be making his first foreign trip as president, to see Mexican President Vicente Fox.

A White House steward entered the Oval Office with coffee. Bush motioned to his guest to stop talking while the steward was in the room. Mike was impressed. Bush cared about security.

At the end of the briefing, Bush brought up the trip again.

"Are you coming with me?" the president asked.

From that point on Mike or alternate CIA briefers traveled with Bush on every trip. They saw him six and often seven days a week, whether at Bush's ranch in Crawford, Texas, his parents' home in Kennebunkport, at Camp David, or in the White House. The contrast with President Bill Clinton could not have been more striking. After the first six months of his presidency, Clinton dis-

---

*Because he is now undercover, Mike's last name is not used here.

pensed with CIA briefings. He read only the President's Daily Brief, a compilation of intelligence reports prepared overnight by the CIA.

George H. W. Bush, a former director of Central Intelligence (DCI), had told his son after his election that the most important item of the day was the intelligence briefing. Meeting face-to-face with the DCI was also important, the former president said. When Bush chose Andrew H. Card Jr. as his chief of staff, he quoted his father's advice and said: "Make sure that happens. I want to see the CIA director and talk with him."[1]

Since the founding of the agency in 1947, no other president had wanted to be briefed by the CIA when he was out of town. Over time, no other president would come to rely so much on the CIA.

The first time Mike gave Bush a briefing was on January 4, 2001 at the president-elect's 1,600-acre ranch. Bush told him then what he expected from the CIA: "There are people planning to do things that put U.S. security at risk," Bush said. "They are trying to keep this secret. I expect the CIA to uncover those secrets and tell me. Second, I want the CIA to inform my decisions. I'll judge you on how well you do that."[2]

Mike, in his forties, had been with the agency since 1980. During that time, he had helped produce the President's Daily Brief, which capsulized the CIA's hottest intelligence.

"He gets it," Mike thought to himself.

More than two years later, on March 19, 2003, George J. Tenet, the director of Central Intelligence, told Bush that a CIA agent in Iraq knew that Saddam Hussein was in a bunker called Dora Farms. As Tenet briefed Bush, the agent called in more details on Hussein's movements. Based on that intelligence and the CIA's conclusion that Hussein continued to develop weapons of mass destruction, Bush ordered a strike on the compound and an invasion that obliterated Hussein's regime three weeks later. While the strike did not kill Saddam Hussein, the regime's command and control disintegrated after the blow.

"We went right to the heart of their inner being," Tenet told me. "Psychologically, that had to have a big effect."

Before Tenet became DCI in July 1997, the CIA was risk averse, awash in self-doubt, and mired in political correctness. After the attacks of September 11, 2001, Bush ordered Tenet to lead the war on terror. The agency would use its full complement of techniques—from human spying and interception of communications to satellite and reconnaissance plane surveillance—to find terrorists all over the world. In the war in Afghanistan, CIA paramilitary teams and U.S. Special Forces would hunt down terrorists and kill them. Now, not only was the agency in the forefront of confronting the gravest threat to the United States since the Soviet Union, its mission had changed. Besides warning of threats and pinpointing them, it had a license to kill.

Never in human history had a country relied so much on intelligence. Yet the question remained: Could the CIA be trusted? And even with its new powers, was the agency capable of winning the war on terror?

1

After John M. Deutch resigned at the end of 1996, President Clinton nominated national security advisor Anthony Lake to succeed him. Lake withdrew his name after Republicans on the Senate Select Committee on Intelligence questioned his handling of personal stock transactions, his tough mindedness, and his politics.

Clinton then turned to George Tenet, forty-four. Also a Democrat, Tenet had been staff director of the Senate Select Committee on Intelligence, then became staff director for intelligence programs at the National Security Council (NSC). In July 1995 he was named deputy director of Central Intelligence, and in December 1996, acting CIA director. Finally, on July 11, 1997, Tenet became director of Central Intelligence, which placed him over both the CIA and the fractious American intelligence community. He was, as one CIA wag put it, the accidental DCI.

Traditionally, DCIs were WASPs with Ivy League backgrounds. Tenet's father John emigrated from Greece through France and Ellis Island just before the Depression. His name was

Tenetis. When he entered France, immigration authorities listed his name as Tenet.

"When he got to Ellis Island, he didn't speak English, so Tenet is what stuck," Tenet said.[3]

Starting with nothing, John Tenet managed to save enough to open the 20th Century Diner in Queens, New York. George's mother Evangelia fled southern Albania, an area once part of Greece, to escape Communism. Somehow she persuaded the commander of a British submarine to take her out. She still spoke little English.

Tenet's first language was Greek, and the dinner table talk at home created an interest in foreign affairs. "I don't think I woke up every day wondering if I was going to be James Bond," Tenet said.

Tenet attended the Georgetown University School of Foreign Service and obtained a master's degree from Columbia University's School of International Affairs. At age twenty-nine he joined the staff of Senator John Heinz of Pennsylvania, where he worked on national security and energy issues. In 1985, he became a staffer on the Senate Select Committee on Intelligence. Almost four years later, he became staff director, managing forty employees.

"He could be forceful," said L. Britt Snider, who worked for Tenet on the committee and later became his special counsel at the CIA. "He could come down on you. But he was always upfront, always played things straight."

"Probably a hundred conversations he had with me started . . . with his saying, 'You're not going to want to hear this, but . . . ,'" said Senator David L. Boren, who had been Tenet's rabbi, naming him staff director of the committee and recommending him to Clinton to head that president-elect's transition team on intelligence. Boren said, "Sometimes he would start with, 'I can tell this isn't a good day to tell you this,' and then he'd go ahead." His candor made him ideal for his future job of CIA director, Boren added.

As staff director, Tenet was in charge of the investigations into CIA abuses in the late 1980s.

"From the vantage point of the committee's investigations, Tenet experienced firsthand the corrosive effect of the Iran-Contra affair on the agency and on the credibility of the DCI," said Paul Joyal, who was one of his staffers. "People were needlessly lying and obfuscating, and it was all going to come out anyway. George would never allow such deception and short-term risky operations to occur on his watch."[4]

Later, as staff director for intelligence programs at the NSC, Tenet became known for his political savvy. Intuitively he sensed what each Washington bureaucrat wanted and how to bob and weave through the thicket of egos to accomplish his aims, all the while keeping a low public profile. Tenet understood the press, and he understood Congress.

"Tenet had all the experience on the Hill, in the White House," said John C. Gannon, a former head of the CIA's Directorate of Intelligence, the analytical side of the agency. "He developed relationships, and he worked them."

As a staffer, Tenet had never managed an agency. Yet as deputy DCI under Deutch, a member of the NSC when R. James Woolsey Jr. was DCI, and someone who had had access to the CIA's secrets going back years, Tenet had a unique perspective. Tenet witnessed firsthand the gaffes of some of his predecessors. Because of those gaffes, the CIA was in turmoil. Since 1991, no one had held the job of DCI more than two years. The agency's morale was shattered and its future was in doubt. Tenet vowed not to repeat those gaffes and to transform the agency into an effective force against terrorism.

A graduate of Stanford and a Rhodes Scholar with a law degree from Yale, James Woolsey had been undersecretary of the Navy before President Clinton asked him to be DCI. He had no experience in intelligence. Nor did Clinton know much about him. Clinton had met Woolsey only twice, briefly, before deciding to nominate him. When Warren Christopher, Clinton's transition chief, summoned Woolsey to Little Rock in 1992, Woolsey thought the trip was to advise Clinton on possible nominees.

"Clinton wants to talk to you about the CIA," Christopher told him.

When he met with Clinton, they swapped stories about the University of Arkansas football team. Woolsey was from Oklahoma; he had relatives who lived in Arkansas. Woolsey did not know he was Clinton's choice as DCI until a Clinton aide asked him to attend a 12:30 P.M. news conference introducing Clinton's national security team. Woolsey called Christopher and asked him about the press conference.

"He wants you to be CIA director," Christopher said.

"Okay, I guess," Woolsey responded."[5]

Woolsey was the only child of Tulsa lawyer and Civil War buff Robert Woolsey. In a eulogy of his father, Woolsey described him as having a "command presence as well as lightheartedness." He was "famous for his perseverance" and had a "litigator's stubbornness." The same could have been said of Woolsey. Brilliant and well respected, he tended to view his job as representing a client—

in this case, the CIA. In his relations with Congress, he came off as a litigator.

As general counsel of the Senate Select Committee on Intelligence, Britt Snider felt that, from the beginning, Woolsey had difficulty relating to his congressional overseers.

"Woolsey had been told by the chairmen of both the intelligence and appropriations committees that they could not support an increase in the intelligence budget that year," Snider recalled. "But at his very first appearance before the intelligence committee, Woolsey said that if he didn't get the increase the president had asked for, it would basically amount to the end of western civilization as we know it. He showed no willingness to compromise whatsoever."

Woolsey's dogmatic approach infuriated Senator Dennis DeConcini, the Arizona Democrat who was chairman of the committee. When Senator Ted Stevens, who was ranking Republican on the Appropriations Committee, attempted to suggest there might be room for compromise, Woolsey put him down as well.

"After that hearing," Snider said, "DeConcini asked me what Woolsey thought he was doing. 'That is not the way you treat members of Congress,' he said."[6]

Clinton, meanwhile, treated Woolsey like a pariah. Clinton had no interest in intelligence or the CIA, as evidenced by the fact that, six months after he became president, he dispensed with CIA briefings. Moreover, some at the CIA thought that, while Woolsey mastered each issue as if he were preparing a legal brief, Clinton sensed that he had no depth of knowledge about intelligence or world affairs. Clinton did not invite Woolsey to daily CIA briefings and eventually stopped the briefings as well.

Woolsey loved to tell the story of the plane that crashed into the White House. "They said it was just Woolsey trying to get an appointment with Clinton," he said.[7]

"I didn't have bad relations with Clinton," Woolsey told me. "I just didn't have any relations with him. Clinton was interested in balancing the budget, health care, NAFTA. He did not want to accomplish much in the foreign policy arena."[8]

If Clinton kept Woolsey at arm's length, Woolsey's congressional critics demanded his presence.

"I had 205 appointments on the Hill in 1993," Woolsey said. "Congress was in session 195 days."

When Woolsey became DCI on February 3, 1993, he received a briefing on the status of the Aldrich H. Ames case. It would turn out to be the biggest spy case in CIA history. What made the case so appalling was that Ames should have been fired years earlier for his drinking and poor performance. The case highlighted how self-protective and unaccountable the Directorate of Operations (DO), which runs spies, had become.

Ames had begun working for the CIA as a case officer in 1962. During his assignment to Mexico City twenty years later, Ames met Maria del Rosario Casas, a Colombian cultural attaché, and recruited her to work as an agent. They began an affair which led to Ames' divorce from his wife and his marriage to Rosario.

By 1983 Ames had been named chief of the counterintelligence branch in the Soviet/East European Division within the Directorate of Operations. In 1985 Ames began working with a joint FBI-CIA squad within the FBI. Called COURTSHIP, this squad recruited KGB officers to work for the United States. Later, Ames was assigned to the CIA's Counternarcotics Center, with responsibility for the Balkans.

Because Ames' job in counterintelligence required him to review files and ask questions not only at the CIA but at the FBI and other sensitive agencies, he was in a better position to help the Russians than even the director of Central Intelligence.

Over the years, the FBI had observed Ames meeting with Soviets. He had not reported the contacts as required by CIA regulations. Whenever the FBI asked the CIA about this, the agency would ask Ames to explain why he had met with Soviets. Ames would ignore the requests. No one pursued the matter.

When assigned to Italy, Ames was drunk at work at least three times a week. At headquarters, he would pass out at his desk. At a joint picnic of FBI and CIA employees at Langley, Ames became inebriated and misplaced his wallet. An FBI agent found the wallet, which contained notes on a classified operation. Classified material is not to be removed without elaborate controls and security procedures. Again, no action was taken against Ames.

In 1976, when Ames was visiting New York, he left his briefcase with classified documents in a New York subway. The documents identified a Soviet agent he was going to meet as part of his work. The FBI recovered the briefcase from a Polish émigré who found it several hours after Ames had lost it. Embarrassingly, an FBI agent returned it to the Soviet branch of the CIA's New York station, where the agency recruits diplomats and scientists to spy overseas. When Ames later requested a transfer to New York, Ken Millian, the New York station chief, blocked it.

"I told headquarters he was a jerk, and I didn't want him," Millian said.[9]

But after Millian left, Ames continued to be sent on temporary assignment to New York, where Ames allowed Rosario to stay at a CIA safe house, even though she was a foreign national.

"Ames said it had been approved by headquarters," Janine

Brookner, who was his supervisor, said. "I knew they had not approved it. I told him, 'I want her out of here and you out of here.' "[10]

Brookner reported Ames to headquarters, but no action was taken against him. The response of the Directorate of Operations (DO) to Ames' sloppiness and violation of rules was to shuffle him into even more sensitive positions. He was a trusted member of the club.

As intelligence operations went awry and assets—agents working for the CIA—were "rolled up" and executed, the FBI and CIA began looking for a mole in their midst in the late 1980s. In 1993, from a Soviet agent who was code-named AVENGER, the CIA learned enough details about a mole in the CIA to narrow the focus to Ames.

AVENGER—a KGB officer—instructed his girlfriend to enter the American embassy in Moscow, ostensibly to obtain a visa. Through her, the CIA arranged to meet with him. Before AVENGER narrowed the field, the CIA listed Ames as a possible spy, in part because he had access to most of the compromised information. But efforts to investigate Ames were amateurish. The agency checked Ames' credit card bills for a month and found they amounted to $3,000. That happened to have been a slow month for Ames and his wife. Normally, they charged $18,000 to $30,000 a month. Rosario owned five hundred pairs of shoes and 150 packages of pantyhose that she had never opened. In one single year, they paid $18,000 in credit card finance charges.

The CIA examined real estate records to see how Ames paid for his home. When no mortgage was found, the CIA twice returned to the recorder of deeds' office to try to find a record of one. Anyone familiar with land records knows that a mortgage cannot be overlooked: It is either recorded or it is not.

In trying to determine if Ames' wealth might have come from Rosario's family in Colombia, the CIA station there asked a local source, who said her family was wealthy. A few weeks later, the agency fired the contact for giving incorrect information on another matter. No one thought this worth passing on to those who were then investigating Ames.

In August 1992, the CIA found a correlation between the timing of three of Ames' meetings with Soviets and cash deposits he made to his bank account in 1985. Yet no one yanked Ames' security clearance, and the investigation of his finances dragged on for three and a half years.

As it turned out, Ames had received $2.5 million from the Russians since 1985. It was a measure of the value of his information. Never before in U.S. history had any known spy received anywhere near that sum. The closest figure was the $1 million received by Navy warrant officer John A. Walker Jr., who collected the money over an eighteen-year period. Ames collected more than twice as much in just over eight years.

In all, Ames betrayed more than a hundred CIA operations and wiped out the CIA's assets in Moscow. The Soviets executed ten of their own and sent others to prison. Ames not only compromised current assets, he impaired the ability of the agency to recruit new assets for years to come. Aware of how negligent the CIA had been in protecting its own agents, any potential recruit would have to think twice about cooperating with it. Despite the damage, because Ames did not have access to all records, the CIA's Soviet assets based in other countries remained intact.

On the morning of February 21, 1994, FBI agents arranged to have a CIA counternarcotics official ask Ames to come to CIA headquarters. As Ames drove his Jaguar to Langley, Agent Michael Donner followed him and turned on a flashing red light that sat on his dashboard. He turned on his siren. Ames stopped a few feet short of a SWAT truck that was driving in front of him. Gun in hand, Donner raced to the driver's side. Ames rolled down his window, and Donner held up his badge and pulled a Benson & Hedges cigarette from Ames' lips.

"FBI," he said. "You're under arrest."[11]

Donner opened the door and yanked Ames into the street.

"For what?" Ames yelled. "For what?"

"For espionage," Donner said. "Put your hands on the roof of your car."

"What!" Ames cried. "This is unbelievable. Unbelievable!"

In return for Ames' plea, John L. Martin, the Justice Department's chief spy prosecutor, agreed to recommend a much lower sentence for Ames' wife. Both defendants agreed to be debriefed by the government and undergo polygraph tests on the truthfulness of their statements. On April 28, 1994, Ames and his wife pled guilty. After Ames cooperated, he got life without parole. Rosario was sentenced to five years and three months in jail.

It was a victory not only for the FBI but for Martin, who presided over espionage prosecutions for twenty-five years and had always fought the CIA's penchant for covering up its embarrassments by fighting prosecutions of spies. Instead, the CIA would offer to make them double agents or even to pay them off if they would keep quiet, thereby granting them immunity from prosecution and avoiding a public trial.

"That was the kind of foolish trade the CIA always wanted. It was part of the gobbledy-gook of 'interdicting' or 'neutralizing' spies," Martin told me. "The fact is, you can prosecute spies, then get your damage assessment after they're convicted and before they're sentenced. When you offer them immunity up front, as the old counterintelligence boys used to do it, you're giving everything away and getting very little in return. Moreover, if you find after granting immunity that the person has been lying to you, there's nothing you can do. On the other hand, if you get him to plead guilty as part of a plea agreement, you can require him to tell what he knows before sentencing. If he lies, you can tell the judge he's lying, and the sentence will be harsher."

As the Soviets arrested and executed KGB officers compromised by Ames, they replaced them with new officers who pretended in some cases to spy for the CIA. As it turned out, since 1986, the CIA had known or suspected that some of these agents were controlled by the Russians and therefore were double agents, yet the agency passed along ninety-five of their reports to the White House and Pentagon without any disclosure that the source was tainted. In fact, in thirty-five cases, the CIA was sure that the source was a double agent. The CIA rationalized forwarding the reports by saying they were thought to contain good information. Yet, later analysis revealed that the reports overemphasized the Soviets' military capabilities, leading to overspending by the Pentagon, according to a CIA report.[12]

"A reports officer decided it was good information, so he forwarded it without disclosing that it came from controlled agents," Frederick P. Hitz, who investigated the case as the CIA's inspector general, told me. "In the Ames case, as in this one, there was hubris. Absolute secrecy corrupts absolutely," Hitz said.[13]

Reflecting similar arrogance, Ames rationalized obliterating CIA assets in Moscow by saying, "I had come to the conclusion that the loss of these sources to the United States government, or to the West as well, would not compromise significant national defense, political [or] diplomatic interests."[14]

After Ames was arrested, the CIA mounted a campaign to show off its good detective work. The agency let analysts who had worked the case talk to the press, giving the impression that they had solved the case. While it was true that a CIA agent had been the key to exposing Ames, most of the CIA's analysis was useless. What counted, in the end, was AVENGER's information, which the FBI, with the help of the CIA, then used to close in on Ames.

A cavalcade of former CIA officials appeared on television expressing lack of surprise about the case: Spying would continue regardless of whether the Cold War was over, and there was not much to be done about it. The roll-over attitude was why the CIA had been duped in the first place. While it was true that spying, like bank robberies, will always continue, it was not true that nothing could be done about it. In the Ames case, as in others, warning signs pointed to security breaches. Based on poor performance alone, Ames should have been transferred to a less sensitive position. He should have been fired for violations of security rules. Yet Ames was not even disciplined for violating agency regulations. No investigators were called in to probe his activities or to find out how he could live so well on an annual salary of $69,843.

As a new DCI, Woolsey could have sent a message that the CIA's laxness would no longer be tolerated.

"The managers responsible for Ames should have been canned," John N. McMahon, a former CIA deputy director, told me.[15]

Instead, despite the repeated bungling of CIA officers in charge of supervising Ames, Woolsey perpetuated the DO's self-indulgent, self-protective culture by giving the supervisors what amounted to slaps on the wrist: He reprimanded five active and six retired CIA officers. No one was fired; no one was forced into retirement. Once officers joined the exclusive club that constituted the CIA's DO, they believed themselves immune from accountability to the outside world. Woolsey's response only confirmed that attitude.

A day after Ames' arrest was announced, Woolsey met with CIA employees in the Bubble, the agency's seven-thousand-square-foot dome-shaped auditorium near the front entrance to the main building. Woolsey said those most responsible for mishandling Ames had left the agency. "Some have clamored for heads to roll in order that we could say that heads have rolled," Woolsey told the employees. "Sorry," he said. "That's not my way. And in my judgment, that's not the American way, and it's not the CIA way."

Woolsey put out an explanation of why he himself had refused to take a polygraph test, which other directors like William Webster had taken. Besides the fact that he was a political appointee and thus did not have to, Woolsey said he remained "skeptical" of the polygraph's effectiveness. Woolsey's position sickened many CIA officers, who pointed out that they, too, had questions about the efficacy of the polygraph but yet were required to take the test or lose their jobs.

While the polygraph was not perfect, it clearly served as a deterrent. The fact that Woolsey would not take the examination, then defended his decision even after the revelation of the biggest security breach in the agency's history, symbolized the arrogance that had led to the Ames case in the first place. But it also underscored how effective the CIA was at domestic propaganda. For, contrary to initial news reports and to the impression Woolsey conveyed, the polygraph was stunningly accurate in Ames' case.

Twice, according to an FBI review of his charts, Ames failed polygraphs. In 1986, he failed when he said he had not been approached by a hostile intelligence service. In 1991, he failed when he said he had not had unauthorized meetings with foreigners. Yet the CIA misread the results of the first test and passed him. The

CIA concluded that Ames failed the second test, but the agency allowed him to retake the test when he offered an explanation for his failure—that he was nervous because of various contacts he had had with people around the world. When he had trouble with a question about undisclosed assets, the examiner accepted his explanation that he was nervous because he received money from his wife's family. In other words, the CIA's polygraph program looked for ways to explain away signs of deception. No one put together the fact that Ames had failed the first time and the fact that there was an ongoing counterintelligence investigation of him.

"He was a sloppy spy, but once you have a blue badge, you're in," former Inspector General Frederick Hitz said, referring to building passes for employees. "Ames was going nowhere, but they left him in the front line despite a record that was less than mediocre in terms of alcoholism, late reports, and other serious problems. Janine Brookner reported the fact that he brought his girlfriend, who was a foreign national, to a safehouse. She was indignant. She wanted him transferred. Nothing happened. Our team wondered, how can this be? Nobody felt responsible."[16]

Woolsey's weak response to the Ames case appalled Hitz. Still the litigator, Woolsey acted more like a lawyer defending the agency than a manager responsible for its proper operation.

"My opinion was Woolsey should have taken strong disciplinary action," Hitz said. "That would have underscored the need to impose accountability."

Woolsey later realized he should have taken a polygraph test himself, and he did so.

"In retrospect, I should have done it immediately," Woolsey said.

As Woolsey continued to vacillate, Congress came down on him.

"Woolsey did nothing much on Ames," Snider said. "De-Concini could not accept that."

Even the CIA turned on him. For all its self-protectiveness, the DO was horrified by the Ames case. The last thing case officers wanted was to be seen as being soft on spying.

At an offsite meeting of eighty senior CIA officials, Leo Hazelwood, the CIA's executive director, asked Peggy Donnelly, the chief of the agency's Information Staff, to address the group, which included Woolsey, on the attitudes and morale of the employees. Donnelly said the rank and file were not happy with the handling of the Ames case, implying that Woolsey had not handled the matter properly. Most of those present stood and applauded.

Beset by leaks that the White House wanted him out, stiffed by his own president, reviled by members of Congress, and now criticized by the people he was trying to defend, Woolsey concluded two weeks later that he was not wanted. After barely two years on the job, he resigned.

2

LIKE MANY DCIS, John M. Deutch, President Clinton's nominee to replace James Woolsey, did not want the job. Unlike other DCIs who did not want the job, the fifty-six-year-old Deutch made no secret of it.

A former MIT provost and deputy secretary of Defense, Deutch had always aspired to be secretary of Defense. When President Clinton pushed him to head the CIA, Deutch took the job reluctantly. He became DCI on May 10, 1995.

After Woolsey's gentlemanly reprimands of those who had done nothing about Aldrich Ames' conduct infuriated Congress, Deutch made it clear he would not tolerate the DO's self-protective culture. While toughness was overdue, Deutch failed to balance it by demonstrating that he valued the agency and its mission and recognized the importance of the DO and its spies. Deutch made it clear that he thought human collection was secondary to technical collection. In retrospect, as the need to penetrate terrorist organizations became clearer, it was an attitude that was chilling.

"I'm a technical guy," Deutch told an interviewer. "I'm a satellite guy. I'm a SIGINT [signals intelligence] guy."

As a chemist, Deutch felt comfortable with the certainty of science: If two chemicals are mixed together, they always react the same way. A chemical formula is neat, clean, unassailable. Gathering human intelligence was exactly the opposite. It was fraught with uncertainty and entailed far greater risk than collecting technical intelligence. Ultimately, the job of the DO was messy. Because it committed espionage in other countries, the DO could create big diplomatic and political trouble—flaps, the CIA called it.

Managing human collection required patience and people skills, something not found in textbooks. When he was at the Pentagon, Deutch married his second wife, Pat, by taking her to the courthouse during a lunch break. He had no time for sentimentality.

"Intelligence is an art, not a science," said Jack Devine, who was acting chief of the DO. "You can't expect the laws of physics to work."[17]

"HUMINT is serendipity," said James M. Simon Jr., a former assistant DCI for administration, referring to the abbreviation for human intelligence. "Even though the DO tries systematically to recruit agents with access, one cannot always anticipate who will agree to spy, whether they will have the right access, and whether they will know what is needed."[18]

Not only did Deutch fail to understand the DO, he would tell fellow guests at Washington dinner parties that the military was far superior to the CIA. He described the DO as defensive, pedantic, arrogant, and less competent than its military counterparts. At a meeting with the *New York Times* editorial board, Deutch bluntly made the same points. A watered-down version of his comments made its way into a piece about him in the *New York Times Magazine* published on December 10, 1995. According to the article, Deutch did not find many first-class minds in the ranks of the DO.

"Compared to uniformed officers, they certainly are not as competent, or as understanding of what their relative role is and what their responsibilities are," Deutch told the *Times*.

"He thought the military was more accountable," an aide said. "They had a strict chain of command. Deutch loved the military mind set. Their mission was clear. Deutch thought the DO had pulled the wool over Woolsey's eyes."

As might be expected, Deutch's comments infuriated the spies and hurt morale at the CIA. Running through the CIA was a strong sense of patriotism. Its mission was to protect America, to warn of threats. CIA officers who served overseas risked imprisonment, torture, or death. Living a lie was not easy. While CIA officers usually told their wives of their true employment, children did not learn their father's or mother's occupation until their retirement. They often thought they were losers.

"In a twenty-eight-year career, I had eight different covers," said former CIA officer Herbert F. Saunders. "I did not reveal my true employment to my parents until after my retirement. I would visit them in Boston on the way to a foreign tour, ostensibly employed by one agency. A few years later, on the way back through at end of the tour, I would casually confide that I had a very attractive offer from another agency. When I finally revealed the truth, my mother said, 'Well, that's a relief. Your father thought you were having difficulty holding a job.'"[19]

Deutch was publicly calling such CIA officers dummies. Besides being offensive, it was not true. Despite the fact that they could receive far more pay in private industry, some of the finest

minds in the country served in the CIA. While Deutch was a
warm, patriotic man who teared up when giving awards to DO
officers, he seemed to need to bolster his own ego by knocking
others.

"You could not tell Deutch he was wrong," said Peggy Donnelly, one of his staff chiefs. "He knew everything."

After Deutch's comments appeared in the *Times,* William Lofgren, chief of the CIA's Eurasian Division, confronted him in his
office. Lofgren was outraged. Deutch had taken away the organization's pride. He had no comprehension of the effect of his comments, nor did he appear to care.

"You obviously don't know much about this agency," Lofgren
said. "This will have a huge impact on morale. It was stupid."

"Well, I did it," Deutch said, as if that made it right.[20]

To make matters worse, Deutch brought in a small circle of
aides from the Defense Department, including Nora R. Slatkin,
who was named executive director. Slatkin, forty, had been an
assistant Navy secretary in charge of overseeing a $26-billion pro-
curement budget. With no experience in intelligence, she was given
final responsibility for selecting station chiefs and running operations. No previous executive director had been given that responsibility. Even though Slatkin carried out Deutch's orders, he
berated her and blamed her when things did not go his way.

"Deutch would humiliate Nora in front of us," a former senior
CIA official said. "He would make her cry in front of us. He would
blame her for things like the fact that his subordinates did not
support his policy positions. He would say, 'How *dare* you allow
this to happen?' "

"Deutch and Nora had a pathological relationship," said one
of Deutch's staff chiefs. "He was an egomaniac and treated her

like a child. She seemed to look to him as a father figure. She was bright and capable but did what he told her."

As if to underscore his disdain for the CIA, Deutch promoted the idea of moving the National Photo Interpretation Center (NPIC), which had spotted Soviet missiles going into Cuba, into a new agency called the National Imagery and Mapping Agency (NIMA) within the Pentagon. Before that, Woolsey had pushed for less CIA control of the National Reconnaissance Office (NRO), which builds, launches, and operates satellites. Deutch agreed with Woolsey.

Both changes, which were implemented, gave the military more control over intelligence. Yet the entire rationale for establishing the CIA as a separate entity, reporting directly to the president, was that intelligence collection should be independent. If the agency were under the control of the Defense Department, the military would influence it to favor its pet projects. Over the years, that proposition had been borne out. For example, the Defense Intelligence Agency, which is part of the Pentagon, repeatedly overestimated the number of missiles and bombers the Soviet Union had. If the Soviets were portrayed as besting the U.S., the Pentagon could make a better case for higher budgets so it could catch up. In contrast, over the years, the CIA's estimates had been far more accurate than the DIA's.

"Deutch was aggressively ignorant," said a former CIA official. "If he didn't know something, it must be unimportant and was therefore without merit or interest."

Besides HUMINT and other abbreviations for types of intelligence collection, the DO was a master at RUMINT. RUMINT is circulation of rumors and leaks to discredit those who have crossed the clandestine service.

"Deutch aggravated the DO, and they leaked stories about him," a former aide said. "That put Deutch on the defensive. It made him push even more. Deutch was brilliant, but he had a big ego. He needed to be loved and to be shown he was wanted."

If Deutch damaged the CIA by undercutting morale, he also diminished its effectiveness by creating a risk-averse atmosphere. When Representative Robert G. Torricelli, a New Jersey Democrat, claimed a Guatemalan CIA asset was involved in the slaying of an American innkeeper in Guatemala and the killing of a Guatemalan guerrilla married to an American lawyer, Deutch imposed a rule requiring special approval before a CIA officer could recruit a spy who was not an upstanding citizen. If a potential asset had been involved in so-called human rights violations—a euphemism for having knocked someone off or having engaged in torture—or had had substantial criminal violations, the DCI or top agency officials had to sign off on the recruitment, a process that could take a month or two. The idea was that if it came out that the CIA had a notorious figure on its payroll, the publicity would make the CIA and the U.S. look bad.

Yet, that kind of person was exactly what the CIA needed to penetrate organizations like al Qaeda. Placing restrictions of that sort on recruitment of spies was like requiring FBI agents to obtain high-level approval to recruit Sammy Gravanno, who murdered nineteen people, before he could present evidence against John Gottti and the Mafia. Who else would know about a Mafia boss' crimes besides another murderer? As it turned out, the CIA's Guatemalan asset was not involved in the killings after all.

The CIA was under fire from other quarters. Representative Maxine Waters, a California Democrat, was convinced, based on a series in the *San Jose Mercury News* that was flawed on its face, that the CIA had been supporting the sale of crack cocaine by

Nicaraguan contras to blacks in south central Los Angeles. After investigations by the *Los Angeles Times*, the *Washington Post*, the *New York Times*, and CIA Inspector General Hitz demonstrated that the allegations were bogus, Waters continued to insist that the CIA "aided" the drug lords in bringing cocaine to the U.S.[21]

As the CIA became a whipping boy, Senator Daniel Patrick Moynihan called for the dismemberment of the agency, a move that would have sent America's intelligence capability back to where it was before Pearl Harbor.

Deutch vehemently defended the agency on the cocaine issue, going so far as to attend a town hall meeting in Watts. But his rule on recruitment of assets had a chilling effect. Deutch pointed out that no proposed asset ever was, in fact, rejected because of human rights violations. But that was beside the point. The rule implied that assets who were bad guys were less desirable than those who were squeaky clean. It was like telling police officers to obtain special approval from headquarters before making an arrest. The extra hassle of obtaining approval meant many CIA officers simply avoided anyone with a history of problems.

When Deutch told employees in the Bubble that case officers would have to obtain special approval to recruit assets with unsavory pasts, he added that he wanted them to continue taking risks. The contradiction brought snickers from the audience.

Aside from Deutch's misplaced emphasis on avoiding risk, because of the collapse of the Soviet Union, the CIA's mission no longer seemed critical. To be sure, the CIA was still needed to uncover new threats, such as efforts to develop weapons of mass destruction. The agency tried to make itself relevant by uncovering economic secrets and fighting drug cartels. But without a real enemy, the CIA lost its focus.

Milt Bearden, who was in charge of what was the Soviet/East

European Division when the Soviet Union collapsed, even said there might not be a need to accept lower-level Russians as defectors.[22] Yet the SVR, the Russian Foreign Intelligence Service that succeeded the KGB in December 1991, continued to spy aggressively on the U.S.

"It wasn't just that we became risk averse," said Paul J. Redmond Jr., who was chief of counterintelligence. "It was that we drifted out of the recruiting business almost entirely."[23]

"We forgot we were an intelligence service," said Lofgren, who was chief of the Central Eurasian Division, which included Russia. "The people were more concerned about our relations with the NSC, State Department, Defense Department, and Congress. We really lost sight of our middle name and why we existed."[24]

In particular, Lofgren said, "The human rights violation rule had a chilling effect on recruitment. If faced with two possible recruitments, are you going to go after the one with a human rights violation or the other one with no human rights violation?" The result was that "people retired in place or left," Lofgren said. "Our spirit was broken. At the CIA, you have to be able to inspire people to take outrageous risks. Deutch didn't care about us at all."

As deputy director for operations, Deutch chose David Cohen. Cohen had spent most of his career at the CIA as an analyst, rising quickly through the ranks to become the associate deputy director in charge of the Directorate of Intelligence (DI). At one point, Cohen was chief of the National Collection Division, which recruits agents in the U.S. to spy overseas and also develops contacts with scientists and business executives who can help the CIA by reporting on foreign developments. While that job fell within the DO, Cohen's role was to be a manager, not a spy.

A slim, self-deprecating man, Cohen was well-liked and respected for his sharpness and analytical abilities. But he was still an analyst, and his selection in 1995 to head the DO sent shudders through the clandestine service. It was like naming an Army officer to head the Air Force.

Given the fact that the DO was under attack for failing to stop Ames' spying and for assorted other transgressions, Cohen, fifty-three, thought that Deutch had had little choice but to bring in someone from outside the DO. At the same time, Cohen respected the DO and thought he understood it. His game plan was to protect the DO from within the agency and without, while reforming it.

In February 1995, six months before Cohen took over, France had expelled a CIA officer after catching her trying to obtain secrets from a French government official. The Paris station had failed to take the usual precautions before the meetings in the suburbs of Paris to insure that the officer was not under surveillance. The French Directorate of Surveillance of the Territory (DST) had recorded the meetings.

By agreement, the CIA does not spy on Great Britain, Canada, and Australia. However, every other country of interest to the CIA is fair game. In turn, some forty countries—including such unlikely ones as Israel, France, Greece, Indonesia, Taiwan, and South Korea—spy on the U.S. When friendly countries catch a CIA officer spying, the practice is normally to lodge a protest with the State Department and quietly expel the officer.

In this case, France, whose hostility to the U.S. had grown since the end of the Cold War, chose to embarrass the U.S. by making the case public. The U.S., in turn, had become more irate about France's practice, through its Department of Economics, Science, and Technology, of stealing secrets from visiting American businessmen by breaking into their hotel rooms and copying material from their briefcases. An intercepted French document listed fifty companies that the French were targeting, ranging from Allied Signal and Bankers Trust to TRW and United Technologies.[25]

In view of the changed political climate, Cohen thought the DO should have been extrasensitive to the need for proper tradecraft. While inevitably CIA officers will be rolled-up from time to time, there was no excuse for failing to take the basic steps taught in CIA training. The flap was unnecessary, Cohen thought. It was sloppy tradecraft.

"If you're going to get caught, do it for the right reasons," Cohen said. "We now live in a hostile environment. Make sure your protective socks are up."

The CIA put out a cover story that its officer was trying to obtain economic secrets. In fact, as the French well knew, the officer had sought codes to secret. French communications links. France was wheeling and dealing with Iraq, among other rogue states, and the CIA wanted to know what kinds of deals they might be cooking up.

Cohen decided the DO's standards had to be raised. Yet he found his hardest job was not improving operations but defending the DO from Deutch. Cohen considered his first encounter with the DCI telling. After an impressive committee named by Deutch recommended Cohen to be deputy director for operations, Deutch was to meet Cohen for lunch in the director's dining room.

"Deutch walked in and said, 'What school did you go to?' " Cohen recalled. Deutch had gone to Amherst and had a Ph.D. from MIT.[26]

"Northeastern," Cohen said.

Cohen felt lucky to have attended college in the first place.

The son of a truck driver from Dorchester, a working class section of Boston, Cohen had $250 in the bank for the first semester. When it came to paying for the second semester, his father told him he had no money.

"I told the school I couldn't pay, and they gave me a $125 grant and the rest in loans," Cohen told me. "They continued to do that until I graduated."

After Cohen told Deutch which college he had attended, Deutch responded, "That's all right. I have an honorary degree from Northeastern."

When Cohen became chief of the DO, the number of case officers had been slashed 25 percent compared with the number in 1991. Only seven recruits were enrolled as career trainees to become case officers. Even though the spies took the greatest risks, Cohen found that personnel in administration were being promoted faster than operations officers in the DO.

"Congress, the White House, the American people had sent the message: You are a dying service," Cohen said.

Cohen decided to call a meeting in October 1995 of all station chiefs at Camp Peary, the facility known as the Farm where the CIA trains recruits outside of Williamsburg, Virginia, a fact the agency still will not confirm.

"Let me tell you what you have achieved," Cohen said at the meeting.

Cohen ticked off dozens of DO success stories: removal of weapons-grade plutonium from a former Soviet republic; the destruction, with the help of the Drug Enforcement Administration, of the Medellin and Cali drug cartels; recruitment of sensitive assets in key countries. His idea was to build morale.

"That was a slam dunk," Tenet, then the deputy DCI, told Cohen.

In the evening, Deutch gave a talk. He played his part perfectly, telling the officers how important he thought they were.

"I'm not here to beat you up," Deutch said.

Two months later, Deutch's hurtful quotes about the CIA and the DO appeared in the *New York Times Magazine*.

"Deutch betrayed them with those remarks," Cohen said. "It allowed everyone to start picking on the carcass of the DO."

In Cohen's view, Deutch and the aides he had brought in from the Pentagon—with the notable exception of Dennis R. Boxx, a savvy PR person—saw themselves as "creditors." They were there either to acquire the assets of what they considered a bankrupt agency or to dismantle it. It was Cohen's job, he felt, to stop those efforts, while making the reforms he considered necessary.

As a matter of course, Deutch would propose ways either to cede CIA operations to the military or to have the military oversee CIA operations. For example, he decided the Predator, an unmanned aircraft that James Woolsey had championed, should probably be moved to the Defense Department. In Kosovo, Afghanistan, and Iraq, the Predator proved to be one of the CIA's most successful efforts.

"We had put together the Predator almost with spit and glue," Cohen said. "The Pentagon spent billions to develop unmanned aircraft that crashed. The fact that the Predator was so successful infuriated the creditors," Cohen said.

One day Deutch walked into Cohen's office and put his feet up on Cohen's desk.

"I've been thinking," he said. "Is the UAV [unmanned aerial vehicle] program really part of our core competence? What do you think about moving it to the Pentagon?"

Cohen gave Deutch his stock response: "Let me think about that one," he said.

As one of the "creditors," Nora Slatkin, the CIA's executive director, would tell Cohen she wanted to be briefed on operations and planned appointments of officers. Because she did not have the background to understand the issues, she would end their meetings by saying, "I'll get back to you." Cohen then went ahead with his plans. It seemed to Cohen that Deutch and his aides thought their job was to hold meetings.

While Deutch did not himself demand it, some around Deutch wanted CIA officers to call him "Mr. Director" and stand when he entered the room. That brought unfortunate comparisons with the last DCI who insisted that CIA officers stand, Vice Admiral William Francis Raborn Jr., a naval aviator who served from 1965 to 1966.

After he was sworn in, Raborn bought more than a dozen newspapers and spread them out in his office on a Sunday, according to a former CIA security officer who was with him. "He was trying to learn about the world situation," the former officer said.

"Raborn was testifying before Congress," recalled former CIA officer Herbert Saunders. "He kept mixing up North Korea and South Korea. He finally said, 'Damn, I never can get North Korea and South Korea straight!' You could have heard a pin drop in the hearing room. Then he continued to mix them up."[27]

"Despite sweeps conducted by our security officers, Raborn was very worried about listening devices that might be planted in hearing rooms on the Hill," said Richard J. Kerr, a former deputy DCI. "At one point, he stood on a chair and grabbed a wooden pointer just before a hearing. He began jabbing with the pointer at a very large glass chandelier to see if it contained any microphones. The chandelier was soon swinging wildly as we tried to get him off the chair."

"Raborn was an idiot," said former CIA analyst Mel Goodman. "One of his briefers told me that Raborn said to him, 'Libya is landlocked, right?' "

"On three sides, sir," the briefer said.[28]

"Raborn was almost incoherent," S. Eugene Poteat, a former CIA scientific officer, said. "He would sit at a table and bounce his leg up and down. The table would vibrate. We would try to keep a straight face."[29]

While Deutch's people never got CIA officers to stand, the efforts to impose military formality symbolized Deutch's approach. It was antithetical to the CIA, which viewed itself as a think tank and referred to its headquarters in McLean, Virginia, as The Campus.

"Unlike the military, the CIA is a civilian agency where a person's ideas are more important than his rank," said James Simon, a former assistant DCI for administration. "We are fractious even after the boss has spoken. The military is the opposite."[30]

Dr. Ruth David, whom Deutch brought in from Sandia National Laboratories to head the Directorate of Science and Technology (DS&T), found Deutch was open to disagreement. But most found his manner intimidating and his fixation on the DO's blemishes paralyzing.

"In a briefing about technical collection, a young analyst made a statement about the degree of randomness involved," a former CIA official said. "Deutch challenged his statement, and they began trading equations. You could tell that Deutch suddenly realized the analyst was right. Instead of conceding, Deutch exclaimed, 'Bullshit!' and stormed out of the room."

When Paul Redmond, who was associate deputy director for counterintelligence, objected to Deutch's idea of implanting components of the Defense Intelligence Agency in every CIA division,

Deutch told an aide, "I don't want that monkey back in my office until he changes his mind."[31]

Deutch eventually dropped the idea, and Redmond was never barred from Deutch's office.

"Deutch is warm, brilliant, courageous, and was willing to make decisions that might be unpopular, but at the CIA he was not deft bureaucratically," said Anthony Lake, who dealt with him as Clinton's national security advisor. "He enjoys banter and sees that as part of friendship, but it was misinterpreted as a put down. He didn't understand that his style of thinking an issue through by debating it could be seen as intimidating."[32]

While the one-upmanship, second-guessing, and negativism led to even more risk aversion in a business that requires risk, Cohen thought Deutch only accelerated a trend that had started years earlier. Cohen recognized that, as an analyst from the DI, he himself was a symbol of that trend. He would never be accepted by the DO.

"Operations was not Cohen's field, and I felt sorry for him being in that job," said William Lofgren, who reported to him as chief of the Central Eurasian Division.

In the end, Cohen thought the Directorate of Operations never understood how much he had done to keep Deutch from damaging it even more.

Deutch finally incurred the White House's displeasure, not because of his handling of his job, but because of his candor at a congressional hearing. In September 1996, Deutch was asked if Saddam Hussein was stronger than after the Gulf War. Going against the administration line, he said he was.

Clinton aides said Deutch was "making our lives harder." Tony Lake, as Clinton's national security advisor, sharply rejected the efforts of some who wanted to muzzle the agency, but he argued to Deutch that Saddam Hussein was clearly weaker militarily and that Deutch should have been more specific in his testimony. Soon, Deutch lost his bid to be secretary of Defense, his dream job, during Clinton's second term.

In the end, Deutch disgraced himself by placing seventeen thousand CIA files, including files classified TOP SECRET/CODE-WORD and those referring to highly sensitive covert operations, on his unclassified home computers. One such file was a memo to Clinton and Al Gore. It noted that the information was so sensitive that Deutch was sending it to only a few other people, including FBI Director Louis Freeh and Secretary of State Warren Christopher.[33] Because the computers connected to the Internet, and because Deutch often gave out his e-mail address, foreign intelligence services could easily have downloaded classified material from his computer.

Agency technicians discovered the security breach in December 1996 when they visited Deutch's house as he was preparing to leave the CIA and asked to keep his agency computers. In a classic sweetheart deal, the CIA agreed to give him a no-fee consulting contract for one year simply to allow him to keep the three Macintoshes.

As inspector general, Britt Snider launched an investigation and gave a copy of his report to Congress and the Justice Department. Snider noted that the CIA initially conducted its own internal investigation of Deutch's use of home computers, but he concluded the review was a sham. The actions of Slatkin, Deutch's executive director, and Michael O'Neill, his general counsel, had the "effect of delaying a prompt investigation" of the matter, Snider's report said.

"It was apparent from our investigation," Snider told me, "that Deutch felt he could do pretty much as he pleased. What's more, nobody really wanted to challenge him."[34]

Initially, the Justice Department declined prosecution. However, Tenet, as deputy DCI, yanked Deutch's security clearances. After questions were raised about whether Deutch had been let off for doing essentially what Los Alamos scientist Wen Ho Lee had done, the Justice Department reviewed the case again. In fact, Lee's situation was quite different from Deutch's. Over seventy days, Lee downloaded sensitive files equal to 430,000 pages of information from the laboratory's classified computer system and transferred them to his unsecure desktop computer and to tapes. Nine of the fifteen tapes were missing.

Before Justice could decide whether to prosecute Deutch, Clinton pardoned the former DCI. By then, he had returned to MIT's Chemistry Department. Because he could no longer obtain a security clearance, he could not act as a consultant on classified issues.[35]

In a characteristic parting shot, Deutch told the *Washington Post*, "Everybody says it's a job I've been pushed out of, but I would recall it's a job I was pushed into."

3

In some ways, Tenet and Deutch were similar. Both emotional men, Tenet and Deutch would greet friends with bear hugs. Because Deutch had pushed him for the job of deputy DCI, Tenet felt loyal to him.

"John Deutch gave me my opportunity to be the deputy director," Tenet said. "He got me in the business. I have enormous fondness for John."

According to Deutch, Tenet once approached him quietly in his office in the middle of a meeting with some foreign dignitaries. Tenet asked if the guests could be ushered out so he could give the DCI an important secret message. Tenet's message, after the room cleared, was that Deutch had forgotten to zip up his fly.

"It was at that point that I knew I had a uniquely loyal deputy," Deutch would later say.

But Tenet shuddered at Deutch's gaffes and thought his approach to his job was wrong and counterproductive. If employees "don't believe that you believe in them and the mission, you can articulate all the strategy you want and nothing will happen.

You can't do it by yourself: They have to implement it," Tenet would say. "If you take the job of director, and they think you are looking for the next job, and you don't really care about it, you're dead."[36]

Instead of calling him "Mr. Director," Tenet tried to call him nothing. He avoided Nora Slatkin. Yet, as Deutch's deputy, Tenet was in no position to remake the boss. Tenet left to others the handling of Deutch's security breaches with the home computers. It fell to Snider, as inspector general, to investigate both Deutch and the role of CIA management, including Tenet, who was by then DCI. Back when Fred Hitz resigned as inspector general, Tenet asked Snider to take the job. Snider had worked for Tenet on the Hill, and Tenet brought him to the CIA as his special counsel. They were colleagues, not social friends. At first, Snider said he was not interested in the inspector general job, but after Tenet came back to him several times, he accepted.

"I pointed out to him that if I became IG, there would inevitably be times when I'd have to criticize him," Snider said, "and that, regardless, I was going to follow the facts wherever they might lead. If that meant criticizing him, so be it. He told me he wouldn't have it any other way."

After he finished his investigation of the Deutch case, Snider reminded Tenet of this earlier conversation. "The report was critical of George," Snider said, "but not overly so. He was relying upon other people to handle the Deutch matter for him, and for the most part they let him down. But, you know, he was in charge. It was his responsibility ultimately to see that things were handled correctly, and they weren't. When I pointed that out to him, he said, 'Fair enough.'"[37] Snider's report said Tenet "should have involved himself more forcefully" to ensure a proper resolution of Deutch's computer issues.

"When George had to strip Deutch of his security clearance, it was hard," a Deutch aide said.

As DCI, Tenet agreed with Deutch that the CIA's security and discipline needed tightening, but his management style was entirely different. He would bounce a basketball down the CIA's corridors and drop in unannounced on CIA officials. He would ask roguishly, "What's going on? What's up? What do you hear?" Without time to filter their thoughts, employees often blurted out the first thing that came to mind, giving Tenet a sense of their moods and attitudes.

Tenet had a gracious way of making people feel important, and he lacked pretense. In a 1999 speech at Benjamin N. Cardoza High School in Queens, where he went to school, he referred to himself as the "short, fat guy from Little Neck." He wanted everyone to call him "George." With his wavy hair, Tenet looked like James Cagney or a young J. Edgar Hoover. He had large, soft brown eyes that made people open up. The fact that Tenet had the mouth of a New York City policeman further elicited candor. He talked straight and expected straight talk in return.

"George's speech was always pretty colorful," Snider said. "He is a passionate Greek-American."

Everyone who knew Tenet worried about his tendency to gain weight. At the NSC, he was taken to the hospital after an apparent heart attack; it was never officially diagnosed. After that he lost weight but soon regained it. A cigar smoker, he took to chomping on unlit cigars. In years past, on an overseas trip, he occasionally lit a cigar, admonishing those with him not to tell his wife, A. Stephanie Glakas-Tenet, who worried about his health.

Tenet met Stephanie, who grew up in Maryland, in college. She was the roommate of a friend of his. "We developed a friendship first," he said. "Then I fell in love, and we got married."

Tenet called Stephanie the best part of his life. He was devoted to her and to their teenage son, John Michael. With agency wife Julie Sussman, Stephanie, forty-six, wrote *Dare to Repair,* a home repair guide for women. Despite having a job that he described as 24/7, Tenet was fiercely dedicated to maintaining a normal home life. A college basketball fanatic, he attended Georgetown games with his son. He cleared off his calendar to attend his son's lacrosse games and would invite him for pizza in the CIA's cafeteria.

"We don't go out a lot, don't entertain a lot, we don't do the Washington social circuit," Tenet said.

Besides the news, Tenet watched *The Agency* on Saturday nights and *Alias* on Sunday nights on TV. He liked to see how the agency was portrayed.

Tenet found inspiration in *Gates of Fire* by Steven Pressfield. An historical novel, the book is about the military stand of an elite group of three hundred Spartan warriors against a force of two million Persians intent on conquering Greece in 480 B.C. Internal bickering and politics had allowed the Persians to make inroads. Led by King Leonidas, the hand-picked force of Spartans sacrificed itself at the narrow mountain pass of Thermopylae, buying the Greeks a few crucial days so the Persian forces could be neutralized. Courageous and patriotic, the Spartans overcame their own weaknesses but, in a bloody battle that lasted seven days, died to the last man. The standard of valor they set by their sacrifice inspired the Greeks. Eventually, they defeated the Persians, preserving the beginnings of western democracy.

To tell the story, Pressfield created a fictional squire named Xeones. Wounded and left for dead, Xeones was saved by the surgeons of King Xerxes of Persia, who was intent on learning what would impel the Spartans to make the ultimate sacrifice for their country. Xeones revealed that the men of Sparta were ordinary men with inner strength that came from devotion to their families and loyalty to their fighting brothers. The Spartan women, who considered themselves equal to the men, spurred them on, telling their sons to come home victorious or not at all. The fact that Tenet's wife Stephanie was a Spartan made the tale a little more real for him.

When he was under stress, Tenet snacked. When his CIA security officers drove him, he would tell them to let him off while he picked up a bag of Dunkin' Donuts. He preferred to ride in an SUV rather than a limousine. He was always on the phone, making calls in the car or as he waited for his donuts. In his office he kept a bowl of fruit which he offered to visitors and munched on himself. He often jogged on the CIA grounds in the morning and occasionally held meetings still wearing his running suit and baseball cap.

"I think he's always been a complex person," Snider said. "Ambitious, but never really a self-promoter. He never took himself too seriously, and he never sought the spotlight. While he's gregarious with people he knows, he actually seems rather shy around people he doesn't know. He's tough-minded but doesn't like to lock horns in controversies or turf battles if he can avoid them. He's fun to be around, but someone who's deadly serious about what he's doing."

Unlike John Deutch, Tenet admired the CIA, respected its traditions and history, and loved the spook world. Tenet attended the funerals, gave speeches at anniversaries of major events, and made it a point to meet regularly with former DCIs like Richard Helms. Despite Helms' involvement in some of the agency's fiascoes, he was seen as a professional who supported the troops. Tenet's embrace of him sent a message.

"George Tenet had political savvy and intuition," said Lloyd

Salvetti, who was chief of staff to David Cohen and to his successor Jack G. Downing. "He saw potential consequences."[38]

"Most of the other DCIs I worked for had personal, political, or policy ambitions," Dave Cohen said. "They saw the job as a stepping-stone. Tenet had no other agenda but the agenda of the CIA."

Tenet often alluded to the CIA's early days and the spirit of "boldness, action, and teamwork" that marked its beginnings.[39] It was important, he would say, to "know your history—to know where you did well and where you didn't." Only by understanding those roots, Tenet felt, could he change the CIA's course.

William J. Donovan called it an "unusual experiment." The best and the brightest—graduates of Harvard and Yale and partners from J. P. Morgan—would be recruited to embark on a dangerous mission: to penetrate the enemy, learn its secrets, and disrupt its operations through covert means, including sabotage and assassination.

The enemy at the time was Nazi Germany and Japan, and Donovan's organization was the Office of Strategic Services (OSS). But the OSS, founded in 1942, would lead through several incarnations to the Central Intelligence Agency and its latest mission of fighting terror. While Donovan, a New York lawyer and politician, never became director of the CIA, his spirit and vision shaped it. A fearless fighter in World War I who looked like Walter Cronkite, Major General "Wild Bill" Donovan is considered the father of the modern spy agency.

"He was impossible, he was unreasonable, he was totally thoughtless," Eloise R. Page, who became Donovan's executive secretary in 1942, told me before her death in 2002. "After I had been working all day, I would get a call at 11 P.M. He would say, 'I'll send a driver. I need to give you some dictation.' He would give me dictation to 3 A.M. I would go home, sleep, and be at the office at 7 A.M. He would still be there, and he would ask if I had typed up the material he had dictated."

If Donovan was demanding, he was also "brilliant and imaginative," Page recalled.[40]

At its peak, the OSS employed thirteen thousand people. Because its upper ranks consisted of the elite of American society, insiders dubbed the OSS "Oh So Social." The agency borrowed heavily from the techniques of the British intelligence services.

"We mimicked MI5 and MI6," Eloise Page said.

The OSS is best known for supplying officers to so-called Jedburgh teams, consisting of guerrillas who parachuted into France to support the resistance against the German occupiers. The teams coordinated airdrops of arms and supplies, engaged in hit-and-run attacks and sabotage, and assisted the advancing allied armies, much as the CIA would later operate against the Taliban in Afghanistan and against the military in Iraq. The OSS also tried, albeit unsuccessfully, to centralize government intelligence functions with an analytical section known as Research and Analysis.

At a time when America was fighting for its survival, Donovan infused the organization with his "can-do" spirit. The OSS developed silenced pistols, an explosive powder packaged in bags of flour, a device for derailing trains, and a remote-controlled speedboat designed to detonate against enemy ships. When shoveled into a furnace by unsuspecting workers, an explosive device concealed in a fake lump of coal would detonate and blow up a factory.

On June 6, 1944, 176,000 allied troops landed on Normandy beaches, beginning a systematic defeat of the Germans. Looking ahead, Donovan proposed to President Franklin D. Roosevelt an "intelligence service for the post-war period." In contrast to the OSS, which reported to the Joint Chiefs of Staff, Donovan envisioned a "central authority reporting directly to you."

The CIA's mission would be simply defined: to prevent another Pearl Harbor. In the weeks before December 7, 1941, U.S. military agencies had picked up alarming signs of a possible attack. Intercepted messages showed that Japan had been putting its diplomats on alert for war. The Japanese ordered their consulates in the U.S. to destroy all but the most crucial codes, ciphers, and classified documents. The high command was padding its radio messages with old or garbled messages to make decoding more difficult.

If they had been considered together, such indications of imminent war would have been enough for President Roosevelt to place the U.S. military on immediate alert and disperse ships at Pearl Harbor. But the strike caught the military by surprise, and 360 Japanese warplanes sank or seriously damaged eight American battleships, fourteen smaller ships, and two hundred aircraft. The attack killed 2,388 people, a toll exceeded only by the September 11 attacks on the World Trade Center and Pentagon.

In the parlance adopted after September 11, there was a failure to connect the dots. Yet that was not necessarily enough to thwart an attack. What was needed was a penetration of the enemy— whether the Germans or Japanese during World War II or al Qaeda in the war on terror. Such a penetration usually entailed inserting spies into the heart of an organization or government so that its innermost plans and secrets were passed along to the other side.

After several predecessor organizations were tried and failed, the CIA was created by Section 107 of the National Security Act of 1947, which President Harry Truman signed into law on July

26. The agency was established on September 18, with Rear Admiral Roscoe Henry Hillenkoetter as its director. He was the third director of Central Intelligence but the first director of the CIA.

In considering the idea of a CIA, Congress was influenced by a joint congressional investigation of the Pearl Harbor disaster. The study concluded that a unified American intelligence system was needed to prevent another such attack. Yet the CIA was charged with more than unifying the collection and analysis of intelligence. As part of its mission, the CIA would gather its own intelligence using all available sources—spies, planes, and later surveillance satellites, intercepted signals and communications, and open source material, such as newspapers and radio broadcasts.

While not spelled out in the act, the CIA would also undertake covert action meant to influence or topple governments and political parties through secret funding, training, propaganda, and paramilitary action. That authority, as Clark Clifford wrote in *Counsel to the President,* stemmed from an all-purpose clause that provided that the CIA shall "perform such other functions and duties relating to intelligence affecting the national security as the National Security Council may from time to time direct."

At the time, there was a "strong and growing worry in the top echelons of the government about the growing influence of the Communist philosophy, particularly in scholastic groups, worker organizations, and political organizations in Europe," Lawrence R. Houston, who helped draft the legislation creating the CIA and was its first general counsel, told me before his death in 1995. "Something had to be done. I was of the opinion that if it were done, it should be done by CIA."[41]

In the year that the CIA was established, B. F. Goodrich introduced the first tubeless tires, and New York City subways raised their fares from five to ten cents. Jackie Robinson signed with the

Brooklyn Dodgers, and Peter Paul introduced Almond Joy to go with its Mounds bar. But far more significant was an article signed "X" in the July issue of *Foreign Affairs* advocating a policy of containment and deterrence toward the Soviet Union.

The anonymous author was George F. Kennan, the new head of the State Department's policy planning staff. His strategy would govern relations with the Soviet Union until the end of the cold war, and the CIA would be a critical component in the prosecution of that war.

4

—————

At first the CIA housed its offices in thirty-three buildings all over Washington, many of them temporary wooden structures around the Reflecting Pool in front of the Lincoln Memorial. Because the floors would not support them, vaults for storing classified information would occasionally come crashing down on floors below.

Headquarters was a brick building with white ionic columns next to a Navy medical building at 2430 E Street NW in Washington. It was bounded by a skating rink, a gas works, and a brewery.

In 1955, President Dwight D. Eisenhower signed a bill authorizing $46 million for the construction of the CIA headquarters complex in McLean, Virginia. On September 20, 1961, the first employees began moving into the new building, a 1.4-million-square-foot structure of concrete and glass. In 1985, construction began on an addition at the rear of the compound behind the old building. Completed in 1988, it nearly doubled the size of the agency's quarters.

If the agency had impressive headquarters, its mission remained virtually impossible: to penetrate the Soviet Union, a police state that initially denied entry to foreigners.

"Even the most elementary facts were unavailable—on roads and bridges, on the location and production of factories, on city plans and airfields," said Harry Rositzke, the first chief of the CIA's Soviet division.

"We had identified our enemy as the Soviet Union. But we didn't know anything about it," Donald F. Burton, a CIA Soviet analyst, said. "The first real big question we had was how big is the Soviet Union? They had stopped any information. There was a great experiment, a new system. We didn't know if it was working or not. How big were they relative to us in terms of their GNP? Were they growing rapidly or were they standing still?"

In desperation, the CIA dropped Russian émigrés by parachute behind Soviet borders, hoping they could transmit back information on the Soviet military. In those pre-satellite days, the CIA even deployed balloons to float automatic cameras fifty thousand feet over the country.

In Moscow, surveillance was so tight that it was almost impossible for CIA officers based in the American embassy there to recruit agents. In the spy business, there was a crucial distinction between *officers* and *agents*. Intelligence agency employees who recruited spies were called intelligence officers, case officers, operations officers, or simply operators. They were considered patriots by their own country. The people they recruited—ranging from officials or intelligence officers of foreign governments to limousine drivers who chauffeured them—were called agents. They were considered traitors by their own countries. Colloquially, both agents and intelligence officers were known as spies.

CIA case officers were assigned to the Directorate of Operations (DO). Also known as the clandestine service, the DO was the heart and soul of the CIA. It broke the laws of other countries to obtain classified information. In that respect, the directorate's mission differed from that of the State Department, which sought information that was not secret and could be obtained legally.

Usually, CIA officers operated under diplomatic cover, meaning they posed as State Department or military officers and, if arrested, could be expelled but not prosecuted. While in that role, they could assume other identities, often using disguises. Other CIA officers operated without diplomatic immunity. Called NOCs, for nonofficial cover, they usually purported to work for private companies. They were at the mercy of foreign countries and could be imprisoned for life if caught committing espionage.

The Soviets wove a cocoon around the Americans in Moscow that made it virtually impossible to recruit agents. The KGB would exploit any weakness, any vulnerability, any hidden desire, to ensnare American embassy employees in a subtle but deadly trap. By the time an American realized what had happened, he was subject to blackmail and terrified of discovery.

The first step in this process was sizing up or assessing each employee assigned to the embassy. The Soviets wanted to get a feel for each individual. Then they could decide on their approach. What better way to do that than by assigning KGB officers and informants to work in the embassy right alongside the Americans?

At first blush, it seems inconceivable the Americans would allow it. Neither the CIA nor the State Department would allow a Soviet national even to sweep the floors at their headquarters in Washington. Nor had the Soviets ever allowed an American to work inside their embassy in Washington.

But, over the years, the Soviets manipulated the Americans so they actually *wanted* Soviets to work inside the embassy. When they came to Moscow, the Americans experienced culture shock. Besides a lack of consumer goods, everything from looking up a telephone number to hiring a plumber took an inordinate amount of time, and everything was controlled by the government. Just buying tickets to the Bolshoi Ballet was like applying to college. To buy a book or a dress, they had to wait in three lines—one to look at the item, one to pay for it, and one to pick it up. There was no such thing as fast food. Going to a restaurant required reservations. If the Americans wanted to go for a ride in the country, they needed Soviet government approval, entailing delays and often ending in rejection.

The Soviets used these powers to control the Americans. If the Soviets disapproved of an American initiative, or the FBI had just arrested a Soviet spy in New York, the Soviets would make life tough for the Americans, perhaps denying a visa to a repairman who could fix the embassy's elevators or claiming planes that were half empty were booked. If the Americans were behaving themselves, they might get their Bolshoi tickets a little faster and their trips within the Soviet Union approved a little quicker.

The Americans gradually adapted by letting the Soviets have their way. For the most part, the same diplomats populated the embassy year after year. Soviet specialists who spoke Russian fluently, the diplomats would do a tour in Moscow, return to Washington to work on the Soviet desk, then do another tour in Moscow. Over the years, they accepted the Soviets' contention that it was easier and cheaper to employ Soviet nationals at the embassy to cut through Moscow's bureaucratic jungle. And which Soviets would the Americans employ? Those chosen by the Soviets, of course. Only Soviets supplied by UPDK, a state agency controlled by the KGB, could work in foreign embassies in Moscow.

The Soviets used these employees to spy on the Americans, to plant bugs, to assess who might be vulnerable to recruitment, and to make sure CIA officers failed at recruiting spies in Moscow. The KGB also wanted the Soviet workers in the embassy to compromise the Americans directly. Like motorcycle riders going without helmets, the Americans recklessly allowed the Soviets to place KGB "swallows" in their midst—enchanting young women used to entrap the Americans in compromising relationships.

"We used sexy artists, musicians, dancers," former KGB Major General Oleg Kalugin told me. "We said, 'This is a great opportunity to help your country!' "

For years the FBI and CIA warned the State Department of the dangers and tried to pressure it to replace the Soviets with Americans. Since they ran the embassy, the diplomats called the shots. They sabotaged the intelligence community's efforts by suggesting they were part of a plot to break relations with the Soviets.

Thus it was not surprising that the CIA's first major recruitment of a Soviet intelligence operative came not in Moscow but in Vienna, in 1952. There, Lieutenant Colonel Peter Popov of the GRU, the Soviet military intelligence agency, offered to spy for the agency. Besides giving away identities of Soviet intelligence officers, Popov delivered to William Hood, his case officer, one of the Pentagon's highest priority targets—a copy of the 1947 Soviet Army field regulations.

The CIA's biggest break came in 1961, when Colonel Oleg Penkovsky, a Soviet GRU officer, approached the British in Moscow after a CIA officer, thinking he was a KGB plant, rejected his overtures.[42] When he visited London the following year, Penkovsky began spying for the west in an operation conducted jointly by the CIA and British intelligence. For sixteen months, he provided MI6 and the CIA with running accounts of Soviet military strategies, the capabilities of the missiles that touched off the Cuban Missile

Crisis in October 1962, and details of KGB and GRU operations targeted against the U.S. In addition, he gave the CIA a series of articles from a top secret military magazine which asked Soviet military leaders to express their views on policy. The articles provided insight into the Soviet military mind.

By the time Penkovsky defected, a sinister force had gripped the CIA. James Jesus Angleton, the chief of CIA counterintelligence, had begun propagating the theory that all Soviet defectors were double agents sent to uncover American secrets. A thin man with a sallow complexion, Angleton had graduated from Yale. He bred orchids, wore a black homburg, and drank heavily. He frequented La Niçoise in Georgetown, where he drank I.W. Harper bourbon with a few cubes of ice, chain-smoked Virginia Slims, and insisted that the chef remove any white-colored mussels before he ate them. He wanted only those with orange-colored flesh, according to Michael Bigotti, who waited on him and became the restaurant's manager.[43]

Besides his counterintelligence duties, Angleton delegated to himself the job of maintaining liaison with Israeli intelligence. It was through that link that the CIA obtained a copy of a secret speech made by Nikita Khrushchev in February 1956 denouncing former Soviet leader Josef Stalin as a despot. The CIA publicized the speech, scoring a tremendous propaganda blow against the Soviets.

Angleton's paranoid outlook and his tendency to label as spies those who disagreed with him so intimidated the agency that recruitment of agents virtually stopped.

"We were blind after Penkovsky and Popov were gone," said William F. Donnelly, a CIA case officer who became chief of internal Soviet and East European Operations. In that job, Donnelly directed CIA spying that targeted the Soviet bloc from within those countries.

Like Senator Joseph R. McCarthy, who without any evidence labeled government employees Communists, Angleton accused everyone from the Paris station chief to CIA directors of being moles. After becoming DCI, James Schlesinger asked Sam Hoskinson, an assistant, to meet with Angleton and find out what he was doing. In his book *From the Shadows,* Robert M. Gates, who later became DCI, said Hoskinson told him that he found Angleton "seated behind his desk, blinds drawn, a single desk light on."

As Angleton chain smoked, he wove Soviet conspiracy theories, finally concluding that Schlesinger was one of "them." When Hoskinson told Angleton that he would have to tell Schlesinger what he had said, Angleton glared at him.

"Well, then, you must be one of them, too," Angleton said.[44]

By talking in riddles, Angleton managed to convey the impression that he knew far more than he did. To add to the illusion, he spoke of the world of counterintelligence as a "wilderness of mirrors," as if only he could unravel its mysteries.

"I spoke to Angleton six times," said Angus Thuermer, a longtime CIA spokesman. "I never quite understood what he had said."[45]

As with Joe McCarthy, the secret to Angleton's longevity was fear. Angleton kept huge files full of names of CIA officers who had come under suspicion based on Angleton's amateurish theories. Anyone who called his bluff could become a target.

"People were always afraid that he had something on them," said Samuel Halpern, who was executive assistant to the chief of the DO, then euphemistically called the Directorate of Plans.

"Angleton had been mesmerized by Golytsin," said Rolfe

Kingsley, who was to head the Soviet Division, referring to Anatoli Golytsin, who defected from Finland in 1961 and claimed all other defectors were fakes. "Angleton saw a mole under every chair. If you had something successful, he said it was a Soviet throwaway. It couldn't possibly be true. Angleton was a brilliant guy. But he was a menace."[46]

"MI5 analyzed Golytsin's information and said it was good until 1962, but he made it up after that," said Donald F. B. Jameson, a CIA officer who debriefed him. "He manipulated Angleton beautifully."[47]

"Angleton was conned by Golytsin," said Richard F. Stolz, a former CIA deputy director in charge of the DO and the first station chief in Moscow.[48]

Angleton was equally naive about Harold A. R. "Kim" Philby, the master Soviet agent who was a high-ranking officer of MI6, the British Intelligence Service. Over weekly lunches at La Niçoise and Harvey's, a favorite of J. Edgar Hoover, Angleton confided to Philby many of the CIA's secrets, and Philby passed them on to the Soviets.

"Our discussions ranged over the entire world," Philby later wrote of his lunches with Angleton after he had defected to Moscow. "Who gained most from this complex game I cannot say. But I had one big advantage. I knew what he was doing for the CIA, and he knew what I was doing for SIS [British Secret Intelligence Service]. But the real nature of my interest was something he did not know."

Angleton would continue to poison the air until William E. Colby, as director of Central Intelligence, finally fired him in 1974. But in 1967 a group of senior case officers working the Soviet and East European target revolted, led by Jack Fieldhouse.

"We literally walked out of a meeting called by Soviet Division management to indoctrinate us in Angleton's thinking and make us cautious about recruiting," Donnelly said. "Richard Helms, who was director of Central Intelligence, quietly sided with us and shortly thereafter replaced the leaders of the Soviet Division."

To make sure Angleton could not interfere with recruitment, Kingsley met with Helms, whom he had roomed with in Germany when they were both in the OSS. A graduate of Williams College, Helms became a foreign correspondent in Europe for United Press. With another reporter, he interviewed Adolf Hitler. While Helms later stood up to Richard Nixon during the Watergate scandal, he was the consummate bureaucrat, skilled at tradecraft and loyal to the CIA and its people but unwilling to take a stand on controversial issues. In meeting with him, Kingsley pointed out that Angleton had claimed that Moscow knew everything that went on in the Soviet division within twenty four hours.

"I told Helms that if the KGB knows everything, maybe Angleton's counterintelligence staff is compromised," Kingsley recalled. "I said I want to shut off his access to our reports. That's how I put it to Helms, and Helms agreed."

"Rolfe Kingsley saved us from Angleton," Donnelly said.

After the revolt, the CIA aggressively pursued new recruitments of Soviet and East European agents around the world. In 1970, Colonel Ryszard J. Kuklinski, a Polish army officer, began giving the CIA astounding access to Soviet and Warsaw Pact military plans in Europe. By the time he fled Poland in 1981, he had turned over thirty-five thousand pages of secret documents. A Polish intelligence colonel who secretly was a KGB officer revealed spying by half a dozen KGB agents, including Harry Houghton and Gordon Lonsdale in the United Kingdom. A technician assigned to develop photographic plans for Soviet missiles turned over the negatives to CIA operatives in Moscow.

Under Donnelly's direction, the agency learned to operate under surveillance. While being followed by KGB officers, an agent would drive with his wife to the country for a picnic. At a curve in the road, she would throw an object out the window. It might be a yogurt container or a piece of wood. Concealed inside would be cash or instructions for an agent. Through similar stratagems, a CIA officer would retrieve the item, sometimes aided by electronic beams emanating from the object. Because the KGB assumed CIA officers were males, Donnelly expanded the use of female officers.

While the CIA adopted many tricks from the British MI6, it developed a range of techniques of its own. One was the simple use of a revolving door in an office building or store to temporarily hide the activities of an agent. When the agent emerged from the revolving door, he could place a chalk mark on a wall to signal that he was about to make a drop of material. Because the surveillance agents were temporarily delayed from following him, he was "black" and could make his mark without being spotted.

In dropping off secret documents, the simplest methods were usually best. Documents might be deposited in the crook of a tree or under a bridge. By using these so-called dead drops, a CIA officer who picked up the documents avoided being seen meeting with an agent who had dropped them off. To signal that documents were ready to be picked up or that a meeting was desired, a CIA officer or agent would leave a particular window open at night, make a chalk mark, leave a wad of chewing gum at a particular location, draw a shade half way, or park a car with its front wheels angled to the curb.

The CIA deployed operatives to break into the communications rooms of foreign embassies to steal secret codes. At one point or another, the agency compromised the communications of most countries of interest to the CIA. The agency dug secret tunnels to eavesdrop on telephone conversations. Through sewers, it wire-tapped lines of military offices in Moscow, then retrieved the taped conversations by driving over a manhole and electronically com-manding the devices to disgorge their take. That way, counter-audio technicians, as they were called, would have difficulty locating the wiretaps. To train officers to plant the devices, the CIA created sewers in Virginia replicating the Moscow sites.

"We found we could operate in Moscow," Burton L. Gerber, a former Moscow station chief and later head of the Soviet and East Bloc Division, said. "We had fantastic numbers of recruit-ments."[49]

Over the years, the CIA was able to intercept conversations of Kremlin leaders in their cars. A listening post disguised by the CIA's Office of Technical Service as a tree stump was installed to monitor electronic signals from Soviet SA-5 missile sites and trans-mit them to a U.S. satellite. While the KGB caught the officer installing the tree, other similar devices were productive. The CIA even tried to teach crows to follow infrared beams so that the birds would affix listening devices to windows. The devices picked up mainly traffic noise. The CIA also experimented with using bugs embedded in crickets and in mice. An electric charge would kill the mice when they reached their intended target.

While using animals as bugs never produced much, the CIA regularly bugged rooms by training laser beams on simple objects like dishes or ceramic or glass lampshades. The beams picked up vibrations from the objects and beamed conversations back to CIA officers. The CIA developed a method to introduce laser beams into fiber optic strands as fine as human hair. The laser beams turned the end of the strand into a microphone, creating an almost invisible bugging device. To further conceal them, the ends of the strands could appear inside a hole in the wall smaller than a pin hole. Thus, these bugs were essentially invisible and undetectable electronically.

Robots planted other bugging devices in inaccessible areas like air-conditioning ducts. Silicone masks and counterfeit passports created by the CIA were so authentic-looking it was impossible to tell that they were fake. By feeding rigged designs for technical innovations like computer chips to the Soviets through a double agent code-named FAREWELL, the CIA was able to harm the Soviet economy. When the Soviets built silicone chips and computers based on the designs from FAREWELL, they found that they eventually stopped working.

"The whole effort to operate against the Soviets depended on getting out from under the Angleton influence," Donnelly said.

In the meantime, the KGB's successes rivaled the CIA's. Quoting from the KGB's 1967 annual report from Yuri V. Andropov, the head of the KGB, former KGB Major General Oleg Kalugin told me the Soviet intelligence service recruited 218 agents that year, including sixty-four with access to U.S. secrets. Of the total, forty-eight—including eight diplomats—were recruited inside Russia. That same year, the KGB read 152 secret communications systems from seventy-two capitalist countries and decoded 188,400 classified documents, according to the report, submitted in May 1968.

"My directorate, the Foreign Counterintelligence Directorate, alone ran 524 recruitments in 1979," Kalugin said. "Most of them were employees of foreign intelligence security organizations, including some retired CIA officers. Some have yet to be caught." Kalugin added, "We considered Angleton to be a useful idiot."[50]

For all the harm he did by closing off potential sources of information, ignoring tips and unfairly accusing CIA employees of consorting with the enemy, Angleton—whose job was to prevent penetrations of the CIA by the other side—never did catch a spy. During Angleton's tenure, Karl Koecher, a Czech intelligence service officer, became a CIA employee and was given sensitive translating tasks. Koecher compromised Aleksandr D. Ogorodnik, a high-ranking Soviet diplomat then working for the CIA. Ogordnik's information about the deliberations of Soviet leaders was so important that it was circulated directly to U.S. presidents. Yet Angleton never had a clue about this major spy case within his own agency.

"Angleton was like a dog nipping at the wheels of a speeding car," said John Martin, the former chief of the Justice Department's counterespionage section. "He never caught up with the car, and if he had, he wouldn't have known what to do."

"Angleton did a disservice to a lot of agency officers whom he thought were spies," John McMahon, who served with him and became deputy CIA director, said. "Colby did a gutsy thing by firing him."

In interviewing Angleton in April 1987, a month before he died, I brought up the case of Karl Koecher. All along, there really had been a mole in the CIA, but it was not Angleton who caught him. While a high-level translator at the CIA, Koecher was working for the Czech Intelligence Service, which was an arm of the KGB. Claiming themselves to be defectors, Karl and his wife Hana Koecher had come to the U.S. from Czechoslovakia in 1965. A brilliant Renaissance man, Karl developed an elaborate legend or cover story. Pretending to be a rabid anti-Communist, he claimed that Czechoslovakia Radio in Prague fired him because of his biting commentary about life under the Communists. Karl obtained excellent recommendations from U.S. professors and used them for his application to the CIA.

Hana acted as his courier, providing him with cash she obtained from the Czechs when she traveled as a diamond merchant. Like Rudolf Abel, Koecher was an illegal who operated without benefit of diplomatic cover. If arrested, he and his wife could be prosecuted.

Aside from his translation duties, Koecher had an unusual way of obtaining classified information—attending sex parties. A redheaded man of slight build with a greying mustache, Koecher introduced his wife to mate-swapping. A gorgeous blonde with huge blue eyes, Hana liked it so well that she became a far more avid swinger than he was. Karl and Hana regularly attended sex parties and orgies in Washington and New York. They frequented Plato's Retreat and the Hellfire, two sex emporiums in New York open to anyone with the price of admission. They also enjoyed Capitol Couples in the Exchange, a bar in Washington, and the Swinging Gate in Jessup, Maryland. Known as the Gate, it was a country home outfitted with wall-to-wall mattresses and equipment for engaging in acrobatic threesomes.[51]

Because of her extreme sexual proclivities, Hana quickly became a favorite on the orgy circuit. Hana liked to accompany Karl to Virginia's In Place, an elite private club organized in 1972 by a suburban Virginia real estate man. For the club, the man rented a spacious home in Fairfax, Virginia, just minutes from Koecher's CIA office in Rosslyn, Virginia, across the Potomac River from Washington. A favorite form of entertainment was the bunny hop. Men and women would dance naked in a line and then fall on the floor, where they had group sex with anyone who landed nearby. A double bed in the recreation room was also used for group sex. Anyone who wanted to joined in.

Hana was one of the most active party goers. Described by one of her partners as "strikingly beautiful" and "incredibly orgasmic,"

Hana would have sex with three or four men at a time. Karl and Hana had a wide circle of married friends with whom they swapped spouses. On the side, they each had their own affairs going.

If both spies enjoyed swinging, they also found the orgies a good way to meet others who worked for the CIA or other sensitive Washington agencies. Because security rules at agencies like the CIA banned such activities, participants placed themselves in a compromising position in more ways than one. The Koechers took full advantage and picked up valuable information from other party-goers who were officials of the Defense Department and White House, as well as the CIA.

Through his translation duties, Karl was able to piece together the identity of Ogorodnik. A critically important CIA asset, Ogorodnik—code-named TRIGON—worked for the Soviet Ministry of Foreign Affairs in Moscow. He provided the CIA with microfilms of hundreds of classified Soviet documents, including reports from Soviet ambassadors.

Once Koecher tipped the KGB in 1977, the Soviet spy agency conducted surveillance of Ogorodnik and caught him photographing documents. He agreed to confess and asked his interrogators for pen and paper. "By the way, for some years I have written with the same pen, a Mont Blanc pen," he said. "I think it's on top of my desk. If one of your people happens to go near my apartment in the next few days, I'd like to have it."

The KGB delivered the pen, in which the CIA had concealed a poison pill. Ogorodnik opened the pen and swallowed the pill. Within ten seconds, he died.

From a defector, the FBI learned about the Koechers and arrested them. After Karl pleaded guilty in a secret court proceeding in New York, the Koechers were swapped on a snowy day in Feb-

ruary 1986, with John Martin there observing, crossing the Gli-
enecker Bridge, which joined East Germany with West Berlin. It
was the same bridge where the United States exchanged U-2 pilot
Francis Gary Powers for KGB officer Rudolf Abel more than
twenty years earlier. Under the terms of an agreement, the Koechers were barred from ever entering the United States again.

Subsequently, during five days of interviews in Prague in April
1987, Karl Koecher told me that attending the orgies was useful.
"Even knowing that somebody attends parties like that—maybe a
GS-17 in the CIA—is interesting stuff," Koecher said. "Or you
just pass it on to someone else [another intelligence officer], who
takes over. That's the way it's done."

The group sex was "just the thing to do at that time," Hana
Koecher said airily as we toured the museums with my wife Pam.
"All our friends somehow went to a little club or something. So
we went there, too, to see how things are."

Thus, Koecher had done great damage to the CIA. Yet, when
I brought up the subject with Angleton, the spy catcher showed
no interest in the case. For Angleton, it seemed, it had all been a
game: Koecher had not been the mole he was seeking. Therefore,
he was of no interest.

5

IF THE CIA was becoming more successful at human spying, it still had no reliable way to assess the Soviets' military capability. The Soviets were masters of deception. At military parades, they created the appearance that they had more bombers and missiles than they actually possessed by running the same ones around the block. The ruse led to claims that there was a "bomber gap" and later a "missile gap" between the Soviet Union and the U.S.

Haunted by Pearl Harbor, President Dwight D. Eisenhower asked MIT President James Killian in July 1954 to study U.S. military and intelligence capabilities. It was the height of the Cold War, when Senator Joseph McCarthy accused the secretary of the Army of concealing evidence of Communist infiltration. In that same year, Univac shipped the first electronic computers to businesses, and RCA introduced the first color television sets.

Killian formed the Technological Capabilities Panel, which recommended greater use of science and technology to improve collection. In particular, the panel's recommendation supported development of high-flight reconnaissance, a capability that would form the cornerstone of the CIA's Directorate of Science and Technology (DS&T).

On November 24, 1954, Eisenhower approved the U-2 project proposed by the Killian Committee and gave the go-ahead to Clarence "Kelly" Johnson of Lockheed Aircraft to develop the spy plane. Allen Dulles, the pipe-smoking CIA director, chose Richard M. Bissell Jr., a brilliant Yale economics professor, to head the project.

Like many of the CIA's pioneers, Bissell came from privilege. The son of the president of Hartford Fire Insurance Co., Bissell traced his roots to George F. Bissell, who settled in Connecticut in 1636. Bissell took his first steps at the Hotel Villa d'Este on Lake Cuomo in Italy. He attended Groton, where he become friends with Joseph Alsop, who later would become an influential columnist. Bissell attended Yale and the London School of Economics. He received a Ph.D. in economics from Yale.

Having headed the Marshall Plan for the reconstruction of Europe, Bissell met Dulles, who urged him to join the CIA. Bissell was already a friend of many of the CIA's leaders, who traveled in the same Georgetown social set.

In August 1954, Bissell wrote to Dulles from his yawl, the *Sea Witch,* accepting his invitation. Four months later Bissell was placed in charge of developing the U-2 that would take photographs at seventy-five thousand feet. On July 4, 1956, the U-2 made its first flight over the Soviet Union. The plane gave the first accurate assessment of that country's military capabilities and debunked the notion that the Soviets had more bombers—and later missiles—than the United States. That, in turn, saved the country tens of billions of dollars that otherwise would have been spent trying to catch up with the Soviets. The U-2 also spotted Russia's first test site for full-scale intercontinental ballistic missiles in Kazakhstan. It was the crown jewel of Soviet space technology.

"Khrushchev was aware of it [the U-2] almost from the beginning," Bissell told me before his death in 1994. "Their radar was
tracking it. A number of times they made diplomatic protests,
privately, very privately. It was clear they didn't want to admit we
could fly an aircraft over their territory, and they couldn't do a
damn thing about it."[52]

Eisenhower was reluctant to approve further flights before a
four-power summit meeting scheduled for Paris. At the urging of
Bissell, he authorized them to continue until May 1, 1960. On
that day, the Soviets finally shot down the U-2 with an SA-2
missile and captured the pilot, Gary Francis Powers. As instructed,
Powers had ejected himself from his seat, but he was unable to
press the button that would destroy the plane, which came down
in large pieces.

While the CIA had given Powers a pin coated with shellfish
toxin concealed in a silver dollar if he chose to commit suicide, no
one at the CIA envisioned that he would ever survive a shoot
down. Bissell had told Eisenhower that the aircraft would disintegrate on impact, and the Russians would have only the wreckage.
Based on that shaky assumption, when the Soviets announced that
the plane had been shot down, Bissell foolishly decided that the
CIA, through the National Aeronautics and Space Administration,
should issue a cover story that a NASA weather research plane was
missing near Turkey, where the U-2 had begun its flight.[53] The
State Department issued a statement saying it would be "monstrous" to claim that the U.S. was trying to fool the world about
the real purpose of the trip.

As the truth leaked out, an embarrassed President Eisenhower issued a public statement on May 11 about the need to "protect the United States and the free world against surprise attack."

Before he would proceed with the Paris summit, Soviet leader Nikita Khrushchev demanded that Eisenhower promise not to resume the flights. He wanted Eisenhower to "pass severe judgment" on those responsible. At the summit, Eisenhower refused. Khrushchev lost his temper, and the summit was over before it began.

After serving time in a Soviet prison, Powers was exchanged in February 1962 for Rudolf Abel, the KGB illegal. John McMahon, who was the case officer for the pilots and would later become deputy CIA director, recalled that James Angleton was convinced that Powers had been turned by the Soviets. He opposed allowing him to return.

"Angleton thought Powers gave the Soviets everything," McMahon said. "We told Powers he could say he was with the CIA but should not reveal the plane's altitude or the fact that the British supplied some of the pilots and were partners with us. He protected that information."[54]

Angleton pressured the State Department to oppose returning Powers, but McMahon met with the State officials who were willing to go along with Angleton. "I told them Eisenhower and then Kennedy had approved the exchange, and I said I would begin taking the names of the people at the meeting. That was the end of the opposition," McMahon said

By August 1956, the CIA had begun development of the SR-71 supersonic spy plane to replace the U-2. The plane, which made its first official flight in April 1962, flew at more than three times the speed of sound at eighty-five-thousand feet. Eisenhower also authorized the CIA to develop CORONA, a satellite reconnaissance system. After thirteen tries, it made its first successful flight on August 10, 1960. But the Soviets beat the U.S. when they launched Sputnik with the Soviet SS-6 rocket on October 4, 1957. Sputnik was the first earth satellite placed in orbit. Its surprise launch created an atmosphere of crisis in the government and shook American self-confidence.

That year, New York's last trolley car was retired from service across the Queensboro Bridge. New York State police found fifty-eight Mafia members meeting in Appalachin, New York, forcing FBI Director J. Edgar Hoover to admit that there was a Mafia. P. Lorillard introduced Newport cigarettes.

Having become an officer in the OSS, Eloise Page, William Donovan's secretary, became an officer in the CIA. Initially she headed a CIA unit that clandestinely interviewed Soviet scientists. From them, she had learned the precise details of the satellite launch, months before it occurred.

"We knew when it would launch, its apogee, and its size," Page said. "The person in charge of the CIA committee which passed on such information would not believe it. He said it was a Soviet deception. So the White House was surprised. It went down as an intelligence failure."[55]

To analyze and interpret photos taken by the U-2 and spy satellites, the CIA created the National Photographic Interpretation Center (NPIC). The center was started by Arthur C. Lundahl, a brilliant former Navy man and University of Chicago graduate who had gone to work for the agency in 1953. For many years, NPIC was located on the four top floors of the Steuart Motor Co., a huge, factorylike brick building. Later it moved to the Washington Navy Yard at First and M Streets SE in Washington. Called Building 213, the center was a seven-story concrete complex that consisted of three cubelike buildings covering two city blocks.

At first the photointerpreters used nothing more than magnifying glasses and measuring devices to help them analyze aerial photographs. Slowly they built up a library of images that would allow them to pinpoint changes by comparing one frame with a similar frame shot earlier.

"You look at a place and then what was it like last year or yesterday," Lundahl told me before his death in 1992. "It's like looking at a movie. The frames are farther apart, but you can infer much more of the intentions by seeing the changes on the ground than by doing it one frame at a time."[56]

For the most part, NPIC concentrated on strategic intelligence and research that could be used to predict long-range trends. Tactical intelligence, which could be used to pinpoint targets for bombing missions, fell to the military.

At a time when television networks broadcast in color only a few hours a week, NPIC used computers to help analyze the take from satellites. As William E. Burrows described them in his book *Deep Black,* the computers inside Building 213 were "routinely being used to correct for distortions made by the satellites' imaging sensors and by atmospheric effects, sharpen out-of-focus images, build multicolored single images out of several pictures taken in different spectral bands to make certain patterns more obvious, change the amount of contrast between the objects under scrutiny and their backgrounds, extract particular features while diminishing or eliminating their backgrounds altogether, enhance shadows, suppress glint from reflections of the sun, and a great deal more."[57]

The computers could even analyze smoke coming from smokestacks and determine, through spectral analysis, what was being burned. With infrared, which senses heat, not only could analysts see inside buildings, they could tell, hours after its departure, that a plane had been on a runway.

The most critical need when NPIC was started in 1961 was to determine what missiles the Soviets had. It was NPIC that counted Soviet missiles during the missile gap debate, demonstrating that there was no gap at all. NPIC went on to use the same techniques to uncover the Soviet missiles being sent to Cuba. By then, NPIC knew what the erectors and transporters for the missiles looked like and what kinds of crates they were shipped in. Even though canvas covered the missiles before they were deployed, their length, shape, and width gave them away. NPIC analysts developed expertise in interpreting missile packaging.[58]

"There was a science of cratology," Lundahl said. "Also they had shelters for steamrollers and other heavy equipment, so we had shelterology. Cuban troops slept in one kind of tent, Soviet troops in another kind."

"The moment of truth for cratology came on October 10, when the first photographs of IL-28 crates en route to Cuba reached headquarters," said Thaxter L. Goodell, a CIA analyst. "Taken on September 28, these showed the Soviet ship *Kasimov* carrying ten crates which could only be for IL-28 bombers. . . . On the heels of persistent reports pointing to Medium Range Ballistic Missiles on the island, they led to the October 14 flight of the U-2, which brought back the first photos of ballistic missile installations."[59]

Based on its experience in analyzing missile deployment in the Soviet Union, the CIA was able to tell President Kennedy how long it would take for the missiles in Cuba to become operational.[60] This was supplemented with information from the manuals to the missiles provided by Colonel Oleg Penkovsky, the Soviet intelligence officer who began spying for the British and CIA in early 1962. Finally, on October 16, 1962, Lundahl presented Kennedy with photographs that convinced him that the missiles really were there. On that basis, Kennedy confronted Khrushchev and, by threatening retaliatory strikes, got him to remove them. It was one of the CIA's greatest triumphs.

"We gave our leaders answers, gave real substance to our national estimate, gave enlightenment when there had been darkness," Lundahl said. "I think we avoided nuclear war a couple of times, particularly in Cuba when people knew exactly what the facts were. We provided a basis for the Strategic Arms Limitations Treaty. Generally, the whole litany of our national intelligence was moved steadily into a technical arena, where the scope and speed and detail of information kept track of world events. People from the president on down became accustomed to this kind of service."

While the Soviets were masters at human intelligence or HUMINT, the Americans were masters at scientific and technological intelligence.

"We knew virtually everything they were doing—how many missiles they had, when they were trying to deceive us," said Gene Poteat, the former high-ranking DS&T officer. "We knew where they had built an underground bunker for Soviet officials to protect against a nuclear hit."[61]

Nor did the Soviets have the analytical ability of the CIA.

"The Soviets had more information on the U.S. than they could assimilate," Richard Kerr, the former deputy DCI, said.[62] "You could have given them our technical collection capability and they would not have known what to do with it."

"In the end, we ran the Soviets out of money," said R. Evans Hineman, who was deputy CIA director in charge of the DS&T. "Had we been blind, who knows what would have happened?"[63]

"The Soviet leadership understood that they would simply be incapable of keeping up the arms race with the United States," former KGB officer Kalugin said.

6

An agent must clandestinely photograph documents, deliver covert messages to his case officer, receive cash, and arrange meetings. Of greatest importance, the agent must have a way to signal in an emergency that he or she needs to leave—or exfiltrate—the country. Through its Office of Technical Service, the DS&T developed state-of-the art devices that CIA case officers used to carry out these missions and to bug rooms, tap phones, and disguise themselves.

Several hundred CIA employees—including engineers, cabinetmakers, woodworkers, leatherworkers, and physicists—secreted bugs or created secret compartments in everything from kitchen cutting boards to felt-tip pens. Oil filters, videotape cassettes, tool boxes, toy trains, batteries, cigarette lighters, basket covers, teddy bears, chess sets, paintings, wallets, statues, hot plates, and toilet kits have all been used for such clandestine purposes.

In the 1960s, OTS assigned three dozen officers to research and deploy secret writing techniques. By the end of the Cold War, the CIA was using almost undetectable quantities of chemicals within visible messages to communicate secretly on paper.[64]

Spinoffs from DS&T research led to long-lasting batteries, beepers, and miniature tape recorders produced by private industry. The CIA's efforts to automatically spot changes in military installations photographed by spy satellites led to mammography.

OTS audio officers routinely placed bugs in ambassadors' offices, the homes of foreign intelligence officers, the hotel rooms of treaty negotiators and United Nations delegates, the meeting room where OPEC held its deliberations, and the cars of possible terrorists. Trade negotiation meetings were usually bugged as well. When foreign countries built new embassies overseas, the CIA obtained the plans and planted bugs in the offices most likely to be used by top officials.

With the FBI and the National Security Agency (NSA), the CIA placed bugs in a Boeing 767 used by the president of China—the Chinese version of *Air Force One*—while it was in the U.S. for retrofitting, according to an FBI source. Those devices were quickly discovered, and the Chinese government disclosed the incident early in 2002. Because of the need to develop new technology and replace large portions of the interior, the operation cost more than $10 million, an intelligence official familiar with the project said.

Bugging an official's office might require four to six months of work. An agent who has access to the office might be recruited to photograph the leg of a desk and cut a chip of wood from it. At Langley, OTS would make a replica of the leg and conceal within it a bug. The type of wood and stain would be matched perfectly to the chip. Then the agent would remove the original leg and install the new one.

To bug a top Soviet nuclear scientist, the CIA arranged for a scientific organization to give him an award. The plaque contained a highly sophisticated bug that transmitted to a remote relay. The relay, in turn, transmitted the signal to a satellite that beamed the scientist's conversations back to the CIA. It was a Trojan Horse operation, widely used in a number of countries.

The CIA equipped officers with electronic scanning devices for detecting the communications of anyone trying to follow them. When airplanes were hijacked, OTS officers supplied items like cases of Coca-Cola containing electronic bugs. When the hijackers demanded drinks, they were given the bugged items. By picking up their conversations, the CIA could learn if the hijackers were about to kill passengers or were making empty threats.

Besides bugging, OTS wiretapped lines in every country in the world. OTS officers either installed the taps themselves or used a recruited agent in the telephone company switching office. In some countries, the local security service cooperated by arranging for the wiretap.

OTS operated its own secret printing plant at CIA headquarters. It could age papers, procure foreign paper, and forge foreign driver's licenses and foreign birth certificates. Each DO officer had multiple identities backed up with passports, driver's licenses, credit cards, and credit histories.

"In the late seventies, we realized we were dealing with a dangerous world," said Herbert F. Saunders, who was deputy director of OTS. "Americans were under surveillance, not only in the Soviet Union but in countries like Somalia, South Africa, Zimbawe, Egypt. We had to work in back alleys in dangerous places. We needed additional tradecraft."[65]

The CIA approached John Chambers, a Hollywood special effects artist who made the masks for the 1968 version of *Planet of the Apes*. He offered to sign on as an unpaid consultant, and he later set up a school for CIA officers.

Under Chambers' guidance, the CIA developed sophisticated face masks made of silicone. Called advanced disguise, they were created by artists who painted minute details like facial hair and pimples on the silicone.

The CIA recruited Robert Barron, one of the artists, from the Pentagon, where he was an illustrator and art director of two Navy magazines. It seems Barron had to park his car in a lot fifteen minutes away from work, so he duplicated a Pentagon parking permit so he could park in the Pentagon lot. A former girlfriend turned him in. When he went to his car one afternoon, two military security cars were waiting for him.

A judge fined Barron fifty dollars, then whispered, "Damn good job." Three months later, a man who said he was from a government agency called Barron and said he would like to talk with him about his artistic skills. Soon, the CIA made him an offer.[66]

At first Barron fabricated movie ticket stubs, credit cards, and driver licenses. Then he helped develop the CIA's silicone masks and the Jack-in-the-Box. A CIA officer trying to avoid surveillance might have his wife drive him into the country at night. At a bend in the road, he would jump from the car, leaving in his place the Jack-in-the-Box, a dummy with a face like his that unfolds from a briefcase.

Before going overseas, some operations officers were fitted with several disguises. They might wear a disguise when breaking into an embassy or house to steal codes or documents. If a case officer was about to try to recruit an agent, he might wear an advanced disguise or a "light disguise"—a wig and glasses, a mole on a cheek, perhaps a beard or mustache—so that, if the potential recruit turned down the offer, he could not readily identify the case officer who made it.

Sometimes the simplest methods were best.

"I might walk out of the embassy at the end of the day with a suit and tie and long hair and my briefcase," a former operations officer said. "I might go into the bathroom of a hotel and take off my coat and tie, put them in a briefcase, put on a sport shirt, wet my hair and slick it back, and walk out with maybe my raincoat draped over my briefcase. If I am arrested, I don't have any spy gear. If you use spy gear, you are in trouble. If you are arrested and they peel your face mask off, you have a lot of explaining to do."

Because of electronic listening devices designed by the OTS, a number of embassies in foreign countries have been penetrated. The OTS supplied the installers—called audio operations officers—who were often assisted by officers from the local stations. One installer was an extremely supple Japanese-American who stood four feet, nine inches tall and weighed just eighty pounds. He wormed his way into air ducts in order to plant bugging devices.

"The installers are guys willing to climb a fence in the middle of the night. If they're caught, they're in deep shit. They might spend fifteen hours on a job," a former OTS officer said. "It is not a simple thing to do. They may need to drill a hole in a wall and put in something that will transmit for years. If the target sees a hole, he tends to get suspicious. So they may have to replaster the wall and match foreign paint that is six years old."

Penetrating the code rooms of foreign embassies was one of the CIA's most challenging tasks. It was the job of the CIA's Systems Procurement Group within the DS&T's Office of Technical Collection, which worked with NSA to intercept signals intelligence.

Not to be outdone, the Soviets, taking advantage of American gullibility, turned the new U.S. embassy in Moscow into a giant listening device. During embassy construction in the 1980s, the State Department essentially gave the Soviets access to its components. Construction materials were stored in a "secure" warehouse that employed Soviet workers. The department let the Soviets form the precast concrete and girders for the new embassy in their own plants, and the materials were not rigorously checked for electronic bugs before they were installed on site. Ultimately, the new embassy was found to be riddled with hundreds of different kinds of bugging devices.

"The State Department said, 'We'll take the bugs out later after the new embassy is built,' " William Donnelly said. "But it turned out the bugs were part of the building."

So contemptuous of American security practices were the Soviets that they arranged different colored bricks in a wall of the new embassy to read from a distance "CCCP"—the Cyrillic letters for "USSR."

The CIA was often criticized for failing to predict that Mikhail Gorbachev would allow the Soviet Union to crumble. But the CIA does not have a crystal ball and cannot read minds. Until the Soviet leader decided to allow the Soviet Union to disintegrate, there was no way to divine his thinking.

Instead, it was the job of the CIA's Directorate of Intelligence (DI) to bring together the fruits of the two other directorates, make sense of the intelligence, and come up with forecasts so that the president and policy makers could prepare for likely scenarios.

Along with HUMINT, an abbreviation for human intelligence, the DI analyzed information from IMINT, SIGINT, and MASINT. IMINT is the collection of imagery, which can be derived from visual photography, radar sensors, infrared sensors, lasers, and electro-optics. SIGINT is the interception of electronic signals, including communications and other electronic data streams. MASINT, a newer category, stands for Measurement and Signature Intelligence, which is technically derived intelligence that detects, locates, tracks, identifies, and describes the specific signature of fixed and dynamic target sources, such as radar, laser, optical, infrared, acoustic, nuclear radiation, and radio transmissions.

Throughout the 1980s, the CIA issued a series of warnings in intelligence estimates and intelligence memoranda that the Soviet Union was in dire straits. But the agency never imagined that the entire system might implode. Nor did the CIA detect Soviet biological weapons programs producing hundreds of tons of anthrax bacteria and smallpox and plague viruses.

"We detected the fact that things had not been working for the Soviets for a long time—their force readiness, their economy," said James Hirsch, a former CIA deputy director in charge of the DS&T. "But we never predicted their collapse."[67]

It is always easier to assume that the status quo will continue. Far less career risk is involved. Without hard data on Gorbachev's intentions, for example, anyone who predicted that he would release the Soviet grip on eastern Europe and allow East Germany to reunite with West Germany may well have been referred to the agency's Office of Medical Services for psychiatric consultations.

"We understood the Soviet economy," said Richard Kerr, the

former deputy DCI. "It was going downhill in a big way. If you said it would implode, Caspar Weinberger, the Defense secretary, and others would have said you're crazy."[68]

"Did the CIA underestimate the percentage of Soviet GNP going to defense? Yes," former DCI Robert M. Gates told me. "But did we generally portray a Soviet economy in trouble and one less and less able to support this superstructure of the military and intelligence? I think we did."[69]

In September 1962, the CIA said placing ballistic missiles in Cuba would not fit into the Soviet Union's known behavior patterns, and Nikita Khrushchev "would not do anything so uncharacteristic, provocative, and unrewarding." Prompted by contradictory and fragmentary eye-witness reports of such a deployment, the incorrect estimate was produced about a month before photographs taken by a U-2 on October 14, 1962, showed conclusively that the Soviets were moving missiles into Cuba.

The CIA presented the estimate to the president, despite misgivings by John A. McCone, the DCI, who called and cabled his doubts from his honeymoon on the French Riviera. McCone was a successful businessman who expected straight answers and managed the CIA firmly. To McCone, it made sense that the Soviets would use Cuba.[70]

The CIA's mistaken estimate was a good example of what is known in the intelligence business as "mirror-imaging"—assuming that leaders of another country might think the same way Americans thought. While an estimate cannot predict events with certainty, it can lay out possibilities and assign probabilities, allowing smart policymakers to develop options to cope with the most likely outcomes. Yet it is not unusual for heads of state to ignore intelligence, as Joseph Stalin did in 1941 when told that the Nazis were about to invade the Soviet Union, costing the Soviets tens of thousands of lives.[71]

"The most important thing was not whether we were right or wrong about the occurrence of events, but that we helped the people making policy decisions by giving them background information," Edward W. Proctor, a former CIA deputy director for intelligence, said. "Sometimes you give them information that is right, and they make the wrong decisions. Sometimes you give them information that is wrong, and they make the right decisions for different reasons. Sometimes you give them information that is right, and they make the right decisions. Sometimes you make a prediction on something coming up, and the policymakers take an action which, in effect, makes your prediction wrong, but it was the right thing to do based on your prediction. The whole purpose is to help these people make better decisions."[72]

Another example of mirror-imaging occurred in October 1973, when the CIA failed to warn that Egypt and Syria were about to launch major attacks on Israel, the start of the Yom Kippur War.

"We did not predict it, period. We had seen the same thing occur several times before, including a year before, and nothing had happened," Proctor, then deputy director for intelligence, said. "It was a buildup of forces and threats. We did not understand what the purpose was from the Egyptians' point of view. They knew they couldn't win, but it was one way of breaking the deadlock."

Probably the most well-known failure came in February 1979 when the CIA did not foresee that the Shah of Iran might be overthrown. In mid-August 1978, a CIA analyst had reported to President Carter, "Iran is not in a revolutionary or even prerevolutionary situation."[73]

In this case, the Directorate of Intelligence disregarded reports coming in from the operations officers in Iran, who were noting growing opposition to the shah. The analysts assumed that the shah would crush the opposition, as he had in the past. But the shah's bout with cancer had weakened his resolve.

"We were aware the shah had opposition," Stansfield Turner, who was director of Central Intelligence at the time, told me. "One difficulty was it was hard to appreciate that a man who had the backing of the military and SAVAK [the shah's secret police] would be toppled by people parading in the streets. When you make an intelligence forecast, you make an assumption. We thought he would use the powers he had, but he didn't."[74]

Despite political pressure, the DI has always tried to tell it as it is. During the Vietnam War, the directorate repeatedly warned that the war was not winnable. In a June 11, 1964 memo to McGeorge Bundy, President Johnson's national security advisor, DCI John McCone debunked the "Domino Theory," Johnson's rationale for prosecuting the war. "We do not believe that the loss of South Vietnam and Laos would be followed by the rapid, successive communization of the other states of the Far East," McCone wrote.

In April 1965, McCone hand-carried a memo to Johnson. "I think we are . . . starting on a track which involves ground force operations [that will mean] an ever-increasing commitment of U.S. personnel without materially improving the chances of victory," McCone wrote. "In effect, we will find ourselves mired in combat in the jungle in a military effort that we cannot win, and from which we will have difficulty extracting ourselves."

As tens of thousands of Americans lost their lives, Johnson ignored the CIA's conclusions.

7

In september 1997, two months after becoming DCI, George Tenet held a two-day off-site secret meeting in a rustic CIA lodge in Virginia. Like the CIA compound itself, the retreat is surrounded by double chain link fences topped with barbed wire. The fence is marked with the standard signs: "U.S. Government Property—No Trespassing." Sensors detect movement, heat, and sound, sounding an alarm in the CIA's Office of Security when anything approaches the fence.

In attendance at the meeting were a dozen of the agency's top officials. They had seen four DCIs come and go in the past six years. No one had held the job of DCI more than two years. The CIA was adrift, mired in political correctness, weakened by funding cuts, and under attack for failing to detect the spying of Aldrich H. Ames. John Deutch had said publicly that the CIA was a second-rate organization and had imposed rules about the recruitment of agents who had problems with human rights.

Tenet asked, "What are we going to do with the CIA as the

twenty-first century approaches? What are we going to need to deal with the twenty-first century?"

The answer was simple: to improve human intelligence and develop more sophisticated methods of technical collection. After a series of meetings with CIA managers, Tenet, by May 1998, formulated what he called the agency's Strategic Direction, a plan for putting the CIA back in the spy game by focusing on the basics.

"Unless we set out to take charge of our destiny through an aggressive program that requires leadership, commitment, and care for our people, we will no longer be relevant ten years from now," Tenet told employees gathered in the Bubble to hear about the strategy. "This business is becoming very high tech," he said. "But no matter how technical it becomes, our job is—and always will be—the same: We are in the spy business. We steal secrets, recruit agents. We do it better than anybody else, and this will not change."

This time, there were no snickers from employees in the Bubble, as there had been when Deutch said he wanted officers to take risks, even as he described rules to give special attention to, and perhaps reject, assets with human rights violations. Within two months of taking over, Tenet had established himself as a leader who appreciated the DO and would champion the agency's cause. Tenet knew how important it was to support employees, whether they worked for his father's diner in Queens or for the CIA.

"The care and welfare of your people, looking after your customers and making sure your people are happy and you're motivating them, those were great lessons," Tenet told me when I asked about his father's influence on him.

George H. W. Bush, who was DCI from 1976 to 1977, had a similar approach.

"When Bush came in, he said to us at the first morning meet-

ing, 'Boy, they're really beating up on us,' recalled Angus
Thuermer, the CIA spokesman at the time. "The key word was
us. At the morning meeting the next day, Bush said he had been
to the White House. He said he told them, 'I've fallen in with the
smartest guys I've ever met.' In thirty minutes, that was all over
the building."[75]

Back when he was on the Hill, Tenet supported the elder
Bush's efforts to name Robert Gates DCI. A former deputy director for intelligence, Gates was the first DCI after Richard Helms
to come from within the agency. Tenet, as DCI, later named CIA
headquarters the George H. W. Bush Center for Intelligence,
which Tenet dedicated in April 1999. He threw a party which the
elder Bush attended, and Tenet also staged a major Cold War
intelligence conference at the George Bush School of Government
and Public Service at Texas A&M University.

While George Senior was overwhelmed when told Tenet
wanted to name CIA headquarters for him, it was Republicans in
Congress—not Tenet, who was Clinton's DCI—who came up
with the idea and pushed the measure through. After Senator
Boren urged the younger Bush to retain Tenet as DCI, the new
president checked with his father, who said he understood Tenet
was a "good fellow"—a high accolade in the elder Bush's lexicon.

To head the DI, Tenet chose John E. McLaughlin, whom he
would later name deputy director of the agency. An avuncular
man, McLaughlin had been in charge of analysis of Russia and the
fourteen other new states that emerged after the breakup of the
Soviet Union.

Like Tenet and most of his top people, McLaughlin had a
diverse background, but was not of the Ivy League. He received
his B.A. from Wittenberg University in 1964 and an M.A. from
Johns Hopkins School of Advanced International Studies in 1966.

He spent a year on Capitol Hill as staff assistant to Senator Joseph S. Clark Jr., a Democrat from Pennsylvania. During his master's program, McLaughlin had spent a year studying in Bologna. He did additional graduate work in comparative politics at the University of Pennsylvania.

Unlike some of the agency's Ivy League founders, such as Richard Bissell and James Angleton, McLaughlin had an abundance of common sense. A brilliant analyst, McLaughlin had a knack for dissecting a complex subject into clear, understandable pieces. Even when the agency and its findings came under the severest attack, he was totally dispassionate, acknowledging that the CIA was not perfect and that some of its judgments could turn out to be in error. As an unflappable analyst, McLaughlin was the perfect complement to Tenet, whose emotions were close to the surface and who loved operations above all else.

Widely admired throughout the agency, McLaughlin was an accomplished magician. On a bookshelf in his office next to Tenet's, he kept a photo of Harry Houdini. McLaughlin liked to quote Houdini's response when an onlooker asked how the greatest magician of all time had made one of his classic escapes: Shackled, he had been buried in a casket six feet under the ground.

"I didn't panic," Houdini said simply.

One day, Paul Redmond, the counterintelligence chief, was walking down a CIA corridor, and McLaughlin came up to greet him. Reaching into Redmond's ear, McLaughlin pulled out a playing card.

For an educational TV show about the CIA aimed at high school students, McLaughlin tore a newspaper into pieces, then appeared to restore the newspaper to its original state.

"Things are not always as they seem," McLaughlin said after performing the trick.

The producers of the movie *The Recruit* apparently saw the clip. In the movie, they have a CIA recruiter and instructor (Al Pacino) performing the same trick in a bar where he meets with a potential recruit (Colin Farrell).

"Nothing is what it seems," Pacino tells the recruit.

When the leader of a Latin American country visited the CIA, McLaughlin asked him if he could borrow a dollar bill. In front of the man's eyes, McLaughlin folded the bill into small segments, then unfolded it and produced a five-dollar bill. He then reached into his pocket and gave the astonished chief of state a dollar bill back.

"I'd like to hire you as our finance minister," the man said.

Tenet recognized that, as an analyst, David Cohen, whom Deutch had placed in charge of the DO, would never be accepted by the clandestine service. Cohen would always be a symbol of John Deutch's emasculation of the DO. So, as deputy director for operations, Tenet replaced Cohen with Jack G. Downing, a DO officer who had retired two years earlier. Downing, fifty-six, had been station chief in both Moscow and Beijing. A Harvard graduate and Marine officer during the Vietnam War, he read Chinese poetry for relaxation. Tenet described Downing to reporters as a "world-renowned operator" who could run "quality operations that generate unique information." Cohen would become station chief in New York.

"Tenet felt it would close a chapter," Cohen said. "The healing process could begin."

Tenet worked at improving cooperation within the CIA and downplayed and eventually rescinded the silly restrictions that made it difficult for the CIA to recruit agents involved in human rights violations. He refocused the CIA on gathering human intelligence, particularly on terrorists. Even before he took over as DCI, Tenet identified terrorism as the greatest threat to the U.S.

"I think we are already at war [against terrorists]," Tenet told the Senate Appropriations Committee in May 1997. "We have been on a war footing for a number of years now."

"George put counterterrorism front and center on the agency's agenda," Snider said. "He became personally involved and made sure that his troops were. He wanted results, not excuses."

In the Bubble, Tenet promised employees that he would not be another DCI who comes and goes in two years. "This one is staying—as long as God and the president are willing," he said.

As Tenet saw it, it was a privilege to be DCI. "Nothing beats enthusiasm, passion, and caring for people, because if you're sincere about that, employees recognize it," he said.[76]

Yet it would require more than leadership to refocus the CIA. It would take money. For years Congress had been chipping away at the agency's budget. Long-term technical and scientific research and development required commitment of funds for many years. Key technical programs, including a new satellite system called Future Imagery Architecture, had not been funded, or had been funded on a year-to-year basis. The satellites were needed to track terrorists, detect troop movements, and identify nuclear, chemical, and biological weapons in countries like Iraq, Iran, and North Korea. They used traditional high-resolution electro-optical cameras, plus heat-seeking infrared sensors and radar capable of taking detailed images in all weather, to relay images in real time. Because of the shortsighted budget limits, the procurement program for the planned satellites was chaotic, and there was inadequate funding to task the satellites, process the digital data they collected, and exploit their take.

In the same fashion, Congress appropriated money for only one or two Predators at a time. When they were shot down in Afghanistan and later Iraq, new aircraft had to be built at far greater cost per plane than if a dozen or more had been produced at one time. No money had been provided to develop new surveillance methods using waves created by oscillations from physical phenomena. Using such thermal, atomic, and other signatures, it would be possible to look through camouflage, identify the function of underground facilities, and find nuclear, biological, or chemical weapons.

Most important, the DO was limping along. The clandestine service remained at about 4,500 employees, of whom 1,200 were officers. Given the number of possible threats in dozens of countries, it was a ridiculously small complement. The number of DO officers was roughly the same as the number of agents in the FBI's New York field office.

Well before Deutch, Admiral Stansfield Turner had cut the DO by 820 positions. Going back to biblical days, when the Lord commanded Moses to send spies to report on the land of Canaan, gathering human intelligence has been critically important. Yet, like Deutch, Turner, appointed CIA director in 1977 by President Carter, mistrusted the CIA and never quite understood the elementary fact that spy satellites and other technical means could not uncover all secrets. In a telling commentary, Turner told me that he *did* appreciate human spies.

"I never was down on the clandestine side at all," Turner said. "They attributed that to me because I arrived there when it was becoming obvious to everybody that technical intelligence was producing amazing amounts of information . . . Therefore, technical collection was getting a lot more attention. The human side's noses got out of joint. They thought they were the be-all and end-all.

Their positions had changed. They are now gap fillers. You won't risk a human agent when you can get a photo. So you try your technical systems and where they can't get something, you fill in with humans. They didn't like that. They still don't."[77]

It was dismaying that, after almost four years as DCI, Turner still did not recognize that many of the most important secrets could not be obtained with satellites or intercepts. In general, only human spies—Turner's "gap fillers"—can pass along an enemy's intentions, the most important goal of intelligence gathering.

Tenet understood that simple point, and he understood the need to make the CIA accountable. Having been in on investigations by the Senate Select Committee on Intelligence during William J. Casey's tenure as DCI, Tenet was acutely aware of how easily the agency could lose credibility and support.

Under Casey—a lawyer, successful businessman, and former chairman of the Securities and Exchange Commission—foolish and highly risky covert actions were approved, or at least considered. It was a reversion to the CIA's earliest days, when covert action was taken simply for the sake of doing something, without regard to possible long-term consequences.

In the beginning, the DO had many apparent successes. In 1948, the CIA funded the Christian Democrats in Italy, helping prevent Communists from taking over the Italian government. In 1950, Colonel Edward G. Lansdale, who was on loan to the CIA from the Air Force, helped the Philippine leader Ramon Magsaysay overcome the Communist-backed Huk guerrillas. On August 21, 1953, CIA forces led by Kermit Roosevelt overthrew the left-wing government of prime minister Mohamed Mossadegh in Iran after he nationalized the British-owned Anglo-Iranian Oil Co. The CIA and MI6, the British Intelligence Service, handpicked General Fazlollah Zahedi to take power instead and funneled $5 million to him. Three days after the coup, Shah Mohammed Reza Pahlevi, who had fled the country the previous week after a clash with supporters of Mossadegh, was returned to the palace.

In June 1954, the CIA supported the overthrow of Jacobo Arbenz of Guatemala after he nationalized four hundred thousand acres of idle banana plantation owned by United Fruit Company. Arbenz had offered $600,000, precisely what the company had declared as the land's value for tax purposes. Moreover, he had come to power in popular elections. But Washington viewed Arbenz's left-leaning politics and the fact that some of his aides were Communists as reason enough to overthrow him.

Yet in most cases, the effects of covert action were temporary. Arbenz was replaced by even more objectionable and often ruthless leaders who killed more than one hundred thousand civilians over the next forty years. In Iran, the shah lasted more than twenty-five years but was toppled and replaced by the Ayatollah Khomeini in 1979.

"The tensions were often exacerbated by covert action. There was a failure to understand its long-term implications," Lloyd Salvetti, who spent much of his CIA career involved in covert action, said.

"Covert action is usually a last resort," former deputy DCI Richard Kerr said. "That is the worst time to use it."

Buoyed by successes in Iran and Guatemala, the CIA assured President Eisenhower that it could come up with a way to topple Cuban Premier Fidel Castro, who was creating a Communist government ninety miles from the U.S. mainland.

Richard Bissell had been named deputy CIA director for plans, later called operations. In that job, he was in charge of covert action. While Bissell had successfully directed the CIA's overhead reconnaissance projects, he had no experience in either human intelligence or paramilitary operations.

"Bissell didn't know too much about humans," said Sam Halpern, who was his executive assistant in the DO. "He was a brilliant man when it came to things. The U-2 and SR-71 all came out of Bissell. When it came to people, which is the business of the DO, he didn't understand how to deal with them. Nor did he think about long-term consequences."[78]

Bissell's original plan called for creation of a guerrilla force of twenty Cuban exiles who would train from 100 to 150 agents in Florida. They would infiltrate Cuba and align themselves with dissident groups. A few hundred more guerrillas would land on the island and somehow touch off a revolt.

The plan assumed that the Cuban population was ready to rise up against Castro. In fact, there was little popular support for overthrowing him, which was a conclusion the CIA's Directorate of Intelligence (DI) had already reached. One estimate, called "Prospects for the Castro Regime," said Castro remained "firmly in control." Internal opposition was still "generally ineffective," the report said.

Known for his arrogance, Bissell dismissed the estimate, and training began.

Like the CIA, President Kennedy, who inherited the invasion plan from Eisenhower, was obsessed with keeping the operation secret. Yet anyone who gave the question a moment's thought would have recognized what Bissell came to understand only after the needless loss of life—that the invasion immediately would have been linked to the U.S.

"My own personal view is that almost the worst mistake we made on that operation was clinging to the belief that this could be done in a way that was not attributable to the U.S. government," Bissell told me before his death in 1994. "Clinging to the idea that if our tradecraft was good, nobody could connect it to the U.S. government. That was just an utterly unattainable, and a very silly hope. Anything of that magnitude would be blamed on the U.S. government, even if the U.S. had not had a role in it."

Thanks in part to last-minute restrictions imposed by President Kennedy, the CIA did not have the air support to pull off the Bay of Pigs invasion. While the DO kept this covert action secret from other CIA components, the word quickly leaked out to the rest of the world. Even the *New York Times* knew about it but agreed not to publish the story.

Because of Kennedy's concerns, the landing was shifted from Trinidad, a major population center where the guerrillas would stand out, to the Bay of Pigs, a swampy coastal area a hundred miles to the west. To further conceal the origin of the invaders, Kennedy wanted a night landing.

While Bissell recognized that the changes would undermine the chances of success, he did not want to call off the invasion. Bissell feared that the trained guerrillas, by now numbering more than a thousand, would go public. Thus, he locked himself into his own naive scheme.

"Bissell was a risk taker, not a risk manager," said Gene Poteat, the DS&T officer who worked with him. "Bissell was slick. He said it would succeed. He did not talk to analysts. We paid the price."

A week before the April 17, 1961, invasion, the CIA learned that the Soviets knew about the plans and even knew the date of the planned attack, according to CIA documents. Unbelievably, the agency did not call it off. Nor did the CIA inform Kennedy of the compromise.[79]

The day before the first strike against the Cuban Air Force was to take place, Kennedy made an ambiguous comment to Bissell about further limiting the impact of the strike. Bissell responded by cutting the number of aircraft to support the invasion from sixteen to eight. On April 16, with the landing only hours away, Kennedy canceled another air strike. In the end, eight sorties were flown, instead of the forty originally envisioned.

Castro easily cut off the invaders at the Bay of Pigs.

"I heard voices of guys on the beach saying, 'We know you haven't abandoned us,'" John McMahon said. "Charles Cabell, the deputy DCI, was crying in the operations room. We were letting our guys get slaughtered."

Castro's forces killed three hundred of the invaders, and the remaining twelve hundred survivors were captured and eventually traded for $53 million in U.S. prescription drugs and food. Because the invasion violated U.S. treaty obligations, the failure impaired America's credibility with Latin American nations.

Lyman Kirkpatrick, the CIA inspector general, concluded that the CIA's officers "became so wrapped up in the operation that they lost sight of ultimate goals." They created an unruly, ill-trained, crudely supported invasion force whose cover was blown and whose existence had been hinted at in newspaper reports. "Plausible denial"—the ability of the United States to convincingly lie about its role in the invasion—became a "pathetic illusion." The CIA convinced itself that the invasion would magically create an "organized resistance that did not exist."

After the invasion, Kennedy called Bissell into his office. "If this were a parliamentary government, I would have to resign, and you, as a civil servant, would stay on. But being the system of government it is—a presidential government—you will have to resign," Kennedy told Bissell.

Allen Dulles offered his resignation as director of Central Intelligence, and Kennedy accepted it.

"Bissell was not a professional and was so obsessed with secrecy it interfered with operations," Rolfe Kingsley said. "It almost led to the end of the agency."

8

Uɴꜰᴀᴢᴇᴅ ʙʏ ᴛʜᴇ Bay of Pigs fiasco, Kennedy endorsed a plan proposed by Edward Lansdale, who reported to the Defense Department, for the CIA to engage in other covert action aimed at Cuba. Called MONGOOSE, the plan included sabotage against oil refineries and storage tanks. Robert F. Kennedy, the attorney general, in particular pressured the CIA to engage in these activities.

As it turned out, most of the agents recruited by the CIA were double agents who reported back to Castro and thwarted the plans. To embarrass the agency, Castro later ran hours of video on national television of CIA officers meeting with Cuban double agents.

"Castro knew about everything," Halpern said.

The CIA's efforts not only were thwarted, they were absurd. The CIA plotted to humiliate Castro with his own people by trying to get his beard to fall off—something that only someone whose level of maturity had not advanced beyond kindergarten could have dreamed up.

A CIA inspector general's report of August 25, 1967, recounted dozens of other bungled attempts to assassinate Castro or embarrass him with his people. Under one such plan, the CIA would spray the air of a radio station where Castro broadcast his speeches with a hallucinogenic agent similar to LSD. Another scheme was designed to contaminate cigars smoked by Castro with a chemical that would create "temporary personality disorientation." A third idea was to introduce thallium salts into Castro's shoes so his beard would fall out. This, according to CIA plotters, would destroy his public image. Finally, the CIA proposed setting off fireworks that would portray an image of Christ in the sky off the coast of Cuba. This was to show that Castro was in disfavor with God.

"Ed Lansdale wanted to have fireworks that burst in the sky like a star from a submarine. It would look like Jesus Christ and The Second Coming. It was to prove Castro wasn't accepted by the Almighty. That was the kind of idea he would come in with," Halpern said.

The stupidest scheme was to enlist the aid of the Mafia in killing Castro. Bissell, as deputy director for operations, asked Sheffield Edwards, director of security, to contact Mafia leaders for the purpose.[80] Edwards enlisted Robert A. Maheu, a private investigator, who asked John Roselli, an associate of Mafia leaders, to offer up to $150,000 to remove Castro. Roselli agreed to contact Salvatore (Sam) Giancana, a member of the Mafia, and Giancana asked for a lethal pill that could be given to Castro in his food. The CIA produced pills containing botulinum toxin for Castro.

The CIA passed the pills to the Mafia, but the gangsters reported they could not carry out the plot because their source had lost his position in the prime minister's office.

"My philosophy during my last two or three years in the agency was very definitely that the ends justify the means, and I was not going to be held back," Bissell wrote in *Reflections of a Cold Warrior*.

Operating in secret with little accountability, the CIA fostered an inbred culture that tolerated if not encouraged such schemes. Congress largely rubber-stamped the unfocused, juvenile approach. The early directors were the men who kept the secrets, and they were proud of it. They saw no conflict in running a secret intelligence organization within a free society, and they saw no reason to tell the rest of America, including Congress, what they were doing. They asked only—as Helms asked the American Society of Newspaper Editors in 1971—to take it partly on faith that "we, too, are honorable men devoted to her [the nation's] service."

As his spokesman, Helms appointed Angus Thuermer, a former Associated Press reporter and CIA operative. "My job was public nonrelations," Theurmer said. "I never said 'no comment,' but I never had any comment."[81]

Beneath the veneer of invincibility was an often shocking lack of common sense. Arguing against the need for congressional approval of covert action such as the Bay of Pigs invasion, Bissell, the architect of the scheme, told me that the "need for congressional notification has a suffocating effect. You have to tailor the mission to them and their staffs."

"Would not the CIA have been better off to seek congressional approval for the Bay of Pigs invasion, avoiding the calamity and loss of life that followed?" I asked him. No, Bissell replied, "If we had had to do that in the Bay of Pigs, I suspect the operation would have been called off. You could say we would be ahead, but you would do better to cancel every third operation on the principle that that way you will save some grief. You can't run an organization on that assumption."

Congress abetted such arrogant thinking, taking the agency at its word that it was both trustworthy and competent. But when Seymour Hersh of the *New York Times* broke the story in December 1974 that the CIA had been violating its charter by spying on Americans who opposed the war, Congress could no longer look the other way.

The top films that year were *The Godfather, Part II* and *Chinatown*. Patty Hearst, missing since the Symbionese Liberation Army abducted her, showed up during an armed bank robbery. Dr. Henry Heimlich announced his technique for saving people choking on food.

In 1975, a committee headed by Senator Frank Church, an Idaho Democrat, began an investigation that would profoundly alter the way the CIA did business. The committee and a president's commission chaired by Vice President Nelson A. Rockefeller found that the CIA for twenty years had illegally intercepted and opened mail between the United States and the Soviet bloc; had kept dossiers on thousands of Americans and indexed the names of three hundred thousand American citizens with no connection to espionage; had infiltrated dissident groups in the Washington, D.C., area; and had experimented with LSD on unsuspecting Americans, leading to one suicide.

Not only were the abuses improper and illegal, they betrayed a lack of understanding of what America is all about. For what was the purpose of the CIA, if not to help preserve American freedoms, whether threatened by Soviet tyranny or later by al Qaeda? Aside from their impropriety, many of the revelations betrayed a dismaying lack of competence. The CIA had attempted to kill at least five foreign leaders, including Castro, but failed each time. The CIA also developed plans that were never carried out to assassinate Patrice Lumumba, who headed the Congo. Before the plans advanced, Lumumba was overthrown and killed in 1961 by his own people. While the CIA supported the rivals, the agency did not order his murder.

"We never assassinated anybody," Halpern said. "We tried. But we were not very good at it."

After fumbling in Cuba, the CIA went on to try to control elections in Chile. In 1964, the agency spent $2.6 million to support the election of the Christian Democratic candidate, Eduardo Frei, to prevent Salvador Allende's accession to the presidency. In 1970, the CIA tried to mount a military coup in Chile to prevent confirmation of Salvador Allende's victory in the Chilean presidential election. It also spent $8 million to prevent his confirmation—all in vain.

The CIA also became involved in covert action and paramilitary actions in Vietnam, Laos, Cambodia, Angola, Afghanistan, and Nicaragua. In Vietnam, the CIA, along with other government agencies, operated the PHOENIX program, which supplied the South Vietnamese with intelligence on the location of Vietcong in the south. Using that information, the South Vietnamese killed and tortured the Vietcong. Since the U.S. was intervening in a civil war, the CIA's involvement was as controversial and confusing as the rest of the war effort. As William Colby wrote in his memoirs, PHOENIX became "shorthand for all the negative aspects of the war."

On the other hand, in Afghanistan, where the CIA supplied money and weapons to the Afghan mujahedin fighting the Soviets beginning in January 1980, the CIA's intervention was considered successful. The Soviets withdrew in 1989, dealing a blow to Soviet prestige that contributed to the end of the cold war. But in 1996, the Taliban took control of the country and eventually supported Osama bin Laden. Given the success against the Soviets, few would argue, even in hindsight, against U.S. intervention. Rather, after the Soviets withdrew, the U.S. should have stayed the course and helped to create a stable government there. If it had, "it's less likely the Taliban would have come into existence," said Richard Kerr, the former deputy DCI.

It would be easy, as some CIA officers did, to blame the president at the time for urging covert action that was ill-advised or for ordering surveillance of Americans. Contrary to allegations at the time, the CIA was not a rogue elephant.

"They [the White House] were screaming, 'Why can't you get rid of Castro?' said Halpern, who helped direct MONGOOSE. "The White House said, 'Why didn't you get rid of him yesterday?' When you object and object and the orders come, you go do it. But many in the CIA did not object. There was always someone who wanted to go out and do crazy things."

"We cannot overemphasize the extent to which responsible agency officers felt themselves subject to the Kennedy administration's severe pressures to do something about Castro and his regime," the CIA inspector general's report on the plots said. "The fruitless and, in retrospect, often unrealistic plotting should be viewed in that light."[82]

When President Johnson ordered Helms to obtain proof that opposition to his prosecution of the Vietnam War was funded and directed from abroad, Helms pointed out that the necessary investigation "might risk involving the agency in a violation of the CIA charter limiting our activity to operations abroad and forbidding anything resembling domestic police or security activity," according to Helms' memoirs.

"LBJ listened for some fifteen seconds before saying, 'I'm quite aware of that. What I want is for you to pursue this matter and to do what is necessary to track down the foreign Communists who are behind this intolerable interference in our domestic affairs,'" Helms said.[83]

Helms carried out Johnson's order, and it led to many of the abuses exposed by the Church Committee.

"We had directors who were unable to say 'no' to presidents," Rolfe Kingsley said.[84]

But that was not the whole story. In those days the agency often encouraged the White House to think that covert action would work and then developed ill-advised schemes to carry it out. Too often, not enough thought was given to what was to be accomplished, whether it would work, and what would happen if the CIA's involvement became public, as it invariably did. In CIA lingo, such bad publicity is known as "blowback."

"There were really no rules in the early days of covert action," said L. Britt Snider, the general counsel of the Senate Select Committee on Intelligence who became the CIA's inspector general. "While the White House might have approved what the agency was doing in principle—indeed, they might have pushed them into it—they basically left it to the agency to decide how to go about it. As a consequence, you saw a lot of cowboyism during that early period. Indeed, because the covert action area was so freewheeling, I think it assumed a larger role in the first twenty years of the agency's operations than anyone had ever imagined when the agency was created."[85]

"The CIA had the responsibility to dissuade the White House and say, 'This is stupid,'" Richard Stolz, the former CIA deputy director in charge of the DO, said.[86] "You often saw a lack of adult supervision."

Having refused since its founding to let the press in on its accomplishments, the CIA had no popular support when its abuses and bizarre schemes became public. "The bad image the CIA got is partly the CIA's fault," said former CIA officer Gene Poteat. "We could have gone out and explained what the CIA had done right over the years. We never did that."

The Church Committee hearings in 1976 and 1977 led to tighter control of covert action by Congress and the establishment of permanent intelligence committees to oversee the CIA and related agencies. Yet the conflict between the "professionals and the cowboys," as Donnelly, who became inspector general, put it, would continue to plague the spy agency.

The cowboys tended to want to do something for the sake of doing it, often failing in their mission, breaking U.S. laws, and undermining the CIA's credibility with Congress and the public. The professionals recognized that there was no conflict between undertaking aggressive spy operations directed at overseas targets, on the one hand, and obeying U.S. laws on the other.

"A lot of our operations raise ethical and moral questions," said E. Peter Earnest, a former DO officer who became the CIA's deputy director of public affairs. "That is why you want ethical people, not cowboys and bandits." He paused. "At times we may want people who think like bandits."[87]

To this day, many CIA operatives will not forgive William Colby, the director at the time, for confirming to Hersh many of the facts in his story disclosing the CIA's abuses and for complying with congressional requests for the details of the CIA's questionable activities. To Colby, there was no choice. A Princeton graduate with a law degree from Columbia, he had a firm grasp of the Constitution. In a democracy, the people make the decisions through their elected representatives. He had to cooperate with Congress: The survival of the agency depended on it. Yet until his death in 2002, Helms was one of those who saw Colby's action as a betrayal.

"Helms was furious with Colby," said Charles A. Briggs, a former CIA executive director and inspector general. "At the unveiling of the statue of William Donovan in the lobby at headquarters, Colby and Helms were to be seated together. Eloise Page noticed the name plates and put a chair in the middle and sat down."[88]

Given his view of Colby's position, it was not surprising that Helms saw no need for candor with Congress. When Senator Stuart Symington asked him on February 7, 1973, "Did you try in the Central Intelligence Agency to overthrow the government of Chile?" Helms answered, "No, sir." Helms also denied to the Senate Foreign Relations Committee that the agency had passed any money to opponents of Salvador Allende, the self-declared Marxist who had been elected president of Chile.[89]

It later came out that, at the direction of President Nixon, the CIA in September 1970 had tried to mount a military coup in Chile to prevent confirmation of Allende's victory in the Chilean presidential election. The agency had spent $8 million to prevent his confirmation.

Caught in a lie, Helms agreed to plead *nolo contendere* to two misdemeanor counts of violating a federal statute, which made it an offense not to testify "fully and completely" before Congress. He told U.S. District Court Judge Barrington D. Parker, on October 31, 1977, that he found himself in conflict between his oath to protect the CIA's secrets and the need to tell the truth to Congress. Parker fined him $2,000 and sentenced him to a jail term of two years, which was suspended.[90]

Before he died in 2002, Helms explained to me that the wrong committee was asking the questions.

"I felt we had proper relations with the Armed Services Committee, and that's where I ought to be testifying about these things," Helms said. ". . . I have thought about it many times, and I couldn't figure out another way. If I had it to do over, I don't think I would change it," he said.[91]

Helms was a smart man who knew that he could have responded by saying he would like to discuss the issue privately. But Helms saw no need to account to Congress, except on his own terms: By Helms' reckoning, only CIA officers knew what was good for the country. It was a feeling shared by most CIA officers of that era.

"If we had had a more sophisticated view of what needed to be secret, as opposed to what was already known, it would have helped," Briggs said. "We tended to shoot ourselves in the foot."

9

After casey became DCI on January 28, 1981, "John Mc-
Mahon, who was deputy director for operations, warned us that
we had to be careful," recalled William Donnelly, who was deputy
director for administration. "Casey was a nice guy and understood
spying, but was dangerous. He could draw us into ill-advised
schemes."[92]

Like many other DCIs, Casey had wanted another job—secretary of State—and aspired to be a policymaker. He asked for
cabinet-level status, and President Reagan agreed. But Casey never
achieved his goal of becoming a social friend of the president. He
was rarely invited to evening events at the White House, and he
expressed his disappointment to his secretaries.

"Casey was never accepted by Reagan's inner circle," James
McCullough, his chief of staff at the CIA, said.[93] McCullough
believed it was because Nancy Reagan disapproved of his off-color
remarks.

When it came to the CIA's analysis, Casey pushed his right-
wing perspective. Casey thought the world had not changed much

since he was in the OSS. While he listened to countervailing views, some analysts found it hard to stand up to him.

"Casey would argue, and some gave in and rolled over," former deputy DCI Richard Kerr said. "The good analysts are not going to fold."

"Casey was gung-ho and ideological," said McMahon, who became deputy DCI under him. "He wanted to know why analysts came to their conclusions." He called in other authorities, like Claire Sterling. In her book *The Terror Network: The Secret War of International Terrorism*, Sterling suggested that the Soviets were providing the weapons, training, and sanctuary for terrorists as part of the effort to undermine western democracy.

"Sterling fired him up," McMahon said. "Finally, I had to say there is no evidence here, give it a break."

"Casey never understood we were winning the cold war," McCullough, his chief of staff, said. "His weakest point was his contempt for Congress. Casey didn't believe Congress had any business intruding into our affairs. He resented it. That got us into trouble. He was in a time warp."

Casey had "zero patience for what he saw as congressional meddling in operations, and he was especially intemperate when he thought Congress was micromanaging," said Robert Gates, who headed the Directorate of Intelligence under him. When testifying, Casey would often appear bored, "look at his watch, scribble notes, and not work very hard to avoid dropping disdain in answering questions he thought were silly."

At the same time, Casey infuriated the press by demanding leak investigations, often over trivial issues.

"Once, Casey demanded that we find out who had told *Newsweek* that he was out of favor as CIA director and might be replaced," said John L. Martin, who was in charge of leak investigations at the Justice Department. "After a Beirut paper revealed that William Buckley, the kidnapped CIA station chief there, was a CIA officer, the CIA wanted us to send FBI agents to Beirut to find out how the paper got the story."

"Casey would rage about leaks," said John A. Rizzo, the CIA's senior deputy general counsel. "He would scream at Edwin Meese, the attorney general, that he wanted leak investigations."[94]

As a former OSS officer, Casey understood the importance of human spies. His support for the CIA and the perception that he had easy access to President Reagan improved morale at the agency. But while Casey supported the work of the DO, he initially enraged the clandestine service by appointing Max Hugel to be DDO—deputy CIA director in charge of the DO. Hugel had no experience in intelligence. His claim to fame was organizing various ethnic groups to vote for Reagan. Seventy days later, he resigned.

Casey's habit of mumbling, especially when testifying to Congress, was often interpreted as a way of purposely concealing what he was saying. During one hearing, Gates noticed that Casey was mumbling when testifying but then, after faced with probing questions, turned to the person next to him and whispered clearly, "Sometimes I fear for the Republic!"

A voracious reader, Casey haunted Washington book stores searching for the most obscure books he could find on Soviet issues and world affairs. Mostly, it was to satisfy his intellectual curiosity. Casey bought so many books at a time that his security guards usually had to help him carry them all. One aide estimated he spent $40,000 a year on books and magazines alone.

"He was the brightest person I've ever met," said Stanley Sporkin, who was Casey's general counsel at the CIA and became a federal judge in Washington. "He had a photographic memory. He didn't tolerate fools. He couldn't stand long meetings. He would tell people, 'Don't repeat things. I understand,' and he did."

"Casey slept three hours a night," McCullough said. "He would go to a social occasion, come home at 11 P.M., sleep for an hour, wake up, and work. He would call in the middle of the night with routine questions."

Casey often took classified documents to bed with him at night and would forget to retrieve the items in the morning. When CIA security officers picked him up to take him to headquarters, they first searched his sheets.

At the CIA, Casey had a habit of throwing a handful of peanuts toward his mouth. Half of them would meet their intended target, and the rest would fall to the floor.

"I had to brush off dandruff from his suit," said Peggy Donnelly, who was assistant to Casey. "He was aging and would have food on his tie. One day after lunch, he was carrying a manila envelope. He explained that it contained a sample of the food served at lunch. He was going to give it to his wife Sophia so she could duplicate it."[95]

As predicted, Casey got the agency into trouble. While the CIA itself did not arrange it, Casey and National Security Council aide Lieutenant Colonel Oliver L. North Jr. used a few individuals in the agency to help carry out the effort to trade arms for hostages held by Iran. Casey also failed adequately to inform the Senate of an ill-advised and disastrous scheme to mine the harbors in Nicaragua to support the contras who opposed the left-wing Sandinistas. The mines consisted of fifty gallon oil drums filled with black power and a fuse. When hit by a ship, they would create huge waves but likely would not sink a vessel. Buried in his testimony to the Senate Select Committee on Intelligence, Casey said,

"Magnetic mines have been placed in the Pacific harbor of Corinto and the Atlantic harbor of El Bluff, as well as the oil terminal at Puerto Sandino."

It was hardly adequate notice, especially given that Casey usually mumbled. After the mining became public, and it turned out that Japanese, Soviet, British, and Dutch ships had hit the mines, Senator Barry Goldwater, chairman of the intelligence committee, dashed off an angry letter to Casey. Saying the CIA, by mining the harbors, had committed an "act of war," Goldwater wrote, "It gets down to one, little, simple phrase: I am pissed off!"

Senator Patrick J. Leahy said he knew about the mining only because of questions he asked during a CIA briefing. He called the program "absolutely stupid. It will prove at best a harassment to the Nicaraguans and can only diminish the position of the United States in the rest of the world."

Casey then repeatedly lied about his involvement in the scheme, including during congressional testimony, according to the final report of Lawrence E. Walsh, the Iran-contra independent counsel.[96]

"The objectivity, professionalism, and integrity of the CIA were compromised by Casey's attitude and behavior in connection with the Iran venture," Walsh concluded. "To a large degree, the CIA's top professionals were dragged against their better judgment into supporting a questionable venture conducted by the National Security Council staff that lacked competence and expertise in covert operations."

Casey was elated when he learned on Thursday, August 1, 1985, that Vitaly Yurchenko wanted to defect. Yurchenko walked into the American embassy on Via Veneto in Rome after calling one of the American diplomats listed by the KGB as a CIA officer. While the man was not a CIA officer, he had one call Yurchenko back at a pay phone across the street from the embassy.

The CIA officer greeted Yurchenko at the bulletproof Marine security guard post at the main entrance. He asked Yurchenko for identification. Yurchenko proffered his passport. The officer asked for his position within the KGB. When Yurchenko told him, the CIA man tried to suppress a whistle. Yurchenko was deputy chief of the First Department of the KGB's First Chief Directorate, the KGB unit that directed spying overseas. The First Department developed and directed spies within the United States and Canada. Yurchenko was the highest-ranking KGB officer ever to defect to the CIA.

Following a script laid down in special defection kits prepared by the CIA, the officer and a colleague asked Yurchenko if he knew of any imminent plans to attack the United States or its allies. Then they asked if the agency has been penetrated. Yurchenko told them of Edward Lee Howard. Yurchenko knew him only by his code name, Robert. He said the CIA had trained him to go to Moscow but then unceremoniously fired him. Yurchenko had learned from a cable from the KGB's residency in Vienna that Howard had just visited the Soviets there: He was spilling all he knew about the CIA's assets in Moscow. Conceivably, Howard could have known of all the CIA's agents in the Soviet Union. Already he had given up at least three CIA informants, including Adolf G. Tolkachev, whose information on Soviet submarines already had saved the Navy billions of dollars in antisubmarine warfare development costs. Then there was Ronald W. Pelton, a National Security Agency employee, who had entered the Soviet embassy in Washington in January 1980, when Yurchenko was security officer there. Yurchenko did not know his real name either.

But having met him, he could describe him and the type of information he offered—including the fact that NSA was intercepting Soviet military communications through a highly secret undersea tap in the Sea of Okhotsk to the east of the Soviet coast.

In fact, while NSA operated the program, called Ivy Bells, the CIA had developed and directed it. For more than ten years the U.S. was able to intercept Soviet military communications, particularly those involving Soviet ballistic missile tests. Periodically a U.S. Navy submarine, using Navy frogmen, had to retrieve the tapes from a pod on the sea bed.

Based on Yurchenko's information, the CIA officers sent a cable to headquarters listing ten possible spies or penetrations of western intelligence agencies. The cable from Rome said Yurchenko insisted on only one condition to his defection: There would be no publicity about his case. No problem, CIA officers agreed. The agency did not want any publicity about it either. But when Clair George, who was in charge of the DO, told Casey about the defection, he realized the director saw it as a tremendous political and intelligence coup. Potentially, it could wipe out all the recent problems with Congress and a series of embarrassing roll-ups of informants in Moscow. Casey saw Yurchenko's defection not only as a tremendous success in the secret intelligence war, but also as a vindication of the American way of life. After all, if one of the KGB's top spies defected to the United States, what did that say about the Soviet system?

Over the coming months, the seventy-two-year-old DCI would play it for all it was worth. In the race to glory, Yurchenko's only condition to defecting—that there would be no publicity—would be ignored. In fact, when Ralph de Toledano broke the story in his column in the *Washington Times* on September 25, 1985, the CIA did not even try to dissuade the paper from running it. If it had, the paper would have held the story, according to Mary Lou Forbes, the commentary editor. Instead, after delaying several days, a CIA spokesperson called back to say before the column ran that the agency had no comment.

Three months after defecting, Yurchenko had had enough. Not only had the CIA broken its word, the agency had treated him almost like a caged animal. To be sure, the CIA was willing to give him more than a million dollars. The CIA considered his information both credible and critically important. Casey's attitude about Yurchenko's defection notwithstanding, since the agency's founding, the CIA had had a cultural mind set that viewed defectors as despicable traitors to their own country and odious human beings with personal problems.

Often, the negative attitude became self-fulfilling. If one expects trouble, one treats others in a hostile manner that is bound to lead to clashes. That was one reason the CIA used phony names when dealing with defectors. Yurchenko knew his case officer, Colin R. Thompson, as "Charlie," for example. It was not so much that the CIA worried about security. It was that CIA handlers did not want to be bothered at home by defectors with problems adjusting.

In training sessions, Jerry G. Brown, chief of the Security Analysis Group within the CIA's Office of Security, would tell new CIA employees that defectors are "misfits" who betrayed their own countries, not for ideological reasons, but because "they want to play by their own rules." They are nothing more than "spoiled children," he would tell them, as if all the émigrés who came to America to enjoy freedom and opportunity had done so only for selfish reasons.

During most of the time Yurchenko was in the United States

the CIA had failed to provide something as basic as debriefers who spoke Russian. Homesick defectors always felt more comfortable if they could speak their own language. The agency had hundreds of Russian speakers, yet, somehow, arranging for them to interview the man who was likely the most important KGB defector in the history of the agency was too much to ask.

"That was a grievous mistake," Burton Gerber told me.

On top of this cavalier handling, Yurchenko was crushed when the wife of a Soviet diplomat based in Montreal rejected him. Yurchenko had had an affair with the shapely, blue-eyed blonde when he ran security at the Soviet embassy in Washington, where her husband was then based. At Yurchenko's request, the CIA arranged for him to see the woman in Montreal. She would not leave her husband for him.

At 5 P.M. on Saturday, November 2, 1985, Yurchenko suggested to Thomas Hannah, his CIA security guard, that they go to a French restaurant in Washington's Georgetown section. They went to Au Pied de Cochon, a French bistro. The two men stared at each other across the small white table. Yurchenko, forty-nine, was a product of the Soviet Union's best schools, a man of culture and power. Reflecting the agency's attitude toward defectors, the CIA had left Yurchenko in the company of Hannah, who was twenty-six, spoke no Russian, and had only recently begun working for the CIA doing background checks.

After they both ordered the poached salmon, Yurchenko stood and said, "Tom, I'm going for a walk. If I don't come back, it's not your fault."

Hannah did not have time to respond to Yurchenko's enigmatic statement. As a security guard, his training had been minimal, well below the standards of the U.S. Secret Service Uniformed

Division officers who guard foreign embassies. The CIA had given him a .38-caliber revolver but had left him in the dark about what to do if Yurchenko bolted, or ever so politely excused himself.

Carrying the hat and trenchcoat he had just bought, Yurchenko, a man of medium build with almost transparent blue eyes, thinning greying blond hair, and a handlebar mustache, walked out under the restaurant's red awning into a cold, light drizzle. Quickly, he made his way up Wisconsin Avenue, a brightly lit commercial strip. Yurchenko was heading for the new Soviet embassy compound. Known as Mount Alto, the forbidding complex, bathed in mercury vapor lights, is on the second highest hill in Washington.

Hannah thought the KGB officer might have gone for a walk. As he later told his CIA superiors, since he had not paid for his order, he did not want to take off after him. While Hannah had no right to detain Yurchenko, he could have run after him and tried to persuade him that the agency would address his grievances. The thought of leaving his credit card with the waiter never occurred to him. Just before the salmon came, Hannah hurriedly paid for the two $8.95 dishes. He then walked outside and placed a call to Colin Thompson from a pay phone in front of the restaurant. Thompson called Michael T. Rochford, a Russian speaker who was one of two FBI agents assigned to debrief Yurchenko.

To Rochford, Yurchenko was a hero, a patriot who had risked his life to help America. He liked and admired the man, and Yurchenko had sensed this and opened up to him. The FBI taught agents to treat anyone who offered information to the bureau with dignity, respect, and appreciation. Sure, they could turn out to be liars or plants. But there was always time later to corroborate their information. Meanwhile, the important thing was to keep them talking, keep them happy, con them into thinking they were the best thing since sliced bread. FBI agents, unlike CIA officers, used their real names with defectors. It helped promote trust, and FBI agents who struck up lasting friendships with them won the admiration of their bosses.

When Thompson called Rochford, the FBI agent guessed immediately that Yurchenko had returned to the Soviet Union. Cursing silently, he blamed it largely on the CIA's coldness and its unforgivable failure to keep his defection secret.[97]

Rochford and Thompson walked up and down Georgetown's streets. Yurchenko was gone. Two days after he walked into the Soviet embassy at Mount Alto, Yurchenko gave a press conference there. Looking somewhat dazed, Yurchenko spoke in a rambling monologue, claiming the CIA had drugged and kidnapped him, then incarcerated him. The KGB pretended to buy his story that he had been kidnapped. That way, it could avoid the embarrassment of admitting that he was a spy and, according to former KGB officer Oleg Kalugin, send a message to other defectors that they would be welcomed back.

The next day, Au Pied de Cochon brassily began serving "Yurchenko shooters," a drink that consisted of equal parts Stolichnaya and Grand Marnier. By then, Yurchenko was on his way to Moscow.

It was the most embarrassing incident in the history of the CIA up to that point, one that prevented the CIA and FBI from obtaining further information about KGB operations and penetrations. Even worse, from a long-range perspective, it served as a warning to others contemplating defection that the CIA could mishandle them and publicize their defections, allowing the KGB to seize their families' assets.

In the only interview he granted to a western journalist, Yurchenko gave me an elaborate account in Moscow of how the CIA captured and drugged him. But at one point he seemed to forget his cover story, saying that, rather than drugging him, the CIA had simply screwed up.

"All foreign reporters and much of the public in your country thinks the truth is what the CIA told them," Yurchenko told me, referring to leaks indicating he had simply changed his mind about defecting.[98] "They never recognized that it was their mistake—many, many things. It is against their nature to recognize that they made a mistake. They are guilty."

"Interestingly, Casey did not ask that I investigate the leak of Yurchenko's defection, a leak which led directly to his redefection," spy catcher John Martin said. "That told me that Casey had either leaked the information himself or had authorized the leak."

"I am sure Casey wanted it [the defection] known," Gates, Casey's deputy, said. "After all, as usual, he was in hot water with the press and Congress, and publicity about a great intelligence success was politically helpful." Gates added, "Casey was telling everyone in town about Yurchenko's defection. Yurchenko was a real coup."[99]

10

In the fall of 1985, Duane R. "Dewey" Clarridge, the flamboyant chief of the CIA's European Division, met with Casey in his office. There had been three major terrorist incidents that year—an attack by the Abu Nidal terrorist group on the El Al ticket counters in Rome and Vienna, the hijacking by Shiite terrorists of TWA Flight 847, and the hijacking of the Italian cruise ship *Achille Lauro* by the Palestine Liberation Front.

Clarridge warned Casey that terrorist incidents would become more common unless the CIA took stronger action. Casey told Clarridge, the son of a New Hampshire dentist, that President Reagan wanted action. The DCI told Clarridge to take several months and come up with some solutions.

A cigar-chomping DO officer who wore white suits with a handkerchief tucked in the breast pocket, Dewey Clarridge had the reputation of a "cowboy," someone who shot from the hip and came up with occasionally silly ideas.

A case in point was the plan to mine the harbors in Nicaragua. As Clarridge recounted in *A Spy for All Seasons,* he thought of the covert action at home "while sitting with a glass of gin on the rocks." Just what the mining would achieve was never spelled out. If it was to harass the Sandinistas, as the CIA did earlier with Castro in Cuba, it was childish and pointless. By potentially damaging Soviet, British, and other ships, the mining boomeranged on the U.S. When the operation and the CIA's role in it became public, Clarridge berated Congress for the subsequent uproar, saying that he and Casey had briefed Congress on the operation.

"That the mining wasn't highlighted in yellow, spelled out in capital letters, and stuck on the front page of their agenda doesn't mean we were trying to obscure what we were doing," Clarridge fumed.

In 1991, Clarridge would be indicted for lying to Congress when he claimed he did not know about a shipment of HAWK missiles that was part of the Iran-contra affair. Clarridge insisted NSC aide Oliver North had misled him, saying the shipment in question contained oil drilling equipment. At the end of his administration, President George H. W. Bush pardoned Clarridge after the CIA officer's indictment but before his trial.[100]

If Clarridge was in some ways a throwback to the days when the CIA tried to get Castro's beard to fall off, he had as much experience with terrorism as anyone else in the CIA. At one point, Clarridge headed Arab Operations in the Near East Division.

The CIA had been picking away at the terrorism problem since 1967, when it began gathering intelligence on the Popular Front for the Liberation of Palestine. When the agency tracked terrorists to a particular country, it would alert the local security services, which often arrested them. The CIA also provided technological help.

For example, on December 4, 1976, seven South Moluccan

terrorists, armed with explosives, a carbine, pistol, and knives, took over the Indonesian consulate in Amsterdam. Demanding that the Dutch government recognize the Republic of South Molucca in Indonesia, they took hostage twenty-one children who were attending school that day in the building, along with fifteen adults. The terrorists lined a room with explosives and threatened to blow up the hostages. The Amsterdam police decided they would storm the embassy only if hostages were shot.

With the consent of the Dutch government, the CIA dispatched a technician who crawled through a sewer pipe into the embassy's basement. There he planted a listening device in a wall so the CIA could eavesdrop on the terrorists. Several days later, a gun went off inside the embassy. The police were about to storm the building. But the bug picked up the fact that one of the terrorists had accidentally dropped his gun, and it had gone off. The police waited out the terrorists. After fifteen days, they finally surrendered. Each was sentenced to six years in jail. Because the CIA had penetrated the embassy, no lives were lost.

Clarridge concluded that the CIA had a number of problems in dealing with terrorism. The first was that, ever since George Kennan had articulated the policy of containment, the agency tended to take a defensive approach. As great a threat as the Soviet Union was, it was governed by rational leaders who would not risk being annihilated by launching a first strike against the United States.

While the KGB was a force to be reckoned with and executed literally millions of Soviets, it would never try to assassinate a CIA officer. Instead, the CIA and KGB confronted each other according to a set of gentlemen's agreements. In retaliation for a spy incident, the U.S. or the Soviets would expel an intelligence officer, never kill him. Only agents who were recruited by intelligence officers and were traitors to their own country could be prosecuted and imprisoned or executed.

In fact, the KGB and CIA established a secure telephone link to arrange secret meetings on matters of mutual concern. The CIA asked for the KGB's help in determining the fate of William Buckley, the CIA station chief in Beirut who had been kidnaped by Islamic Jihad terrorists in 1984. The Soviets, in turn, asked for CIA help in learning what happened to a Soviet diplomat who had disappeared in India.

In contrast, terrorists were neither rational nor constrained by gentlemanly rules. They were willing to blow themselves up to achieve their goals. They killed innocent women and children. A new approach was needed to deal with them.

Beyond that, jurisdictional rivalries hobbled the CIA's efforts to attack terrorism. The CIA was organized like an array of stove pipes, with separate directorates and geographic divisions. Yet many terrorist organizations operated throughout the world. Analysts who worked on terrorism in the DI or DS&T rarely came in contact with DO officers working the same problem. Beyond a small advisory staff, no one at the CIA had overall responsibility for counterterrorism.

In late 1985, Clarridge got back to Casey with a solution. He proposed a Counterterrorism Center within the DO that would bring together all the directorates to attack terrorism. Casey enthusiastically endorsed the idea.

Earlier, on March 11, Mikhail Gorbachev had become the Soviet leader and began reforms that would culminate in the end of the Soviet Union and the cold war. Thus, 1985 was a watershed year for the agency, when it began a gradual change of focus from fighting the KGB to fighting terrorism.

George J. Tenet gave Vice President Dick Cheney, President Bush, and White House Chief of Staff Andrew H. Card Jr., right, an update in the Oval Office on March 20, 2003, the day after the first air strikes against Saddam Hussein. *AP/Wide World*

Unless otherwise noted, all photos are courtesy of the CIA.

George Tenet met with Vice President Dick Cheney, National Security Advisor Condoleeza Rice, and President Bush in the Oval Office on October 7, 2001, after Bush informed the nation that air strikes had begun in Afghanistan. *AP/Wide World*

George Tenet sat behind Secretary of State Colin L. Powell when Powell presented intelligence outlining Iraqi defiance of United Nations disarmament resolutions to the UN Security Council on February 5, 2003. *AP/Wide World*

George Tenet's office is on the top floor above the CIA's main entrance.

An electronically activated building pass is required to enter or leave the CIA through turnstiles at the main entrance.

After the attacks of 9/11, George Tenet ordered an evacuation of the CIA's old building, left, and the new building, right.

Signs at the Counter-terrorism Center point to sections that focus on Osama bin Laden and Iraq.

Johnny "Mike " Spann, a CIA paramilitary officer, was the first casualty of the war in Afghanistan.

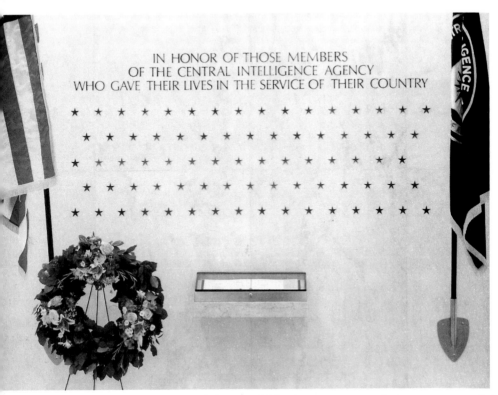

After Johnny "Mike" Spann was gunned down in Afghanistan, a seventy-ninth star was carved into the Memorial Wall in the CIA's main lobby.

William J. Donovan is considered the father of the CIA.

Eloise Page was executive secretary to William J. Donovan, director of the Office of Special Services, and she became the first female to head a major CIA station. *Courtesy of Cecil Wray Page*

Vitaly S. Yurchenko, the highest ranking KGB officer ever to defect to the U.S., returned to Moscow after the CIA mishandled him. *Ronald Kessler*

The author interviewed Karl Koecher, center, the only known Soviet bloc mole in the CIA, and his wife, Hana, after they were returned to Prague in a spy swap. *Pamela Kessler*

Douglas F. Groat's job at the CIA was to break into overseas embassies to steal communication codes. *Ronald Kessler*

John L. Martin, the government's chief spy prosecutor for twenty-five years, often bumped up against the CIA's self-protective attitude. *Olivia Boinet*

To give the CIA more power to counter terrorism, in January 1986 Reagan signed a finding—an authorization to conduct covert action—to allow the CIA to identify terrorists who had committed crimes against Americans abroad and to help bring them to justice. Now, besides letting other countries know about terrorists so they could capture them, the CIA itself could participate with the FBI in their arrest. George W. Bush would later broaden the finding to allow the CIA to capture or kill terrorists as part of U.S. defense.

The concept of a center cutting across jurisdictional lines represented a sea change for the CIA. Convinced that its job was the most important one in the agency, each directorate, like competing sports teams, vied for attention, funding, and status. Each would put down the other directorates. Successful as the technical side was, for example, many in the DO never considered it part of the CIA. Especially in the early days, "The technical people were never part of the family," said Albert "Bud" Wheelon, who was deputy director in charge of the DS&T. "We were illegitimate kids."[101]

Symbolizing the divided approach, for many years CIA headquarters was physically partitioned so that officers of one directorate could not enter corridors of another directorate without an escort. While the separation was designed to compartment secret information, it also served to discourage cooperation.

"What I was proposing was nothing less than a revolution within the CIA," Clarridge recalled. "Each directorate had always been a sacred fiefdom unto itself. Each had always been headed by a deputy director, a monarch of his own domain who guarded his territory jealously, and subordinates with geographic regional responsibilities did likewise."[102]

In 1986 Casey named Clarridge to head the new center. The director promised him twenty-five officers. Six months after he approved the idea, Casey asked to see the new center. Because of

internal opposition, beyond a few cramped offices, the center had
not been established.

"The bureaucracy rejected the idea of working jointly," Donnelly, who was in charge of administration, said. "So nothing really
had happened. To divert Casey's attention, Clair E. George, who
was in charge of the DO, said, 'Let's take a trip to France.' Casey
loved to travel, and he forgot about looking at the Counterterrorism Center. Two weeks later, when they returned from France,
the center had been set up, and we took Casey to see it."[103]

Still, Clarridge said, "The European and Near East Division
chiefs wanted to sign off on every cable. They played games. It
was very painful to get anything done."[104]

Clarridge decided the first order of business was dealing with
the Abu Nidal Organization (ANO). The organization was
founded by Sabri al-Banna, who was born in 1937 in British-ruled
Palestine. During the 1948 Arab-Israeli War, Banna's family fled
to the West Bank. Banna became involved with terrorist organizations, including the Palestine Liberation Organization (PLO). He
took the name Abu Nidal, meaning "father of the struggle" in
Arabic.

In the 1970s and 1980s, Abu Nidal's organization killed or
wounded nine hundred people in twenty countries. While his main
targets were Israel and Jews, they included moderate Arabs, Eur-
opeans, and Americans. In 1974, Abu Nidal broke with the PLO
and Yasser Arafat, accusing the PLO leadership of abandoning the
fight against Israel. Soon, PLO leaders became targets, including
top aides to Arafat in Tunis in 1991.

Besides the 1985 attacks on the El Al ticket counters in Rome
and Vienna, which killed nineteen people, ANO assassinated the
British cultural attaché in Athens, the British deputy high com-
missioner in Bombay, and a Jordanian diplomat in Ankara. In

1986, ANO gunmen killed twenty-two people during a hijacking of a Pan Am jumbo jet in Karachi. Before Osama bin Laden, Abu Nidal was the number one terrorist threat.

Like al Qaeda, ANO used sophisticated tradecraft, secure communications, and compartmentation to keep its operations secret. Because ANO recruited members through known family ties, penetration of the organization was difficult. To prove their loyalty, recruits had to a commit a murder or assault a rival group.

But a DO officer managed to recruit a key source within the ANO, and the analysts put together a comprehensive picture of the organization and its financial backers and arms suppliers. Clarridge decided the best way to deal with ANO was to expose these collaborators. With the approval of Secretary of State George Shultz, Clarridge had the State Department present countries that harbored ANO backers with démarches, the diplomatic equivalent of a demand. When the countries took no action, Clarridge arranged for the State Department to publicize the information in *The Abu Nidal Handbook*.

"The publication of our handbook had the desired effect," Clarridge said. "Governments in Europe squirmed, but they terminated their dealings with Abu Nidal."

With his financial empire under attack, Abu Nidal became paranoid. If a member of ANO reported being approached by the CIA, he would execute him. The CIA fed his paranoia by sowing rumors about members who were, in fact, loyal to Abu Nidal. The result was a bloodbath.

On one night in November 1987, Clarridge recalled, Abu Nidal ordered that 170 of his own members be tied up, blindfolded, and killed by machine gun. Abu Nidal killed another 160 of his members in Libya. Fearing he was crazy, his leadership began to plot against him. Soon, ANO vanished as a threat.

Eventually, Abu Nidal wound up in Iraq, where Saddam Hussein welcomed him as a fellow hater of the U.S. and Israel. In August 2002, at sixty-five, he died in his Baghdad apartment. The Iraqi government claimed he committed suicide by shooting himself in the mouth when security officers came to arrest him for entering the country illegally. But Jane's Terrorism Intelligence Center said Hussein feared that the terrorist would try to overthrow him and ordered him killed.

Now that Reagan's intelligence finding allowed it to participate in the capture of terrorists, the agency, under Clarridge's direction, worked with the FBI to bring Fawaz Younis to justice. Younis, a Lebanese used car dealer who reported directly to the leadership of the Shiite Amal militia, had commandeered a Royal Jordanian jet at Beirut International Airport on June 11, 1985. He overpowered its armed guards and ordered its pilots to fly him and his henchmen to Tunis so he could deliver a message to a meeting of the Arab League. When the plane was denied landing privileges, Younis forced the pilots to fly back to Beirut. After allowing the passengers and crew to leave, Younis had his fellow terrorists blow up the plane as he read a ringing statement on the need to expel Palestinians from Lebanon, his embattled homeland. Three Americans were among the passengers who were released unharmed.

In pursuing Younis, the CIA recruited his friend Jamal Hamdan to help entice him onto an eighty-one-foot yacht the agency had leased. Clarridge arranged to have the yacht, the *Skunk Kilo*, manned by members of the FBI's Hostage Rescue Team off the coast of Cyprus. At Clarridge's suggestion, two attractive bikini-clad female FBI agents joined the crew. When Younis stepped on board on February 13, 1987, agents slammed him to the deck and arrested him.

"He [Younis] confessed in the first thirty minutes we talked to him," said Oliver "Buck" Revell, the FBI agent who was on a larger Naval vessel commanding the operation. "We debriefed him over three days."

Younis was convicted of conspiracy, hostage taking, and air piracy. He is serving a term of thirty years at Leavenworth federal penitentiary in Kansas.

"The Counterterrorism Center represented a huge cultural change," said former DCI Gates, who was then chief of the DI. "Before, we issued analyses to policymakers about terrorist organizations. Now we were operational."

In December 1986 Casey was slated to testify under oath before the Senate Select Committee on Intelligence about his role in the Iran-contra affair. Casey had been stumbling more than usual, and he fell and cut his forehead. At 10 A.M. on December 15, a day before his scheduled testimony, Casey collapsed in his office as an agency doctor was taking his blood pressure.

Casey was taken to Georgetown University Hospital, where he had surgery three days later for a malignant brain tumor. Despite widespread skepticism within the agency and denials by Casey's widow Sophia, Casey had been able to speak haltingly at the hospital, as described in Bob Woodward's account in his book *Veil* of his bedside interview with the CIA chief. In his book, Woodward said he asked Casey in the hospital if he knew about the diversion of funds from the Iran arms deal to aid the contras, a question that has never been answered.

"His head jerked up hard," Woodward wrote. "He stared, and finally nodded yes."

"Why?" Woodward asked.

"I believed," Casey said, then fell asleep.

At the time, CIA officials denied that Woodward could have gotten past CIA security at the hospital. But William Donnelly, who was in charge of CIA administration, including supervision of the CIA security officers, told me, "Woodward probably found a way to sneak in."[105]

With little fanfare, Gates, then Casey's deputy, confirmed in his book that Casey could speak. On Saturday morning, January 24, 1987, Casey had one of his security guards place a call to Gates at the office. According to Gates' account, Casey got on the line and, with considerable difficulty, indicated that he wanted Gates to come see him. Gates followed up with Casey's wife, and she finally called on the morning of the 28th and asked Gates to come and see the director that evening.

Gates told me, "When I saw him in the hospital, his speech was even more slurred than usual, but if you knew him well, you could make out a few words, enough to get a sense of what he was saying. I briefed him on developments at the agency and the White House."[106]

When it became clear Casey was not going to recover, Gates brought Casey a resignation letter on January 29, 1987. Because he couldn't sign the letter, Casey handed it to Sophia to sign. She began to cry, and Casey had tears in his eyes.

"Well, that's the end of a career," Casey said to Gates."[107]

Gates held his hand for a few minutes and left. Casey died in May 1987 at the age of seventy-four.

After Woodward's *Veil* revealed a number of CIA secrets, the Senate Select Committee on Intelligence asked Britt Snider, its general counsel at the time, to look into the matter and advise the committee whether it should request that the Justice Department conduct a formal investigation. In examining Casey's calendar and CIA logs, Snider discovered that Casey, who had always demanded jail time for leakers, had had forty-three meetings or phone calls with Woodward, including a number of meetings at Casey's home with no one else present. With Casey dead, Snider decided it would be pointless to attempt to investigate the leaks presented in Woodward's book.[108]

11

To replace casey, President Ronald Reagan chose William H. Webster. A former prosecutor and appeals court judge, Webster was then FBI director. The Senate Select Committee on Intelligence voted unanimously to endorse his nomination after Webster, in an obvious reference to Casey's approach, promised he would be neither "devious" nor "cute" with the panel. On May 26, 1987, he became DCI, pledging "fidelity to the Constitution and the laws of our beloved country."

Webster was hardly a foreign policy expert, and he often confused "agent" with "officer." But he quickly put a stop to the games Casey had played with Congress, and he restored the CIA's credibility with the public.

"Webster was like night and day compared with Casey," said James McCullough, who was Webster's chief of staff as well as Casey's. "Webster was not well prepared for the job. I had to educate him. He was leery of being co-opted by the bureaucracy. He tended to cut himself off. But he learned the ropes, and he brought a reputation for integrity."[109]

Richard F. Stolz, one of the most admired officers in the DO and the CIA's first station chief in Moscow, had retired because of his disgust with Casey. Webster convinced him to return to head the DO.

"Webster said we need risk takers, not risk seekers," Stolz said.[110]

At the same time, Stolz recognized a need to tighten discipline in the DO. Occasionally CIA officers claimed they had recruited agents, but when they left a post and turned the agents over to a new officer, the agents would say they had never agreed to spy. The same kind of pressure to claim nonexistent recruitments led DO officers to accept as genuine, over a period of more than a decade, thirty-eight Cubans who turned out to be double agents. Major Florentino Aspillaga Lombard, who had worked in Cuban intelligence and defected to the CIA, revealed the deception to the CIA in 1988.

"We got promoted based on the number of assets recruited," said Colin R. Thompson, a former case officer. "It was quantity over quality. More than one case officer made his reputation on fabrication."[111]

Stolz began a program to validate assets.

As DCI, Webster had no patience with the winking and nodding that went on under Casey. Webster fired two employees involved in Iran-contra and disciplined seven others, demoted one, and reprimanded four. That was heresy in the Directorate of Operations (DO), long accustomed to fending off disciplinary action by virtue of its power and ability to persuade.

In a symbolic gesture, Webster moved all the agency's lawyers from a building in Rosslyn, Virginia, to headquarters. Under Casey, only Stanley S. Sporkin, his general counsel, and Sporkin's deputy had been in the main building. Webster more than doubled the number of lawyers to forty.

Unlike most of his predecessors, Webster believed that the CIA had an obligation to account to the American people for its activities. He brought in William M. Baker, who had served as his director of public and congressional affairs at the FBI, to give the press more access to the agency. Baker's directness and suave manner helped restore trust.

"I have to be fully informed so I can say 'no comment' with authority," Baker would quip.

But Webster still had to fight the CIA's culture of secrecy. While CIA officers selflessly commit themselves to living in a secret world where they will never gain recognition, simply knowing a secret is intoxicating, creating a sense of power and entitlement.

"It's prestigious to be in the black world and to know secrets," said Gene Poteat, the former high-ranking CIA scientific officer.

Because of the special conditions of their work, CIA people—especially DO officers—tended to keep to themselves. The secrecy and insularity often conspired to impel the CIA to try to keep secret things that should not be secret.

In late 1990, members of the CIA's Employee Activity Association decided that their store, on the ground floor of headquarters, should sell CIA commemorative mugs, T-shirts, and baseball hats. They pointed out that Cassel's Sports & Awards, a mile and a half away, did a booming business in the souvenirs. Why shouldn't CIA employees be able to buy the mugs at headquarters?

Each of the powers weighed in. The deputy director for administration, Raymond Huffstutler, opposed the mugs. The CIA's effectiveness depended on keeping a low profile. How could undercover officers take home CIA hats and shirts for their kids?

Richard Kerr, the agency's deputy director, had the same reservations. Self-advertisement went against the CIA's grain, he argued.

Others said undercover officers should not be working for the CIA if they were dumb enough to take home CIA mementos. It was an example of CIA paranoia. Anyone could buy the items in the center of McLean, Virginia.

The issue made its way up to the "seventh floor," an inside reference to the DCI's suite of offices, where Webster decided against selling the mugs. The controversy puzzled Webster. Covert employees were not supposed to identify themselves as being with the agency anyway. If they received awards from the CIA, they could not take them home until their retirement. Those who were not in covert capacities would be known to their families and friends as CIA employees. What was all the fuss about? But Webster was sensitive to tradition. If selling memorabilia went against past practice, it was not worth making an issue of it.

What Webster would not tolerate was the contemptuous approach Casey had had toward Congress. Holdovers from the Casey era compiled briefing books with sample questions and answers. The suggested answers gave a narrow response to the questions, avoiding possibly negative information.

"Well, judge, you don't want to say that. You can't say that," one CIA aide told him when discussing forthcoming testimony before a congressional committee. "Only say that if they ask that question."

That kind of attitude never failed to infuriate the former judge. He occasionally raised his voice with subordinates when he was mad. But to those who knew Webster, the most ominous sign was when his eyes became more steely blue than usual, and his lips became thinner, so that his mouth seemed to disappear. It happened a number of times as he made it clear he would not accept anything except complete and honest disclosure.

"He just couldn't stand the CIA's disdain for Congress," Nancy McGregor, one of Webster's assistants at the CIA, said. "He thought it was ridiculous, dated, not in the best interests of the agency, not smart, and not good government. He really believed that Congress was the elected representative of the people. He couldn't stand the grumbling about sharing information with Congress."

Webster found that the CIA's decision-making process was haphazard as well. Plans for undertaking covert action were approved rather informally, and the hard questions often were not addressed.

"Webster wanted the covert action proposals to be reviewed to make sure they would make sense to the American people if they were to be revealed," McGregor said. "It sounds simplistic, but if you think about it, this approach places good controls over the proposals. The people in the agency can't be the sole watchdogs because of the tendency to get too close to the programs. Webster's questions were: Would people understand why and how a particular program was being carried out, or would they say this is crazy, ludicrous, and how could our government be doing something like that?"

Above all, Webster was a lawyer, a man who wanted facts backed up and procedures followed. Too often he found that when he asked the source of a statement the answer was "Johnny Smith on the third floor told me." As a judge, first on the district court level and then on the appeals court level, his opinions had been replete with citations. He wanted the same documentation to back up reports at the CIA, and he established systematic procedures for approving covert action. Each covert action—roughly twelve at any given time—was to be listed in a briefing book with a two- or three-page description and an analysis of its purpose.

The DO was horrified. Somehow, the spies thought the listing, which was contained in a black three-ring binder, would increase the chances of leaks. But once the book became a fixture on Webster's desk, everyone wanted his own copy to enhance his status.

"Most directors are co-opted by the DO," said John C. Gannon, who was in charge of the DI. "Webster was not. He was straightforward, restored the rule of law, and led by example."[112]

Webster was a highly competitive tennis player who recognized that "tennis diplomacy" could win more support in Washington than the most eloquent testimony before congressional oversight committees. He played with everyone from George H. W. Bush, when Bush was vice president, to Katharine Graham, Alan Greenspan, and Zsa Zsa Gabor.

Despite his stern demeanor, Webster had a sense of humor, occasionally signing letters to friends "00-14," doubling James Bond's code number because he was the fourteenth director of Central Intelligence. One of Webster's most treasured possessions, given to him by an assistant at the FBI, was a two-foot-high brown bear dressed in judicial robes, tennis shoes, an FBI T-shirt, and pin-striped pants, its hands clutching a tennis racket.

Under Webster, the Counterterrorism Center began focusing on Peru's Sendero Luminoso, or Shining Path. Founded in 1970 by philosophy professor Abimael Guzman, the Shining Path was a Maoist group that tried to spread a Communist revolution. Guzman instilled religious zeal among his followers and convinced them that they would one day carry their revolution to the hated heart of capitalism, the United States.

At its peak, the Shining Path counted ten thousand fighters and controlled large swaths of Peru's countryside. During the 1980s, thirty thousand people died in the violence generated during a campaign of car bombings, political assassinations, and massacres of peasant communities that refused to support the rebels.

The Counterterrorism Center provided local police in Peru with money, training, and electronic surveillance equipment. Using those devices, the police tracked Guzman in September 1992 to a safehouse in a middle-class Lima suburb. Guzman was placed under arrest, and soon the movement lost its momentum.

Earlier, the Counterterrorism Center and the CIA's Office of Technical Service successfully traced to Libyan intelligence a fingernail-size piece of a green circuit board that was part of the Swiss MeBo MST-13 timing device that detonated a bomb that blew up Pan Am 103 over Lockerbie, Scotland. The plane exploded on December 21, 1988, killing all 259 passengers and crew members on board and eleven people on the ground. OTS matched the timing device to one the Libyans had planned to use in a terrorist operation preempted by the CIA in Senegal.

The coordinated approach proved so successful that Webster set up two additional centers to cut across CIA jurisdictional lines, one to combat narcotics and one to coordinate counterintelligence. The counternarcotics center collected information about narcotics trafficking so it could be used by law enforcement agencies to help obtain arrests and convictions. With the aid of satellites, the center tracked drug shipments on the high seas and pinpointed laboratories and fields where coca and other drug-related plants were grown. As part of the counternarcotics effort, the center tracked money-laundering transactions, intercepting electronic transmissions of bank account information.

12

___

THE COUNTERTERRORISM CENTER applied essentially the same techniques the CIA used to help win the cold war—recruiting agents, analyzing images from spy satellites, and intercepting communications. Critics said those methods would not work. How could American case officers who do not speak the local language penetrate terrorist groups? Even Reuel Marc Gerecht, a former CIA case officer who wrote a lengthy article on the subject in the July/ August 2001 *Atlantic Monthly,* seemed to think that the CIA's approach was flawed.

Focusing on the difficulties of operating in Pakistan, Gerecht said, "Even a Muslim CIA officer with native-language abilities (and the agency, according to several active-duty case officers, has very few operatives from Middle Eastern backgrounds) could do little more in this environment than a blond, blue-eyed all-American." Further, Gerecht wrote, "Case officers cannot long escape the embassies and consulates in which they serve. A U.S. official overseas, photographed and registered with the local intelligence and security services, can't travel much, particularly in a police-rich country like Pakistan, without the host services knowing about it. An officer who tries to go native, pretending to be a true-believing radical Muslim searching for brothers in the cause, will make a fool of himself quickly."

Gerecht quoted a former senior Near East Division operative as saying, "The CIA probably doesn't have a single truly qualified Arabic-speaking officer of Middle Eastern background who can play a believable Muslim fundamentalist who would volunteer to spend years of his life with shitty food and no women in the mountains of Afghanistan. For Christ's sake, most case officers live in the suburbs of Virginia. We don't do that kind of thing."

Gerecht's portrayal reflected a fundamental misunderstanding of how the DO operates. As when they penetrated the KGB, CIA case officers recruited agents who were either members of the target group or who could penetrate it. While case officers learned the local language, what was important was the quality of the native agents they recruited.

"No American case officer, even if he is an Arab who is a native Arabic speaker, is going to penetrate a terrorist cell overseas," said former CIA officer Herb Saunders. "The job is to find a local who is willing to penetrate the cell and tell you what is going on. That's done all the time."

Contrary to Gerecht's thesis, David Manners had no difficulty recruiting. A handsome slim man with luminous blue eyes, Manners grew up in western Massachusetts, where his father was a GE engineer and Manners was an Eagle Scout. After graduating from the U.S. Naval Academy, Manners joined the DO in 1980.

Manners took the usual training at Camp Peary, the CIA's training facility near Williamsburg, Virginia. Camp Peary, which purports to be a restricted military base, has tennis courts, an outdoor swimming pool, boats for fishing in a nearby river, and skeet and trap ranges. At Camp Peary, Manners learned the fine art of spying: how to spot, assess, recruit, and run agents.

Trainees learned through role playing. An instructor would pose as a potential agent, and an officer would try to recruit him or her. In a typical exercise, a CIA employee pretending to be an agent arranged to meet a female officer who was a trainee in a movie theater. During the movie, he placed his hand on her dress and tried to kiss her. The female officer objected. The man persisted. She got up and left. A subsequent critique marked her down for not making plans to get in touch with him again.

Officers were taught to look for clues signaling a target's vulnerability—money problems, a grievance against his agency, or a drinking problem. To sharpen recruitment skills, a tough former Marine, for example, might be told to recruit an instructor posing as a gay man. Above all, officers were taught to do whatever was necessary to protect the life of an agent.

Like other officers, Manners took courses in the detection of explosives, surveillance and countersurveillance, how to write reports, and how to shoot a variety of weapons. Since Manners took his training, Tenet overhauled the curriculum and facilities. To attract the best instructors, he promised them good overseas assignments after doing a tour at the Farm. Now trainees are taught how to run counterterrorism, counternarcotics, and paramilitary operations.

Manners had a soft way about him, and he looked people straight in the eye, establishing trust. He was the kind of person you would want to have a beer with. Eventually, with CIA training, he would speak Polish, Czech, and French; he already knew German. Manners rose through the ranks. After serving in Warsaw he became station chief in Prague.

"He practically got everything they had," said Janine Brookner, who was in charge of the Czechoslovakia Branch.

Eventually Manners became station chief in Amman. In that job Manners directed the recruitment of agents in al Qaeda and in the Iraqi intelligence service.

To recruit a spy, "You have to understand what makes a guy tick and how to manipulate him," he said. "What are his problems—his wife, girlfriend, boss, money? You become the friend he doesn't have. You feed his ego. You agree that his boss is unfair. Then you plant a seed. Perhaps he needs money for private school for his kids. You say, 'I can help.' The process of recruitment can take years. It's not overly complicated. It's all about manipulating people, gaining their trust, finding out what makes them tick, and using them to get the information we want."

If Manners wanted to recruit the aide to a top government official, for example, he would learn everything he could about him, starting with information in agency files.

"I would find out who his kids are, what schools they go to, who his friends are," Manners said. "Perhaps I knew one of the friends, who could make an introduction. If I met with him, I would try to find out what his problems were. Perhaps he is having trouble paying for private school for his kids. We can help. Or his boss is abusive. I would sympathize. You have to appear to be trustworthy. They put their lives in your hands."

Once an asset accepted money, he was compromised. To ensure that he was not spotted meeting with an asset, Manners would spend up to eight hours darting into alleys or having his wife drive him through the country. While he never used it, Manners had a Jack-in-the-Box, a dummy created by CIA disguise experts to resemble him so that he could jump out of a car and leave the dummy in his place on the front seat.

Often, the CIA used operatives from Arab intelligence services like those of Jordan, Syria, and Egypt and other countries to infiltrate bin Laden's organization. They not only developed intelligence but sowed suspicion so that members of the group would kill each other.

"Egyptians, Jordanians, Palestinians penetrated the bin Laden organization for us," a longtime CIA officer said. "It's b.s. that we didn't."

Such liaison with foreign intelligence and law enforcement agencies remained one of the agency's secrets. While these services could be a target of the CIA, they could also be one of its greatest assets. In return for help, the CIA provided them with money, equipment, and intelligence on their adversaries. Over the years, the Jordanians, for example, relied on the CIA to alert them to plots against the king. Over time, the Jordanians became so good at the intelligence game that they were better at detecting plots than the CIA.

In developing assets within al Qaeda, Manners had to be prepared for the possibility that the agent might be tasked to carry out an assassination or bombing. In that case, the CIA might make it look as if the asset had been killed. A decomposed body, with I.D. from the asset planted in its clothes, might be used for the purpose.

The other misconception perpetrated by former CIA officer Gerecht and others was that CIA officers who had diplomatic immunity and were assigned to embassies were useless because they were followed. The Soviets were the best at conducting surveillance. To help track CIA officers, they sprinkled "spy dust" in the American embassy in Moscow. No doubt applied by the Soviets working in the embassy, the dust was a chemical known as NPPD, combined with luminol. As pieced together by the intelligence agencies, the Soviets used the dust to spot Soviets who might be in contact with the CIA. If a suspect had shaken hands with a CIA officer or touched the same doorknob, the dust would rub off on his hands and transfer to his belongings. The Soviets applied a chemical to the desk, filing cabinets, or steering wheel of the suspect. On contact, the chemical made the spy dust turn pink, signaling that the suspect had had unauthorized contacts with CIA officers. The Soviets might then set up video cameras to try to catch the suspect in the act of stealing secret documents.

While Middle Eastern countries were generally not as aggressive, most conducted surveillance of CIA officers. For many years, Israel broke into apartments of CIA officers, just as the French entered hotel rooms to steal secrets from American businessmen.

"We let the Israelis get away with murder," a former CIA officer said. "They followed us in Tel Aviv, entered our homes, and conducted surveillance. We caught them breaking in."

A CIA officer with diplomatic immunity might throw off surveillance by wearing a disguise to make himself look like a lower-ranking embassy employee. When the officer left the embassy looking like the communications officer, local security services likely would not follow him. Besides using officers attached to embassies, the CIA has always used officers who visit countries briefly to conduct their mission. In addition, the CIA used perhaps a hundred officers who are NOCs—those who lacked diplomatic cover and posed as businessmen, scientists, or taxi drivers. Thus, they had no apparent connection with an embassy.

Contrary to Gerecht's implication, "There was no shortage of Arabic speakers in the CIA," Manners said.

At one point Manners recruited an Iraqi who told him about Saddam Hussein's weapons of mass destruction program. When the man's boss threatened to return him to Baghdad for some minor infraction, Manners decided to remove the boss. Manners and several other CIA officers met with the boss in his apartment and offered him $100,000. The encounter was videotaped, and the officers—all wearing disguises—stated they were with the CIA. If the man had taken the money, they would have sent the videotape to his superiors to show that the CIA had compromised him. Iraq would then have removed him, allowing the CIA's prized asset to operate freely without interference from his boss.

When the boss spurned the money, Manners arranged for the Jordanian intelligence service to try to recruit him. The man reported the overture and—because it meant his identity as an Iraqi intelligence officer had been uncovered—the Iraqis sent him home. Manners had succeeded in removing the man as a threat. The Iraqi recruit continued to spy for the agency.

Manners did not think the CIA discriminated against women. However, because of the position of women in Arab societies, using a female CIA officer to recruit a male was usually pointless.

"Talented women can't succeed in the Middle East," he said. "Arabs say they want to go to bed with them."

"In Saudi Arabia women aren't allowed to drive a car," said Janet Lofgren, a former CIA case officer. Although she had a successful recruitment record in other countries and cultures, she did not disagree with the agency's reluctance to send women to countries such as Saudi Arabia.

"The job is tough enough already. If you're two or three steps behind, you're at a distinct disadvantage," she said. "You can have meetings, but recruitment is difficult. We have to send people who have the best chance of success."

While it's assumed that sexual attraction may play a role in recruitment of agents, CIA officers are not supposed to have sex with their agents. But some do.

As a pretty, green-eyed blonde, Lofgren occasionally encountered both CIA officials and agents who tried to take liberties or did not take her seriously. In one case, headquarters dismissed her belief that a Chinese intelligence officer wanted to defect, saying he was merely making a sexual advance. Fending off agents was sometimes more difficult.

"I had a high-level agent," she told me. "I worked with him for two years. At our last meeting in a car, he reached over and grabbed both my breasts. He said, 'I always wanted to do that.'"

"I'm glad you got that out of your system," she responded sarcastically.

Lofgren said she had to handle the situation carefully "so as not to jeopardize the CIA's relationship with an important source." She added, "It doesn't make much difference whether the case officer is male or female. Sexual attraction occurs occasionally, because you're meeting clandestinely, often in cars late at night or in safehouses. The relationship is intimate, even though physical intimacy is rarely involved and is against the rules. The agent's life is in your hands. You're conspiring together. There are elements of danger, risk taking, excitement, and secrecy. How could it not be intimate?"

The OSS employed 4,500 women who served in every position from code clerk to spy, and many of them joined the CIA. Eloise Page, who began as Donovan's secretary in the OSS and became an OSS and CIA case officer, rose to become station chief in Athens. It was the first time a female officer had headed a major station.

Page was an unlikely spy. A debutante, she was born in Richmond, Virginia. Her family traced its roots to Colonel John Page, a founder of the city of Williamsburg who arrived there from England in 1650. Page gave her first piano recital at the age of eleven. After attending Hollins College in Roanoke, she graduated from the Peabody School of Music in Baltimore, thinking she would become a pianist. When Page's mother learned she had become a spy, she asked, "Isn't that a strange profession?" Cecil Wray Page, her cousin, recalled.

At one point, the CIA wanted Page to head a new technology unit to be called the Scientific Operations Branch. "I'll be damned if I'll be the chief SOB," she said. The agency renamed the branch for her.

When she was station chief in Athens, Page packed a gun, a precaution necessitated by the fact that a predecessor, Richard Welch, had been assassinated three years earlier. Like the rest of the CIA's officers, she received acknowledgment only within the agency, which promoted her to one of the highest levels of the DO and gave her a coveted Trailblazer Award on the agency's fiftieth anniversary. Never married, she told her family she was a State Department officer.

Besides the CIA and her church, Page was devoted to her dogs. When one of them, a Golden Retriever named Lionel, died, Page had a local veterinarian freeze him until the ground thawed. She then had him buried in the side yard of her home in Georgetown.

"She had two Episcopalian priests do the service," said Paul Redmond, the CIA's counterintelligence chief, who dug the grave with another CIA officer.

"I didn't care about public acknowledgment," Page told me in her room at Sibley Memorial Hospital after undergoing hip and knee surgery. "I did it because I believed in what I was doing."

At the hospital, Page asked if I wanted a drink. Pointing to a corner of her hospital closet, she directed me to a bottle of Dry Sack sherry concealed from the nurses.

Like Page, Janine Brookner was a pioneer, becoming the first female station chief in Latin America. In one Asian country, she recruited seven key assets in two years, including a government official who saw everything that the chief of state saw. In a South American country, she got a government official to give her secret reports on the country's reserves and oil production.[113]

"She was amazingly successful," George Kalaris, her station chief, said. "She was one of the best officers I had."

But Brookner's career came to a screeching halt when she became chief of station in Jamaica in 1989. Brookner commanded twenty people. She had a helicopter for tracking drug traffickers and a variety of weapons at her disposal. She lived in a tropical house with a swimming pool about ten minutes from the embassy. She had a mongrel dog, Shaughnessy, and a goat. A radio in her bedroom linked her to the CIA station.

By Brookner's account, trouble began after she took action to discipline employees involved in improper behavior. They, in turn, alleged that the blonde, blue-eyed Brookner had engaged in inappropriate conduct, including excessive drinking and being sexually provocative with underlings. Soon, Fred Hitz, the inspector general, launched an investigation. Hitz recommended a reprimand, which she got. It would have meant no promotions for at least two years.

Instead of accepting that, Brookner retained Victoria Toensing, an aggressive former deputy assistant attorney general, to sue the CIA. Hitz, a Princeton and Harvard Law School graduate who had been in the DO, thought the CIA should litigate the case. But Woolsey decided to recommend to the Justice Department that the government reach a settlement with Brookner. Woolsey came to that conclusion after it turned out that one of Hitz's investigators had scribbled disparaging comments in the margins of interviews and reports. One comment referred to Brookner, who is petite, as "Roseanne." Another referred to her as "nurse Jekyll and Mrs. Hyde."

At the least, the comments were unprofessional. At worse, they displayed a bias against her. Toensing and Brookner also obtained an affidavit from a person the investigators said was one of Brookner's principal accusers, saying he had never made such claims and, in fact, had never been interviewed. The government settled for $410,000, plus Toensing's legal fees and expenses of $265,167.

Brookner left the agency and went to law school, becoming a successful lawyer. Her case was widely portrayed as an illustration of the DO's antifemale bias—the CIA's old boy network ganging up on a female officer. In fact, a group of CIA women who alleged sexual discrimination at the agency won a settlement of just under $1 million. But the fact is that the DO did not turn against Brookner and, after she won her case, Thomas A. Twetten, a former head of the DO, and Milton Bearden, who headed the Soviet division, appeared on ABC's *Nightline* to defend her.

The Brookner case became a "star chamber process," Twetten said. She had no choice but to resign, he said. "She was driven to it by [the] inspector general."[114]

On the same show, Gates, who had agreed as DCI to the reprimand of Brookner, said he now realized that the evidence against her was "not complete or that there were serious flaws in the investigation." This "clearly suggests that the original case in the agency was unfair," he said.

"Being in the CIA was an adventure," Brookner told me. "But it was clear after I had sued the agency that I had no future."

———

Like most CIA officers, Dave Manners felt discouraged after Woolsey, then Deutch, became DCI. "After the fall of the Soviet Union we were looking for aggressive leadership," Manners said. "The Soviets were the north star. We had things that needed to be done, but there was a lack of purpose. After Ames, we had outsiders telling us how bad we were. We were presumed to be guilty. A lot of people in the CIA believed it. Every decision was pushed up within headquarters. This started under Woolsey and continued under Deutch."[115]

By definition, DO officers must be risk-takers. Manners saw himself as a man whom people counted on to get the job done.

"We are the brotherhood," Manners said. "We are the ones who really do it."

The negativism from Washington grated on Manners and other spies. To them, the rule requiring special approval to recruit assets with human rights problems symbolized just how risk averse and purposeless the agency had become.

"You said to yourself, why bother with recruiting assets with human rights problems because I'm going to have to paper them to death," Manners said. "Officers said that it's easier not to. We paralyzed ourselves."

After Tenet took over, Manners felt more support. "Anything I needed I received," he said.

As a station chief, Manners was making $100,000 a year, compared with $70,000 for a case officer. Overseas, he had a free house and sometimes a car. But it would take time for Tenet's more aggressive approach to have an effect. Manners had had enough of the bureaucracy and second-guessing.

"As station chief, I spent more time filling out goddam reports on things that had nothing to do with operations," Manners said. "Why would I want to rise in the organization? To be humiliated, punished, maybe indicted?"

In 1998, after twenty-five years with the CIA and the U.S. government, Dave Manners took advantage of an early retirement program and left the agency at the age of forty-four.

13

Ever since the Aldrich H. Ames case came to light the FBI had been pushing for more control over the CIA's security and counterintelligence efforts. In 1994 the FBI assigned Edward Curran, a top FBI counterintelligence agent, to oversee investigations of possible espionage cases within the CIA. Because the FBI is the only agency with the authority to conduct espionage investigations, it could supersede the CIA's internal efforts.

As chief of the Special Investigative Unit under the Counterespionage Group, Curran was shocked to find that CIA polygraphers had concluded that three hundred employees either failed their tests or had inconclusive results. Yet no investigations had been done to determine if any of them was, in fact, a spy. One of those who failed was one of the CIA's highest-ranking officers.

"The mentality was, if you failed it, nothing would happen," Curran said. "And everyone knew that."

Many of the questions that raised red flags were unrelated to espionage—cheating on taxes or child abuse. But other questions related to espionage. On the FBI's recommendation, the CIA changed the tests to focus only on a few questions relevant to spying.

One of the officers who had come up inconclusive on the polygraph was Harold J. Nicholson, a former CIA station chief in Bucharest. The CIA ignored the finding, but later a defector revealed that Nicholson had been working for the Russians since 1994, when he completed a tour of duty as deputy chief of the CIA station in Malaysia. He was subsequently assigned to the CIA's training center at Camp Peary. When he came under suspicion, the CIA moved him to a position where he could be watched.

While Nicholson was at work in August 1996, FBI agents picked the lock of his Chevrolet Lumina van in the agency's parking lot. They found a personal notebook computer and copied the contents of its hard drive. On it were files that had been deleted from directories but still could be retrieved. Presumably, Nicholson had already provided the SVR—the successor to the KGB—with copies of the documents on a diskette. The files included information he had no reason to have: details of a planned assignment of one of his trainees to Moscow, biographical and assignment information on CIA personnel, and a secret report on Chechyna. In Nicholson's office, agents found forty documents relating to Russia, including some classified TOP SECRET/CODEWORD, a category beyond top secret.

In November 1996 FBI surveillance videotapes caught Nicholson copying documents under his desk with a CIA camera. He had torn off their classified markings. The FBI also watched as Nicholson made contact, on a trip to Singapore, with his Russian handlers in the back seat of a Russian embassy car. Back home, the FBI found unexplained cash deposits in his bank accounts.

As it turned out, Nicholson told the Russians the identities of every CIA case officer trained between 1994 and 1996. He also gave them a summary of debriefings of Aldrich Ames after his guilty plea. Over a two-year period Nicholson received $120,000 from the Russians. When FBI agents arrested him on November 16, 1996, boarding a flight to Switzerland, Nicholson was carrying rolls of film with images of top secret CIA documents.

The CIA issued a cover story to suggest that Nicholson had been caught because he failed a polygraph test. The truth was just the opposite: The CIA had done nothing when Nicholson came up inconclusive.

Nicholson pleaded guilty and was sentenced to twenty-three years and seven months in prison. He was the highest-ranking CIA officer ever charged with espionage. Thus, between Ames and Nicholson, the CIA appeared to be a disaster. Yet the FBI had its own mole in Robert Hanssen. While Ames caused the deaths of more agents, Hanssen, arrested in February 2001, did the greatest damage to U.S. intelligence operations of any spy in U.S. history. Among the items he gave up was the U.S. plan for continuing the government in the event of a nuclear attack.

"We should have been looking at our own," Curran said. "Everyone was dragging the CIA through the mud, but there was also arrogance by the FBI."

In establishing an FBI presence at the CIA, Curran had to overcome tremendous bureaucratic resistance.

"When I came in, the CIA said, 'We'll have a committee decide whether to refer a case to the FBI.' I said, 'Time out. I decide what goes to the FBI.'"

Paul Redmond, who was in charge of counterintelligence, wanted Curran to clear investigations with him.

"Redmond investigated the spy who turned out to have been Aldrich Ames for almost eight years and never caught him," Curran said. "He had analysts who were good at analyzing, but they had no investigative sense. When the Ames case broke, the CIA needed a hero, so they chose Redmond, who claimed he and his analysts had solved the case. They didn't," Curran said, referring to the CIA agent code-named AVENGER who actually broke open the case with the help of Redmond's analysts and the FBI.

When Tenet took over as deputy DCI, Curran got full support.

"There was a lot of resistance to our investigations, but Tenet was outstanding," Curran said. "He had biweekly meetings to review ongoing cases. He got involved. He knew what was going on. If it weren't for Tenet, we would have been in trouble."[116]

He also established far greater cooperation with overseas FBI agents, called legats.

"Tenet addressed the legats when they came to Washington," said an FBI agent who was a legat. "He developed an atmosphere that said, 'This is not just our information. It's yours as well.' They gave our counterterrorism sources protection and did countersurveillance when we met with them overseas."

When Curran learned that Deutch had approved a plan to buy off Douglas F. Groat's silence when he threatened to reveal some of the agency's most sensitive secrets, Curran could not believe that anyone could be that foolish.

Groat joined the agency in 1980 after being a captain in the Army and a police officer. At the time the agency was emphasizing hiring police officers. If the CIA had properly checked his background, the agency likely would not have hired him. Unlike their superiors who recommended him, Groat's fellow police officers in Glenville, New York, described him as a strange man who kept what he called logs, noting if their shoes were scuffed or their ties askew. Groat ticketed volunteer firemen for using emergency lights during a drill. The town fired Groat for allegedly mistreating a prisoner, but a court reinstated him.

"This guy was twisted," said Sergeant Daniel Moffett, a Glenville officer for twenty-seven years. "He went beyond the pale."

In August 1982, Groat was assigned to the CIA's Systems Procurement Group, which breaks into embassies overseas to steal codes. At the time, the unit consisted of ten officers who worked in a one-story building entirely devoted to the operation. Near Franconia, Virginia, the building had no sign. Those who worked there called it "The Shop."

Before an operation took place, the break-in artists would engage in careful surveillance of the target, often wearing disguises. They determined what security was in place, whether anyone was in a building at night or on weekends, and what cover stories could be developed in case they were caught. If the building had a video surveillance system, they would develop ways to freeze the pictures so they would not be spotted. The preparations took six to eighteen months. Often, agents recruited by the local station helped, giving them keys to the embassies or inside information on security measures. The CIA might also arrange to have the power to the embassy turned off or might turn in a fire alarm so that those in the embassy would evacuate.

During Groat's nine years in that job, he assisted in sixty break-ins and actually entered six embassies. No one was caught, and the CIA obtained codes almost every time.

Groat's troubles at the CIA began in 1989 when a new boss took over and initiated new policies. It made sense to have the same officers who were to break in conduct the security survey. They were the experts, and they were the ones who would be caught if something went wrong. But the new chief, with his eye on the budget, decided that there was no need to send "black bag" experts to case a location: local CIA officers could conduct surveillance. Groat argued with his boss to no avail.

One weekend in 1991, Groat and his colleagues entered an Asian embassy that was located in another Asian country. They found that a maid and security officer were in the building. While the break-in artists were able to steal the codes and evade the security officer and the maid, Groat blamed his chief for not allowing his team to conduct proper surveillance that would have established that the building was occupied on weekends. The preparation was sloppy and the operation had almost been compromised. Anyone caught in such a situation could be shot. Groat tried to complain to higher authorities. His chief told him to keep quiet.

According to a source familiar with the subsequent investigations, "Groat blamed the CIA, probably correctly, for not planning the operation well. Groat complained and, instead of addressing his complaint properly, the CIA transferred him in October 1991 to a job doing nothing."

In late 1992, the CIA learned that an embassy penetration, which Groat had been involved in, had been compromised. The CIA's tape of intercepted, coded communications to and from the embassy—a European embassy of an Asian country—had simply stopped. Because of the way the system stopped, the CIA knew that the embassy had learned that it was penetrated.

The CIA asked Groat and other officers to submit to lie detector tests. Groat refused to take one. While debating his fate, the agency continued for three years to pay him to report to a desk in an office in Rosslyn, which infuriated him even more. Usually, he left soon after arriving and went to a nearby health club.

In their defense, CIA officials cited the case of Edward Lee Howard, a CIA officer who was trained to go to Moscow but turned out to have a drinking and a drug problem. Howard told a CIA officer he had been thinking of giving information to the Soviets. After he had learned many of the secrets of the CIA's Moscow station, the CIA abruptly fired him. Howard then contacted the Soviets and spilled the beans, ultimately defecting to Moscow. Howard died in 2002 at the age of fifty, when he fell and broke his neck on steps in his dacha outside Moscow.

"We should never have hired Howard, and we should never have fired him as we did," said Burton Gerber, who became chief of the Soviet division after Howard's firing.[117]

In 1993, the CIA put Groat on administrative leave with pay. As the agency let him dangle, Groat traveled around the country in a motor home, leaving phone numbers where the CIA or FBI could call him. He denied to the FBI that he knew anything about the compromised embassy penetration in Europe, and the bureau decided it did not have enough evidence to charge him. But the FBI found he had taken home classified documents, including those listing his activities and complaints. Groat kept the papers—a stack a foot high—in his garage at his home in Manassas, Virginia.

In October 1996 the CIA finally fired Groat, and Groat decided to extort the agency. A handsome man with large muscles and blue eyes, Groat told me that he put it to the CIA this way: "I have no income. I have nothing to offer but what I learned while at the agency. You leave me with no other choice but to use what I have learned while working at the agency to make a living." He later told the CIA that he wanted to become a security consultant to foreign countries.[118]

Because many of the embassies Groat had penetrated were

those of friendly countries, the CIA was particularly anxious to keep the Groat case quiet.

"He had the jewels," said a CIA source. "He knew about penetrations, bugs, codes, everything."

Incredibly, the CIA fell for Groat's scheme. The agency began to negotiate a "contract" that would pay him $50,000 a year for five years, attorney fees, and a full retirement. Groat countered with a request for $1 million.

"They said they could work out something," Groat said. "I gave them a deadline. It was my idea of bringing things to a head."

On March 24, 1997, James W. Zirkle, a CIA associate general counsel, faxed Groat a "contract proposal" outlining the offer of $50,000 a year until Groat was eligible to retire. "It is my understanding," Zirkle wrote, "that you will, through your attorney, make a written proffer concerning information you are prepared to provide us to resolve all outstanding issues regarding the compromise of the sensitive operation that has been the subject of our ongoing counterintelligence investigation." Zirkle said the deal would include a grant of immunity from prosecution, subject to the Justice Department's approval.

The deal, approved by Deutch before he left, reflected the CIA's old mentality, which accepted the proposition that the end justifies the means. It was a dangerous precedent. The comparison with the Howard case was specious. There was a difference between easing the transition from the agency for an employee who had personal problems and caving to an extortion demand from an employee who implicitly threatened to give up classified information.

"When you were in a sensitive position and had sensitive information and threatened to use it, that was the practice: to give them a golden parachute," Curran said. "Groat knew that. He had a lot of information, and they made a deal. Previously, there were warning signs about Groat, and no one took any action. If there was no prosecution, the CIA's dirty linen would not come out."[119]

Yet the CIA's offer was not good enough. Groat noted that the payments could stop if he failed to comply with all the terms of the agreement, including submitting to polygraph examinations. The offer did not require that he pass the tests, but Groat worried about what would happen if he failed. So Groat wrote letters to the security supervisors of thirteen consulates in San Francisco. Saying that his job with the agency had been to "gain access to extremely sensitive information from crypto systems of select foreign countries," Groat informed the embassies, "your country was one of my targets."

While Groat said he would not discuss "when or where I may have been able to gain access to information on your country during my employment with the agency," Groat offered to "upgrade the security of your crypto systems" as a security consultant. The consulates included those of South Korea and several western European nations. Over the course of two days, beginning on March 26, Groat delivered the letters to the consulates. Connie Boggs, his girlfriend then, drove. She knew nothing about what he was doing. Groat subsequently mailed similar letters to four embassies in Washington.

"I was tired of being stalled by the CIA," Groat said.

Some of the embassies turned over the letters to the FBI, which had observed Groat during routine surveillance. The FBI found Groat's fingerprints on a CIA directory listing the addresses of the embassies he visited. Disclosing to foreign countries that they were Groat's targets alone violated espionage laws, which prohibit disclosing classified information to agents of a foreign power. Yet the CIA continued to negotiate with Groat, who said in a letter that while the talks over money continued he would "suspend any and all actions that may interfere with agency intelligence gathering activities."[120] When Tenet became DCI in July 1997, he put a stop to the outrageous negotiations.

"George Tenet stopped the payment that Deutch was going to give Groat," Fred Hitz, the inspector general, said.[121]

On April 3, 1998, the FBI arrested Groat, who was then fifty. He was charged with one count of attempting to extort $1 million from the CIA in exchange for not disclosing to foreign governments how the U.S. intercepted their secret communications. Groat pointed out that he informed the FBI in October 1997, when agents searched his motor home, that he had met with foreign governments to offer his expertise in the field of crypto security. He blamed the CIA for trying to silence him when he complained about the sloppiness that led to the near compromise of the operation back in the summer of 1991.

As part of a plea bargain, Groat was sentenced on September 27, 1998 to five years in jail. He admitted trying to extort $1 million from the CIA in exchange for not revealing secrets. As part of the bargain, prosecutors dropped four additional counts of espionage, including two that could have carried the death penalty.[122]

Groat was in federal prison for four years and was released in August 2002. He now does landscaping for a development where he lives with his second wife, Aleta, whom he met when she was his case manager at the Federal Prison Camp in Cumberland, Maryland.

Despite his plea in court, Groat told me he did nothing wrong. "It was all because some people at the agency were irritated with me," Groat said. He is incensed that he could have retired at the age of fifty, but will now receive retirement benefits based on lower salary levels when he turns sixty-two.

"They still owe me," he said.

In court, Ronald L. Walutess Jr., the assistant U.S. attorney who prosecuted the case, said Groat had found "the perfect extortion method."

Perfect, that is, if the subject of the extortion is a willing victim. To former spy prosecutor John Martin, who had retired from the Justice Department before Groat was arrested, the CIA's negotiations with Groat illustrated just how out of touch with reality the agency could be.

Martin was in a unique position to evaluate the agency's actions. Among the seventy-six spy prosecutions he supervised were those of Navy warrant officer John A. Walker Jr., FBI Agent Earl E. Pitts, Israeli spy Jonathan Jay Pollard, and CIA officers Harold J. Nicholson and Aldrich Ames. Only one of the prosecutions he supervised resulted in an acquittal; all the other defendants went to jail or were exchanged. During his twenty-five years as chief spy catcher, no one ever suggested that Martin acted unethically, improperly, or illegally.

"I'm a firm believer in giving spies their full constitutional rights—then sending them to jail for as long as possible," Martin would say.

As part of his job, Martin had the highest security clearances the U.S. could bestow, clearances so secret they were referred to only by initials. They included TK, for Talent Keyhole, which gave him access to information about spy satellites; M, which was the first initial of a code word for sensitive covert operations; SI for signal intelligence, which gave him access to intercepted and decoded communications from NSA; Byeman, which related to satellite reconnaissance and material from the National Reconnaissance Office; and Q, which was issued by the Energy Department and allowed access to information about nuclear weapons. With the clearances, so long as he felt he had a need to know, Martin had the authority to look at practically any file of the FBI, CIA, NSA, State Department, Defense Department, or White House. In addition, as a member of the Justice Department's Departmental Review Committee, Martin saw the documents that were considered too sensitive to release under the Freedom of Information Act.

"The fact that the CIA was willing to negotiate with an extortionist was outrageous," Martin said. Yet the negotiations fit a pattern. "The CIA never wanted to have a trial because it would mean publicly revealing that the CIA had been penetrated or an employee had gone over to the other side, embarrassing the agency," Martin said. "Usually, the CIA's own deficiencies contributed to the problem. So the easiest thing was to cover it up by not prosecuting. If we took that attitude with bank robberies, we would have one every minute. The CIA could tolerate espionage. It could not tolerate exposing how it happened," Martin said.

Over the years, Martin repeatedly battled the CIA when he wanted to prosecute employees who had become traitors and the agency wanted simply to cover up what had happened. The best example was the case of William Kampiles, who was a watch officer assigned to analyze incoming traffic at the CIA's Operations Center.

Kampiles had sold a top secret manual for the KH-11 surveillance satellite to an agent of the GRU—the Soviet military intelligence service—in Athens. The manual revealed the workings of the sixty-four-foot-long satellite and its capabilities. The satellite tricked the Soviets by transmitting its real time data to other satellites instead of back down to earth as expected. The result was the Soviets did not realize it was a photographic satellite and did not try to conceal weapons or military operations while it passed overhead. Kampiles, twenty-three, got $3,000 for the manual; he could have easily received at least $3 million.

The FBI learned about the case in 1977 from Sergei T. Bokhan, a GRU officer who defected from Athens. As is often the case, the FBI issued a cover story to conceal the fact that a defector had given up Kampiles. The cover story was that Kampiles had written a letter to an agency employee mentioning frequent meetings with a Soviet official in Athens.

When Kampiles returned to the U.S., Martin authorized the FBI to interview him. He told the agents to take a copy of the KH-11 manual with them to show Kampiles. That way, if Kampiles confessed, the agents could have Kampiles initial each page of the manual to demonstrate that he had given it up.

Sure enough, Kampiles confessed to giving up the manual. He claimed his objective was to become a double agent for the CIA, a common defense by those charged with espionage. As Martin instructed, the agents had Kampiles initial the pages of the manual. On his authority the FBI arrested Kampiles in August 1978.

Despite his confession, Kampiles pleaded not guilty. Martin assured the CIA that during a trial the agency's secrets would be protected. As in a previous case involving Andrew Daulton Lee and Christopher Boyce, any sensitive information could be presented to the judge in an *ex parte* submission.

"That was not good enough for the CIA," Martin said. "The agency wanted either no prosecution or prosecution with such unrealistic restrictions that Kampiles would never have been convicted. CIA officials felt the judicial system should bend for them. The CIA had many dedicated, intelligent, sophisticated, and patriotic people, but I wondered if some CIA officers appreciated the constitutional system they were so zealously committed to defending." Bureaucrats in charge of secrets often go into denial when those secrets leak out, Martin said. "Somehow, they think that if they can control any further disclosure, they have managed to contain the secrets. Meanwhile, back in Moscow, the KGB was laughing at our poor security and making more and more inroads into our defense and intelligence operations."

Ultimately, Griffin Bell, the attorney general, had to take the issue to President Jimmy Carter, who overrode CIA objections. Despite the problems, Martin obtained the conviction of Kampiles, who got forty years.

"We introduced the KH-11 manual into evidence. The judge and jury saw the manual, but later we had it sealed from public view," Martin said. "It showed you can do two things at once: convict the spy and protect the secrets."

14

———

ORIGINALLY HIGHWAY SIGNS marked the location of the CIA along George Washington Memorial Parkway in Virginia, but Robert F. Kennedy, who was attorney general and lived nearby at the family's Hickory Hill estate, asked the CIA to take them down.

"Bobbie Kennedy said, 'This is the silliest thing I've seen. Please take the signs down,'" William Colby, the former DCI, told me before he died in 1996. "We pretended that the building wasn't there, even though every pilot used it as a checkpoint going down [to National Airport]."[123]

When James R. Schlesinger became director of Central Intelligence in 1973, he asked Colby why the CIA had no signs. Colby told him the story.

"I think we should have signs," Schlesinger said.

After Schlesinger checked with the White House, the signs went back up. Today highway signs along Dolley Madison Boulevard and George Washington Parkway clearly point to the CIA or the George Herbert Walker Bush Intelligence Center.

While the CIA is said to be in Langley, Virginia, no such town exists. Langley once had its own post office inside a country store. By 1910 the village had been merged into nearby McLean, named for John R. McLean, then the publisher of the *Washington Post* and the principal stockholder in an electric rail line that linked the area with Washington. Because of the rail line there was no need for a separate village so close to McLean. The Langley post office was closed.

On a map the CIA's 225.5-acre compound looks like a giant weather balloon, with its top jutting toward the northeast just below a crook in the Potomac River. The mouth of the balloon forms the entrance to the compound.

Where the CIA's new and old buildings meet is a rectangular courtyard dotted with black plastic picnic tables. In one corner of the courtyard is a major part of an installation by Washington artist Jim Sanborn, who was chosen through a competition of two hundred entrants. It took Sanborn two years to create the work, which included three other pieces within the courtyard and at the entrance to the new building. The cost of the project, called "Kryptos," was $250,000.

The main piece was a sculpture that stands more than six feet high and looks like a scroll. Constructed over a pool of water, it is made of petrified wood, granite, red slate, green quartz, and copper. Letters carved in a curved copper plate at the right of the installation represent a table that can be used to decipher a text cut into the plate at the top left. The text can be deciphered only by using the table and a key word, which is "kryptos."

Sanborn composed the secret message with the help of a fiction writer. The combined messages are said to describe the information-gathering role of the CIA. At the unveiling of the art work in November 1990, the artist gave Webster, as the then DCI, a deciphered copy of the text. Jim Gillogly, a California computer scientist, deciphered much of the text, but ninety-seven characters remain undeciphered.

"Some of the text was in blank verse," Webster told me. "It made little sense to me. I couldn't even summarize it."[124]

As you turn into the lanes leading to the CIA at the main entrance on Dolley Madison Boulevard, Route 123, you are confronted by an array of signs warning that visitors may be searched and that no photographs are allowed. Anyone who is not an employee is directed to a lane to the right, where you must convey your Social Security number over an intercom. If the number matches with a list of visitors cleared to enter that day, you may advance to the next stop, which is the main guard gate, a concrete-and-glass structure. There you must show picture identification. If everything matches, the guard gives you a visitor's badge and a parking permit with a map of the parking lots. The color of the permit changes every day, and it is stamped with that day's date. Everyone assumed that the CIA ran a check on each individual, but in fact, the Social Security number was used only to verify that a visitor had a scheduled appointment.

If anyone tries to enter the compound without permission, the guard can flip a switch and raise a steel barrier that revolves out of the ground. Just in case, the guards are armed with nine-millimeter semiautomatic pistols, rifles, and submachine guns.

Once or twice a day, people who do not have appointments showed up at the entrances asking to see the director or requesting that the CIA stop the satellite signals in their heads. In those cases, their identity is checked. Often, they are intoxicated, have no driver's licenses, or have outstanding warrants for their arrest. The CIA's police officers arrest them, or the Fairfax County police are called.

"Two years before he went to the Capitol, Russell E. Weston Jr. came here," John A. Turnicky, the director of the CIA's Office of Security, said. "He had a story about John F. Kennedy and Clinton trying to kill Marilyn Monroe."[125]

A diagnosed paranoid schizophrenic, Weston shot and killed two Capitol Police officers and wounded a tourist at the U.S. Capitol Building on July 24, 1998.

In December 1996, an intoxicated man driving a pickup truck approached the main entrance on Route 123 and ran through the checkpoint at eighty miles per hour. The guards did not have time to raise the steel barrier that revolves out of the ground. After that, the CIA created a more serpentine route, so vehicles could not develop speed before approaching the gates.

In addition to three hundred uniformed CIA security officers, the agency has twelve dogs trained to sniff out explosives or hazardous materials. In one famous incident, Stanley Moskowitz, then the agency's director of congressional affairs, left his car in the CIA parking garage. Later in the day, the Office of Security asked if he would mind coming down to the garage and opening his trunk. Two dogs trained to locate explosives had fingered it for harboring a bomb.[126] Moskowitz opened the trunk.

"The dogs detected aromatic tennis clothes," said Alan C. Wade, who became director of the Center for CIA Security.[127]

One evening just before Christmas of 1999, a man drove to the entrance at Route 123. Apparently, he wound up at the CIA entrance by mistake. As a guard checked his identity, Maggie, a Lab, came over to sniff. The man panicked and jumped out of the car, dropping packets of cocaine. Since Maggie was not trained to uncover drugs, she began eating one of the packets, as any dog would. The man with the cocaine was arrested. Maggie was in intensive care for four days. She continues to work on the force.

The CIA's dogs—mostly German shepherds and Labs—are kept in kennels outside a home on the CIA's property once owned by Margaret Scattergood. Scattergood bought the property in 1933. When the federal government tried to take the property for the CIA, she got a private law passed allowing her to stay there undisturbed until she died. In the meantime title passed to the government, and she received $54,189 for the property.

The daughter of a wealthy dye maker in Philadelphia, Scattergood was a Quaker and a pacifist. The CIA, in her view, meant war and killing—everything she was against. Scattergood helped civil rights organizations and was corresponding clerk of the Langley Hill Friends Meeting in McLean. But she spent most of her time doling out money from a trust fund set up by her father. She gave to antiwar and other liberal causes and wrote letters to members of Congress urging cuts in the military and intelligence budgets. She also gave sanctuary to refugees from Nicaragua and Guatemala—illegal aliens fleeing the turmoil in the two countries where the CIA was heavily involved. Occasionally they ended up at the CIA's gate as they tried to find Scattergood's driveway, which was off an access drive going to a rear entrance of the CIA.

When the CIA began widening its front access drive in 1983, Harry E. Fitzwater, the CIA's deputy director for administration under Casey, learned that Scattergood was worried that the agency would intrude on her property. For some time, Fitzwater had been concerned about Scattergood's welfare. Since her home extended into the CIA's grounds, it was probably more secure than the White House. But Scattergood was advancing in age. Since her friend Florence C. Thorne's death in 1973, she had lived alone.

Fitzwater had the CIA's guards patrol her property to make sure she was okay.

One day, Fitzwater invited Scattergood and a grandniece, Sylvia Blanchet, to have lunch in the director's dining room and to tour the CIA. After they sipped sherry, Casey dropped in, and they had lunch with him. They discussed Casey's 1976 book, *Where and How the War Was Fought: An Armchair Tour of the American Revolution.*

"My relatives were in jail at the time," Scattergood declared. "They were Quakers and were doing civil disobedience. They don't believe in war and don't believe in killing other people and would rather go to jail and lose everything rather than participate in war."

Scattergood died on November 7, 1986, at the age of ninety-two, after a stroke. She had lived on the property twenty-five years after the CIA occupied its headquarters building—a last show of resistance.

It was at the main entrance of the CIA where a gunman opened fire on CIA employees as they waited at a red light to make a left turn from Dolley Madison Boulevard into CIA headquarters just before 8 A.M. on January 25, 1993. The man fatally shot Frank A. Darling, twenty-eight, a DO officer, and Lansing H. Bennett, sixty-six, a physician and CIA analyst, and wounded three others.

Darling's wife Judy was sitting beside her husband when the gunman struck. One bullet had already hit Darling in the back when he told his wife to get down and stay down. She complied. In the seconds that followed, three more bullets hit her husband, including one that shattered his head.

To Tenet, who became deputy DCI and then acting DCI

while the hunt for the killer continued, nothing was more important than catching the man who had murdered two of his employees that day. Tenet pledged to devote the full resources of the
intelligence community to the effort. Twice, he met with Bradley
J. Garrett, the FBI agent assigned to the case.

Garrett was not your typical FBI agent. He usually dressed
entirely in black, wore Armani and Hugo Boss suits, and walked
with a swagger. From 5 A.M. to 7 A.M., he worked out at Gold's
Gym. But Garrett, who had a Ph.D. in criminology, was a tena-
cious, smart investigator who had developed a reputation for solv-
ing the most difficult murder cases. Robert R. "Bear" Bryant, who
headed the Washington Field Office, considered Garrett one of his
best agents. When told about the shooting, Bryant made sure Garrett got the case.[128]

Witnesses told Garrett the gunman was in his thirties and
looked as if he was from the Middle East. He used an AK-47
automatic rifle. The FBI and ATF canvassed local gun shops to
try to trace the weapon. The owner of a shop in Chantilly, Virginia, recalled that three days before the shooting a Middle Eastern
man had purchased an AK-47.

Garrett pulled the record. Aimal Kasi, an immigrant from
Quetta, Pakistan, had purchased the gun. He listed an address in
Herndon, Virginia, where he rented an apartment with Zahed Ah-
mad Mir, who had recently reported him missing.

When interviewed on February 8, Mir said Kasi was a mild-
mannered man, except when watching CNN shots of the U.S.
military intervening in Moslem countries. He would then become
agitated and denounce the United States.

"Mir said that a week or two before the shooting Kasi said,
'I'm going to do something at the CIA, White House, or Israeli
embassy,' " Garrett told me.[129]

After the shooting, Kasi* told Garrett he was going out of town. He said Mir could keep his personal belongings. As it turned out, a few hours after the shooting, Kasi paid cash for a plane ticket back to Pakistan.

Mir gave his consent to a search of the apartment. Under a sofa, Garrett found an AK-47. Ballistics tests showed it had fired the fatal shots. In a closet, FBI and Fairfax County police found, on Kasi's shoes and jacket, glass from the windshields that had been shattered during the shooting.

Over the next four and a half years, Garrett pursued leads with the help of the CIA. Tipsters came forward to try to obtain the reward money, but most of the information turned out to be useless. Garrett spent a month to two months at a time in Pakistan, where Kasi was believed to be hiding.

In the spring of 1997, several of Kasi's bodyguards, who were being paid by Kasi's family, approached a State Department officer in Karachi. He put them in touch with a CIA officer there. They told her they could pinpoint Kasi's location in return for the reward money, then set at $2 million. The CIA officer decided the bodyguards were legitimate and recommended that the CIA do business with them. Eventually the CIA agreed to increase the reward to $5 million. The agency obtained support for the operation from the Pakistani government.

"For Tenet and the CIA, it was personal," Garrett said.

For days, with the help of Pakistani agents, Garrett, agent Jimmy C. Carter, the local FBI agent or legat, and two members

---

*Initial news reports spelled the suspect's name Kansi, the name he used when he entered the United States. Investigations in Pakistan determined that his name was Kasi. Many knew him as "Mir Aimal," but Mir was an honorific, like "sir," which he bestowed on himself.

of the FBI Hostage Rescue Team conducted surveillance of the Shalimar Hotel in Deri Ghazi Khan in central Pakistan. Kasi, then thirty-three, was said to be staying there.

Since snatching Kasi was considered a covert action, Clinton had to sign an intelligence finding to allow the CIA to carry it out. After the Church Committee hearings, such findings were required to insure that the CIA only engaged in covert action approved by the president. Twenty-four hours before the bust was to take place, Clinton's National Security Council team objected.

"The NSC said, 'Wait a minute. You didn't tell us this could be a lethal operation,' " David Cohen, who was deputy director for operations, recalled. " 'Someone could get killed.' The White House was living in an ivory tower."

After overcoming NSC objections, the CIA and FBI gave the go-ahead. At 4 A.M. on Sunday, June 15, 1997, the FBI agents burst in on Kasi. They were armed with shotguns and nine-millimeter handguns.

Kasi fought but was not armed. Garrett took Kasi's prints. With a magnifying glass, he compared them with the ones he had brought.

"We got him," Garrett announced.

The agent accompanied Kasi on a C-141 cargo plane back to the U.S.

"He said in the plane he didn't like the CIA intervening in the Moslem world," Garrett said. "He mentioned the U.S. bombing in Iraq."

At 6:30 P.M. Kasi was taken off the plane at a secure area of Dulles International Airport, where an FBI SWAT team stood guard. Tenet, Dave Cohen, Winston P. Wiley, who was in charge of the Counterterrorism Center; William J. Esposito, an assistant FBI director over the criminal investigative division, and "Bear"

Bryant, by now an assistant FBI director over counterintelligence and counterterrorism, were there as well.

The capture of Kasi came two weeks before Tenet, having been acting DCI for six months, took over as DCI. To Dave Cohen, it seemed the two events signaled the beginning of the revitalization of the CIA. The day after Kasi arrived, Tenet held a meeting in the Bubble. He played Lee Greenwood's *God Bless the USA*.

Support employees put up posters with a big cross written across a photo of Kasi.

"We could be proud of ourselves again," Cohen said. "We could be proud that we caught this person who had killed two of our own in front of our noses."

Besides helping to restore the agency's confidence, the capture signaled a turning point in relations between the CIA and FBI. Even after J. Edgar Hoover, over some imagined slight, ordered the bureau not to cooperate with the agency, FBI agents and CIA officers quietly cooperated with each other. Since the mid-1990s, an FBI agent had served as deputy to the chief of the Counterterrorism Center. A CIA officer was deputy in the FBI division that dealt with counterterrorism. But the degree of cooperation depended on the personalities of the people involved. After the Ames case, the FBI's move to take control of security and counterintelligence at the agency offended the CIA. Now the FBI had arrested the man who had killed two CIA employees. In the Bubble that day, the FBI agents who captured Kasi got a standing ovation.

On November 10, 1997, a Fairfax County jury of six men and six women convicted Kasi of capital murder. Tenet's wife Stephanie attended the penalty phase of the trial, saying she was there to support the family members of the victims.

Stephanie, who could speak Greek to her mother-in-law, often helped CIA families encountering personal difficulties. On Thanksgiving, she and Tenet would bring pumpkin, apple, and blueberry pies to the CIA officers who staffed the Operations Center on the seventh floor. Stephanie had an uncle who had been in the CIA. After her husband became DCI, another uncle revealed to her for the first time that he had been in the OSS. He was from the old school, Tenet would say. Now Stephanie had a need to know.

"Men, women, and children of the CIA . . . risk their lives every day, not for money and not for recognition," Stephanie told reporters at the courthouse. "Most sacrifice in total anonymity."

Citing the "vileness" of his act, the jury recommended that the judge impose the death sentence. On January 23, 1998, Judge J. Howe Brown Jr. sentenced Kasi to death by lethal injection.

Several times, Garrett visited Kasi on death row at the Greenville Correctional Center in Jarratt, Virginia. Kasi spoke on the phone to Frank Darling's brother and apologized. He also asked Garrett to relay an apology to Bennett's family. However, Kasi maintained he had done the right thing. He drew a distinction between the U.S. and his victims. The individuals were not to blame; it was the U.S. that was at fault. He wanted to teach America a lesson.

"What I did was a retaliation against the U.S. government for American policy in the Middle East and its support of Israel," Kasi, thirty-eight, told Garrett. "It had nothing to do with terrorism."

In fact, while Kasi was not tied to a terrorist group, violence by individuals or groups to further a political cause by definition is terrorism.

Strapped to a stainless steel table with his arms extended, Kasi was rolled into the death chamber at 8:58 P.M. on November 14, 2002. He had asked if Garrett would stay with him, and so he did.

"There is no God but Allah," Kasi said. He then softly began chanting in his native Urdu.

"As they injected him with three drugs to stop his brain activity, respiration, and heart, he held up two fingers," Garrett said. "It was either a peace sign or a victory sign."[130]

To remember the victims, a local resident created flower beds and erected a small plaque on the median strip leading to the headquarters entrance. When the beds became overgrown, Tenet's wife Stephanie, wearing sunglasses, could be seen pulling weeds from around the flowers.

15

In seeking to rebuild the CIA, Tenet drew on the wisdom of his unofficial advisors, the Intelligence Advisory Group. The members, who met with Tenet about every three months, included former DCIs William Webster and James Woolsey, former Baltimore Orioles owner Eli Jacobs, former White House counsel Lloyd N. Cutler, former White House Chief of Staff Howard H. Baker Jr., former ambassador Sol M. Linowitz, former Senators Warren Rudman and Sam Nunn, former Secretary of State Henry Kissinger, and retired Admiral William J. Crowe Jr. Cleared to see classified information, the group reviewed any issue that Tenet felt was troublesome—for example, the behavior of North Korea. By keeping the members abreast of developments at the agency, Tenet sowed goodwill among Washington powers.

Through Eli Jacobs, Tenet heard about A. B. "Buzzy" Krongard. An investment banker, karate expert, and former Marine captain, Krongard had been secretly helping the agency for years. Soon Tenet recruited him, first as his counselor and then as the CIA's executive director, the agency's third-highest-ranking official.

Like many of the early OSS and CIA officers, Krongard did not need a job: He was worth close to $100 million. Alvin Bernard Krongard, whose nickname "Buzzy" came from an aunt who thought he looked like the DC Comics character, had come to investment banking circuitously. Having finished a three-year stint with the Marines, Krongard worked for his father-in-law's label and patch company in Baltimore. When his father-in-law died, Krongard arranged the sale of the company. Hooked on deal making, he joined Baltimore's Alex Brown & Sons in 1971 as a finance associate and worked his way up to CEO. In the process he transformed the company from a regional brokerage house to an underwriting firm that was a major force on Wall Street, with revenues in 1996 of more than $1 billion.

As CEO, Krongard required employees to sign a pledge that they would adhere to his mantra: "Client first, firm second, individual third." He would shepherd a prospectus through the printing process at night to make sure it was done right. He was known for his decisiveness, his sharp analytical mind, and his loyalty.

"If you were in trouble, and you only had one phone call to make, Buzzy is the guy you'd want to call," said Marc E. Lackritz, president of the Securities Industry Association in Washington.

In 1997, Bankers Trust bought the company for $1.7 billion, leaving Krongard with $71 million in Bankers Trust stock and giving him the title of vice chairman of Bankers Trust. He sold his stock after Deutsche Bank bought Bankers Trust in 1999. In his last year with the firm, Krongard made $4 million in salary and bonuses.

Soldier and scholar, Krongard was given to quoting Socrates, Spinoza, Nietzsche, and Hume and expounding on paintings in the Louvre. He graduated with honors from Princeton, where he was an All-American lacrosse player. While working at Alex Brown, he obtained a law degree with honors from the University of Maryland in 1975.

On the side, Krongard was an aspiring James Bond. A black belt in karate, Krongard practiced several martial arts disciplines, including Chinese kung fu. From inside a diving cage in the Indian Ocean off Australia, he punched a great white shark in the jaw. Because of his highly developed muscle tone and control, he was able to withstand body blows to his stomach, a talent he sometimes showed off to guests.

Krongard had a collection of thirty-five guns, including an Uzi. On his ninety-three-acre estate near Baltimore, Krongard regularly honed his marksmanship with his favorite, a nine-millimeter Glock. He engaged in target practice with a local police SWAT team as well. In his 15,000-square-foot home, he would thrust his hands into dry ice to toughen them.

"The joke around here," said Alex Brown colleague Richard Franyo, "is that he never really worked here all along. It was just a front."

A year after Aimal Kasi shot CIA employees on their way to work Krongard worked with the CIA and FBI to try to catch him. Meeting with contacts from Pakistan, he posed as a businessman who was willing to make a multimillion-dollar deal if they could deliver the suspect. In that role, Krongard was a nonpaid CIA contract employee.

Nothing came of Krongard's effort, but Tenet was aware of his help. In late 1997 Krongard invited Tenet to lunch at the Capital Grille, a Washington restaurant that specializes in dry-aged steak and is frequented by members of Congress and lobbyists. Krongard complained about some of his contacts with the CIA, saying the agency was too bureaucratic.

"Why don't you come and fix it?" Tenet asked.

It was exactly what Krongard had wanted to hear. Krongard had made all the money he wanted. Now his desire was to help his country. At the age of sixty-one, Krongard was hired as a counselor to Tenet. So he would not have to commute from Baltimore on weekdays Krongard bought a townhouse near the CIA.

"I'm not sure this second career has anything to do with patriotism. It's self-interest," Krongard told *USA Today* just after joining the CIA in February 1998. "My main job is to be helpful. I'll pick up towels in the men's room if they want."

Instead, Tenet made Krongard executive director of the CIA in March 2001. In that job, Krongard was the chief operating officer, a position just below John McLaughlin, who became the CIA's deputy director in October 2000. Krongard's office on the seventh floor was sealed at night by cipher locks that kept a record of each person who gained access. Motion detectors and heat sensors sounded alarms, bringing two CIA security officers running, if anyone tried to enter.

When I interviewed Krongard in the small conference room outside his office, he was wearing a pin-striped charcoal suit. Instead of the Rambo-like figure I had expected, Krongard, with his grey hair and stern demeanor, looked like the conservative, serious investment banker he had been for twenty-nine years.

On the walls were photos of Krongard with white sharks and a letter he received in 1961 from the agency accepting him as a career trainee. When his wife's parents died in a plane crash, Krongard decided to run his father-in-law's business instead. Krongard was a widower, his wife having died shortly after he joined the agency.

I asked Krongard if I should punch him in the stomach. He stood up.

"Harder," Krongard said after I punched him once.

I punched him again.

"That's all you can do?" he asked, disappointed.

Having spent his life in the business world, Krongard said he was not prepared for the way the government does business.

"It's a total disaster," Krongard said. "It's mind-boggling. There is no competition, no financial discipline, no rigor. You have a budget instead of having a business plan. They give you money first, regardless of how well you are doing. I was the ninth CEO of Alex Brown in almost two hundred years. The CIA had five DCIs in seven years."[131]

Within three weeks of becoming executive director, Krongard decided that the CIA's fourth directorate, the directorate of administration, had to go. The directorate was too powerful, bureaucratic, and sluggish. Before approving new computer hardware or software, the directorate required a review of 136 criteria by six different boards. Krongard decided that, as in private companies, finance, information technology, security, global support, and personnel functions should report separately to top management.

"Buzzy was a breath of fresh air," said James Simon, the former assistant DCI for administration. "He made decisions and had enormous integrity."

"Buzzy seemed to relish throwing little grenades into a discussion," Snider said. "He constantly challenged the prevailing wisdom and asked why things were being done the way they were. He served a very useful function in this regard. Buzzy had been a hard-nosed manager in the private sector and brought the same toughness to his work at the CIA."

Krongard found that the CIA was spending a ridiculous amount of time checking expense accounts.

"We spent more money checking on travel and meals than we could lose," he told me.

Krongard rescinded a rule requiring employees who were out sick more than three days to submit a letter from a doctor verifying the illness. Because most spaces at the agency were reserved, there was not enough parking. Aside from spaces for the most senior management, who parked underground, Krongard declared all spaces open after 9:30 A.M. The chiefs of regional divisions, who were among those affected, were not happy.

Like the rest of the government, the CIA was loath to fire employees who did not measure up. Employees felt entitled, Aldrich Ames being but one example. Krongard tightened up on performance reviews. As a result, twenty-five employees were fired or eased out each year, a significant number for a government agency.

"The biggest death knell for any bureaucracy is not closing the deal," Tenet said. "Buzzy is an implementer. He's a closer."

Krongard saw Tenet at the end of every day, and they went over pending items. He freed the DCI to deal with policymakers, the Hill, and CIA operations, the area Tenet most enjoyed. Once a year Tenet and his top people gave former senior officials who were still involved in the business a classified briefing. Poteat, the former DS&T officer, was amazed at Tenet's performance.

"After one of his deputies answered a question, Tenet would add his thoughts," Poteat said. "I couldn't believe his grasp of everything going on in every directorate, including technical projects. He explained them better than the people in charge."

Poteat had worked for DCIs going back to Allen Dulles. None had mastered CIA operations as Tenet had.

Tenet saw himself as a leader rather than a manager. In fact, he hated the terms "managing" and "workforce." They called to mind herding cattle or, as he put it, some "undifferentiated thing" that needed tending. If anyone was the CIA's manager, it was Krongard.

"The key to success is to pay attention to the plumbing, to the insides of the organization," Tenet said. "The health, care, well-being, promotion, education and training, retention, and compensation of employees. Buzzy imposed discipline on our pay system, security, personnel policies, and education."

To bring the CIA more in line with private sector practices, Krongard moved to replace automatic pay increases based on years of service with raises based on merit. However, because of opposition from members of Congress who represented local employees, he could only implement the changes on a limited basis in a pilot program.

"It's feudal and futile," he said.

For all the obstacles, "I have the best job in the world," Krongard said. "Look at what I've gotten from this country. They won't let me go back to the Marines to pull the trigger. So I'm here instead."

"How much do you make?" I asked him.

For the first time, Krongard looked flummoxed. He turned to William Harlow, the CIA's director of public affairs.

"How much do I make?" he asked.

"You make about $140,000 a year," Harlow informed him.

Besides human and technical collection, the CIA analyzed open source information. When the main target was the Soviet Union, the job was manageable. The Soviets controlled the press, so public information was limited. With the explosion of the Internet and a need to monitor developments relating to terrorism all over the world, the CIA was inundated with information it could not sort, much less analyze. A mosque might have a low-power radio station. The Kurdish press had to be read and official Chinese statements reviewed. Because of the use of e-mail and cell phones, the volume of intercepted communications was growing exponentially as well.

To deal with the problem, Tenet and Krongard got behind an innovative project called In-Q-Tel. Formed by the CIA in February 1999, In-Q-Tel was a nonprofit organization that funded technology to grapple with the CIA's exploding information and help track down the bad guys. The "Q" in In-Q-Tel was inspired by James Bond's Q, who equipped the secret agent with high-tech gadgets like a folding helicopter and an exploding pen.

The idea for In-Q-Tel originated with Dr. Ruth David, director of the DS&T under Deutch, and Joanne O. Isham, her deputy. When she came to the CIA from Sandia National Laboratories in 1995, David was dismayed to find that her desktop did not offer Internet access. In the early days, the CIA was on the cutting edge of technology. Besides developing the U-2, the agency developed the newer, advanced satellites, like the KH-11. The KH-11 spawned the technology that led to high-definition television and digital photography.

"It used to be that everyone in industry wanted to work with the CIA because it always meant an opportunity to work on the leading edge of technology," said Gene Poteat, the former DS&T officer.

By the 1990s, the agency had become almost as bureaucratic and resistant to change as the rest of the government.

"Their business was information, but they weren't living in the information age," David said. "They didn't have the culture, tools, or mind set."[132]

Even if the CIA became more forward-looking, startup firms with innovative technologies avoided the agency because of the cumbersome procurement process. At the CIA, as in the rest of the government, by the time new technology was approved, it was out of date.

"Alex Brown had the reputation of being the number one technology banker in the country," Krongard said. "Consequently, we met, interfaced with, romanced, and cajoled a lot of different people. Their attitude was such that they were not going to put up with the typical government approach to doing business, and yet that was where the cutting-edge stuff was being performed."

As an alternative, Ruth David and Joanne Isham tried to recruit tech whizzes, but that was difficult as well. It was the beginning of the dot-com boom, and new graduates wanted to work for private companies and make millions from stock options. At first David and Isham proposed a research and development center, funded by the CIA, that would pay salaries competitive with private industry. Deutch shot down the idea. Later, after he left the CIA, Deutch invited the two women to lunch at MIT and introduced them to the heads of MIT departments that might supply job candidates for the CIA.

On the trip back to Washington, the two women brainstormed on the idea of a non-profit that would invest in products or companies that were already selling cutting-edge software the CIA might use. By backing new projects at existing companies, the CIA would obtain technology tailored to its needs. At the same time, the companies would be free to market those new products, thus giving them incentives to develop items of interest to the CIA. In effect, the agency would be able to leverage its money.

As they envisioned it, the organization, which became In-Q-Tel, would speed up or even bypass entirely the government's procurement process. Instead of taking years to evaluate a product, it would do so in months. While the CIA would usually classify how it used a program, the technology itself would remain unclassified. In some cases, In-Q-Tel would take an equity interest in the companies.

"For me, it was all about the future of the directorate," Isham said.[133]

In contrast to Deutch, when Tenet became DCI, he enthusiastically embraced the idea. Tenet presented it to Senate and House intelligence committee staffers, saying this was a way for the CIA to "swim in the Valley." He implored them to "take a risk with me."

"Okay, but don't screw it up," one of the staffers said.

Krongard and Tenet put together an all-star board of trustees, ranging from former Defense Secretary William Perry to John McMahon, the former deputy DCI who became president and CEO of Lockheed Missiles & Space Co., and Norman R. Augustine, a former chairman and chief executive officer of Lockheed Martin.

With the backing of Tenet and Krongard, the board chose Gilman Louie, thirty-nine, to run In-Q-Tel. A Silicon Valley legend, Louie had formed his first computer game company while in college. He later helped develop the Falcon F-16 flight simulator game. In 1987 a Soviet representative in Budapest showed him Tetris, a Soviet computer game. With two other companies, Louie bought the rights for $15,000. Tetris became the largest selling computer game of all time; more than a hundred million copies have been sold. After selling the company, MicroProse, to toy maker Hasbro for $70 million (he owned 2 percent), Louie became Hasbro's chief of on-line projects.

As they played a computer game at an Atlanta flight school, a headhunter recruited Louie to head In-Q-Tel. He was then making a total of $1 million a year from salary, bonuses, royalties from Falcon, and a stock option plan. At In-Q-Tel, Louie was paid $407,000 a year, or about three times what Krongard made from his government salary. With a performance bonus and incentive payment, Louie recently made a total of $760,000, still well below what he made at Hasbro.

In-Q-Tel was based in a private office building in Arlington, Virginia, overlooking the Pentagon. The lobby directory did not list it. Inside, a large space that looked like a nursery school classroom was called the "boomerang room," where wonks could toss around ideas. Another room was a laboratory lined with computers where new software could be tried out. In-Q-Tel also had an office in Menlo Park, California, in the heart of Silicon Valley. In-Q-Tel employed fifty people and had a budget from the CIA of $30 million a year. The In-Q-Tel Interface Center, a team at the CIA, integrated In-Q-Tel's work with the agency.

By 2003, In-Q-Tel was funding projects at thirty companies. Among them were Browse3D, which developed a Web browser that showed several pages at once in virtual three dimensional rooms that revealed what lay behind links; Attensity Corp., which developed software that could examine a document and figure out if a reference to "wood," for example, was to a person or to a place; and Tacit Knowledge Systems, which built software that analyzed e-mail and other documents from employees and determined what they were interested in and which other analysts might be interested in the same subjects. One obvious use for such a program would be data mining communications to zero in on potential terrorists. In-Q-Tel also invested in software that displayed information about terrorists by location on a map of the world for use by the CIA's Counterterrorism Center.

Louie and his team haunted computer industry trade shows and conferences looking for leads on new concepts. They also picked up tips from the CIA. Through such a tip, Louie heard about software developed by Systems Research and Development. Based in Las Vegas, the company had a program to spot collusion among gamblers and dealers. It sorted through mountains of data and pinpointed links between people using Non-Obvious Relationship Awareness, or "fuzzy logic." The program detected when a person intentionally transposed his name or tried other ruses to obscure details about himself.

"Casinos want to catch these guys in real time," Louis said. The same would be true for the CIA and terrorists. Soon, In-Q-Tel funded a project that would adapt the casino security program to the CIA's needs.

"We want to get there ahead of time," Louie said. "There was a volume problem. The ability to put pieces together and get actionable intelligence was shrinking. Our mission was to go after technologies that were going to get to market anyway."

Making use of Krongard's financial expertise and contacts, In-Q-Tel persuaded venture capital funds to invest in companies in which it had taken a position. As Krongard pointed out, the CIA was a brand name. If it became associated with a company, it could enhance its prospects. Venture capital funds put about $500 million into companies in which In-Q-Tel had an equity interest. Several companies were on the verge of making offers to buy companies In-Q-Tel had invested in, potentially giving the nonprofit organization a cash infusion of millions of dollars.

Innovative as In-Q-Tel was, the CIA was slow to adopt the new technology it offered. The original idea was that In-Q-Tel was to be an experiment to be evaluated after five years. The few programs actually adopted were considered pilots.

"There was resistance to change," McMahon said. "People liked the software they were using, basically because they were used to it."

All that changed after 9/11.

16

Mike*, the agency's White House briefer, was with Bush in Sarasota, Florida, on September 11, 2001. At 8:15 a.m., in Bush's luxury penthouse hotel suite on Longboat Key, Mike briefed the president on the Middle East and the Palestinian situation. Bush made a call to National Security Advisor Condoleeza Rice and asked her to follow up on some of the points. As the presidential motorcade sped toward Emma E. Booker Elementary School, where Bush was to read to the children, Ari Fleischer received a call. It was just before 9 a.m. "Do you know anything about a plane hitting the World Trade Center?" Fleischer asked Mike after getting off the phone. He didn't.

Perhaps it was pilot error, or the pilot had had a heart attack, Bush thought when told about the first plane crashing into the North Tower. But later, as Bush read to the children, Andy Card whispered to him that a second plane had hit the South Tower.

"America is under attack," Card said.

---

*Because he is now undercover, Mike's last name is not used here.

After thinking about what his response would be, Bush cut short his presentation, apologizing to the principal, Gwendolyn Tosé-Rigell. From a secure phone in an adjoining room, he called Vice President Dick Cheney and FBI Director Robert S. Mueller III. Bush watched videos of the attacks on a television that had been wheeled in on a cart. Flame and smoke engulfed both towers, and people were jumping from windows.

"We're at war," Bush announced to his aides—Card, Fleischer, Karl Rove, and White House Communications Director Dan Bartlett.

At 9:30 A.M. Bush appeared in the school's media center to make a brief statement on TV.

"Today we've had a national tragedy," Bush said. "Two airplanes have crashed into the World Trade Center in an apparent terrorist attack on our country." Borrowing a phrase his father had used more than a decade earlier about Saddam Hussein's invasion of Kuwait, the president said, "Terrorism against our nation will not stand."

The limos carrying Bush and his entourage raced to the airport at speeds up to eighty miles an hour. During the ride, Bush learned that a third jetliner had slammed into the Pentagon. Over a secure phone, he consulted with Cheney, who was in an emergency bunker beneath the White House grounds. The vice president urged him to authorize military planes to shoot down any commercial airliners that might be controlled by the hijackers. Bush called Secretary of Defense Donald Rumsfeld, who had elected to stay in the burning Pentagon, and conveyed the order.

"We're going to find out who did this, and we're going to kick their ass," Bush had told Cheney.[134]

Air Force One took off at 9:57 A.M. and began climbing fast to 45,000 feet, accompanied by F-16s and AWAC radar planes as escorts. Because of Secret Service concerns that terrorists might try to track the plane, no one on board was allowed to make a call from any of the plane's eighty-seven phones. Being with the president, Mike figured his wife would know he was safe.

They flew to Barksdale Air Force Base in northwest Louisiana, where camouflaged soldiers brandishing M-16s surrounded the plane. As extra food and water were brought on board, Bush consulted by phone with Cheney and made another televised statement. Bush looked crestfallen.

After they took off again, Bush, his jacket off, called Mike into his cabin near the front of the plane. The president asked Mike who he thought had done it.

"I would bet everything on bin Laden," Mike said.

From its first briefing of Bush back in Crawford in December, after he became president-elect, the agency had been warning about bin Laden and al Qaeda. In April and May, Mike began conveying reports of chatter indicating that terrorists could be planning a major attack. During the summer Bush asked several times whether the CIA had any information indicating an attack might occur within the U.S. The answer was that, while bin Laden would like to launch a direct attack and had made such plans in the past, including a thwarted plot to bomb Los Angeles International Airport, no intercepted communications suggested it was about to happen. On August 6 the CIA gave Bush a background paper on everything the agency knew about bin Laden and al Qaeda.

On the plane Mike listed some of bin Laden's previous attacks—the ones on two American embassies in East Africa and the one on the USS *Cole*. Bush asked how long it would take to know if bin Laden was responsible. Based on previous attacks, Mike said, it would probably be a matter of days.

Air Force One landed at Offutt Air Force Base in Nebraska, where Bush held a teleconference with members of the National Security Council (NSC) and with Cheney, Rumsfeld, Mueller, and Tenet. Again accompanied by fighter jets, *Air Force One* roared back into the sky at 4:36 P.M. for a return to Washington. Bush, overruling the Secret Service, had insisted that no terrorist was going to stop him from going home.

When the planes hit, Tenet was eating breakfast at the St. Regis Hotel three blocks north of the White House with Senator David L. Boren, the former chairman of the Senate Select Committee on Intelligence. Boren and Tenet were talking about their families when a CIA security officer interrupted the breakfast to inform Tenet of the first attack, then twenty minutes later, of the second one.

"This has bin Laden all over it," Tenet said to Boren.

As his scrambled eggs got cold, Tenet called CIA headquarters on a cell phone and ordered his top officials to meet with him in his conference room. Tenet, forty-eight, felt anger and frustration.

"There was no doubt that al Qaeda was going to come here eventually, and that something spectacular was planned," Tenet told me. "I knew immediately who it was."

As it turned out, a close friend of Tenet and his wife Stephanie had been on the plane that crashed into the Pentagon. One of his high school friends had been on the plane that crashed in Pennsylvania.

"Three thousand of your citizens die," Tenet told me. "I lost two of my friends. My hometown was blown up. This was personal. And it was personal for our workforce in a way that very few people understand."[135]

Usually, Tenet held an 8:30 A.M. meeting of fifteen of the agency's top officials in his conference room each day. Each official contributed news from his or her area, without revealing the most sensitive information or its source. Besides the chiefs of each of the three directorates, William Harlow, Tenet's choice as director of public affairs, attended. If Harlow was not present, his deputy, Mark Mansfield, the director of media relations, sat in for him.

A former Navy captain, Harlow had been officer of the deck aboard the aircraft carrier USS *Midway,* then spent most of his twenty-year Navy career in public relations. He was assistant press secretary for national security and foreign affairs in the Reagan White House and continued in that role under George H. W. Bush. In 1992, he became special assistant for public affairs in the Office of the Secretary of the Navy and ended his military career as deputy director of the American Forces Information Service, where he managed the Defense Department's worldwide internal information efforts.

Harlow was also an accomplished novelist, having written *Circle William,* about a White House press secretary who, with his brother, the commander of a Navy ship, scrambled to prevent a Libyan plot to use chemical weapons against Israel and the U.S. Harlow had a wry sense of humor, which he used to good effect when reporting at the morning meeting on press coverage of the agency.

"CNN is going to say we're morons," he would say, adding, "They're behind Fox."

Leaning over backwards to be ethical, Harlow vetoed listing his CIA affiliation on his novel, but in a broadcast interview, Terry Gross of NPR brought up his day job.

"Does keeping secrets come pretty naturally to you?" Terry Gross asked him.

"No comment," Harlow said.

As director of public affairs, Harlow was in charge of thirty people, including two speechwriters and other specialists who attended to internal communications, community relations, and event planning. That compared with a staff of one in the 1970s, when it was Angus Thuermer's job to say, "No comment."

In those days the CIA had an Alice-in-Wonderland approach: If the agency were actually to deny a charge, the reasoning went, then a "no comment" on other charges would imply that those allegations were true. And, if other intelligence services noticed the CIA talking to the press they would never deal with the agency. Sources and methods must be protected, the CIA would declare, refusing to acknowledge that there were shadings of secrets. Almost anything—including the fact that the CIA had a headquarters building in Langley—could be considered a method in carrying out CIA operations. That did not mean everything about the CIA should be secret. It was unrealistic and self-defeating for the agency to withdraw from American society.

Tenet tried to strike a reasonable balance between the need for secrecy and the need to account to the American people. "We're a secret organization," Tenet said. "We have to maintain that secrecy if we're going to do our business. At the same time, the American people deserve to know just what we're doing and how we're doing it."

Under Tenet and Harlow, the CIA aggressively debunked charges that were not true and occasionally leaked tidbits that made the agency look good. When Chuck Barris, in a book and new movie, claimed he had been a hired killer for the CIA at the same time he was running TV's *The Gong Show* and *The Dating Game*, CIA spokesman Tom Crispell responded, "It sounds like he might have been standing too close to the gong all those years."

If a reporter already had the glimmer of a story, Harlow worked with him to get it straight, while denying untrue charges.

Like the best PR people, Harlow got his message across while giving the reporter material he or she could use. Both sides of the transaction came away happy. Because he leaned over backwards to be honest, Harlow had credibility. Thus, when he asked a reporter not to report a story, or to withhold a fact because it was too sensitive, the reporter usually obliged. But occasionally, Harlow had to report at the morning meeting, "I *told* him it was not true, but he went ahead with it anyway."

Tenet recognized that in Washington, where perception is everything, good press became self-fulfilling. If the agency looked competent, Congress would give it more money, allowing it to do a better job. Tenet looked at the press as an early-warning system: If a politician or someone in another agency were preparing an attack on the CIA, it would be preceded by a negative story in the media.

"Tenet learned in the hardball world of the Hill that outcomes in Washington depend on close working relationships with self-interested power brokers in town, including the media. You continuously need to cultivate allies and outrun your adversaries, at which Tenet is a master," said John Gannon, the former chief of the DI. "Tenet cared a lot about press reaction and would call Bill Harlow at any time of day or night. He skillfully managed the relationship with the press. He strategized. But he rarely gave interviews and does not go on the Sunday TV shows."

In fact, in the six years Tenet had been DCI, he had given only a handful of print interviews—all before 9/11—and never appeared on television. Even when Tim Russert asked him to appear on *Meet the Press* on the fiftieth anniversary of the agency, Tenet declined. His philosophy was that a DCI should be neither seen nor heard. While Tenet appreciated and understood how powerful the press was in shaping Washington's agenda, he had a healthy skepticism of it. The media thrived on controversy and negative stories. They set up phony expectations and then pounced on policymakers for not living up to them. They ran stories suggesting the CIA had been wrong about an issue without accurately stating what the agency's position had been. In Tenet's view, giving interviews and appearing on television would only allow the media and members of Congress an opportunity to create imaginary rifts within the administration.

Reporters would have loved to run stories on disputes between the DCI and the president, or between him and Rumsfeld, with whom he had lunch every other Friday in the seventy-year-old former Navy pilot's office. While there was always backbiting between the Pentagon and the CIA, Tenet and Rumsfeld managed to iron out any disagreements they had. The fact that Tenet saw the president six days a week was all anyone needed to know about the DCI's clout in Washington.

"The only reason the media would want me to appear is to figure out how to drive a wedge between the intelligence community and the policymakers," Tenet would say. "I'm not going to let that happen."

Tenet told me that, as DCI, "You're not a political animal. You're not on prime-time television. You don't go on the talk shows. That's not your job. I don't do TV. I give very few print interviews. I don't believe it's my job to do that."

While Tenet saw the press as a useful tool, he disciplined himself not to let media criticism affect him. He was like a driver indifferent to provocations of the road, while others become apoplectic at every honking horn. At Langley, it was a given that as much as half of what the press reported about the agency was wrong or misleading.

"If you get diverted to worrying about the media, you're losing your focus, and there's nothing I can do about it," Tenet said. "Our business is not a public relations business. If something is egregiously wrong, you have to jump in and tell them. Sometimes they believe us, sometimes they don't. I see people writing with single sources, no corroboration, no one verifying what they wrote. That's not the way we do our business. But that's not my business."[136]

If Tenet was not a media star, the CIA was. The agency was at the core of the counterterrorism effort and a hot subject for movies and television shows. Each month Harlow sifted hundreds of requests for cooperation on everything from news magazine articles focusing on counterterrorism to reality shows based on CIA training. He agreed to very few. In reviewing them, Harlow considered whether the proposed project would help the agency, the track record of those proposing it, how much time would have to be devoted to the project, and how competing media might react.

When a freelance for *Rolling Stone* asked for cooperation on a piece about agency training, Harlow was intrigued. The publication was read by young people who might make good recruits. The reporter had written serious articles in a number of newspapers, including the *Washington Times* and the *Christian Science Monitor*. He was bright and had a seemingly open manner. Harlow was inclined to grant the reporter's request, and he discussed it with the CIA's Recruitment Center. One of the officials recognized the writer's name. Checking, he found that the young man had recently applied to be a CIA officer. The agency had been impressed by him and was about to ask him to agree to a background check and a polygraph.

Harlow analyzed the situation as well as the best seasoned journalists would. Applying for a job while writing a story on an agency is not inherently unethical, although papers like the *Washington*

Post would not allow it. The problem, Harlow decided, was that if the reporter was seriously trying to get a job, he had not been straight with the recruiters, because he had not disclosed he was doing a story. If he was applying for the job in order to do the story, the reporter had not been straight with Harlow.

Either way, Harlow decided not to cooperate. The reporter never knew why. Nor did he get the job.

Because Tenet was having breakfast with Boren on the morning of September 11, Buzzy Krongard was running the 8:30 A.M. meeting. At 8:45 A.M., the senior duty officer of the CIA's Operations Center interrupted.

"Excuse me, Mr. Krongard, but I thought you would want to know that a plane just struck the World Trade Center," he said.

The Operations Center, a huge blue-carpeted room on the seventh floor, was staffed twenty-four hours a day by fifteen CIA officers who faced three television screens that spanned twenty feet. Usually, the TVs were tuned to CNN, MSNBC, and Fox, but they could also be used to view classified images. The center was equipped with sofa beds, in case officers had to sleep there.

Adjourning the meeting, Krongard returned to his office and glanced at the TV monitors. They carried the news that a plane had hit the North Tower. By the time James L. Pavitt, the deputy director in charge of the DO, returned to his office, a second plane had hit the South Tower. Soon the Pentagon would be hit by a third plane.

No one questioned that Pavitt, fifty-six, knew the business. After working as a legislative aide in the House, Pavitt joined the agency in 1973. He served in the DO in Europe, Asia, and headquarters, becoming Dick Stolz's special assistant when Stolz headed the DO under Webster. In 1990 Pavitt was detailed to the NSC as its director of intelligence programs. In 1992 President George H. W. Bush appointed Pavitt special assistant to the president for national security affairs and NSC senior director for intelligence programs.

Like Tenet, Pavitt, a natty dresser who wore double-breasted suits to go with his bushy white hair, reveled in the spy business and its intellectual game of chess. He liked to visit the CIA Museum on the first floor of the old headquarters building. Unlike the International Spy Museum in Washington, the CIA Museum was only open to those cleared to come to the agency. Curated by Toni L. Hiley, it had one of the cryptographic machines that Navy spy John A. Walker Jr. compromised, an OSS bomb concealed in a fake piece of coal, a radio transmitter hidden in a pipe, a scale model of the U-2, an al Qaeda training manual captured by the CIA in Afghanistan, and a rock from Crawford, Texas, retrieved by Mike, the CIA briefer who often saw Bush there.[137]

One of the exhibits catalogued the exploits of Virginia Hall, an OSS officer who was known as the "limping lady of the OSS" because she had a wooden leg, the result of an injury during a hunting accident. So effective was Hall that during World War II the Gestapo circulated a wanted poster calling her "one of the most valuable allied agents in France." It added. "We must find and destroy her."

As the Allied invasion of Europe at Normandy approached, Hall, under the cover of a milk maid, worked with the French underground to establish safe houses and drop zones and to cut electrical lines to telegraph offices, disrupting German communications. With the Nazis still hunting her, she managed to transmit thirty-seven radio messages to London conveying information on German troop movements.

When the war was over, President Truman wanted to present Hall with the Distinguished Service Cross, the only one awarded to a female civilian during the war, at the White House. Saying the publicity would compromise her future intelligence work, she declined. From Paris, she cabled that she was "still operational and most anxious to get busy." Instead, Donovan discreetly gave her the award, now on display in the CIA Museum. Hall continued to work for the CIA until 1966.[138]

After returning to his office from the morning meeting on September 11, Pavitt sent a message to all stations: "I expect each station and each officer to redouble efforts of collecting intelligence on this tragedy."

Mary,* the CIA's New York station chief, called him. The New York station was at 7 World Trade Center, a forty-seven-story building in the shadow of the Twin Towers. Marked with a U.S. Army Logistics sign, the office consisted of forty employees, of whom half were case officers. Another contingent of roughly half that number was based at the United Nations. Weakened by the destruction of the South Tower, 7 World Trade Center would crumble later that day.

Mary and Pavitt agreed that bin Laden was behind the attack. Its scope, temerity, degree of planning, and viciousness fit his way of operating. Since the early nineties the CIA had been tracking him. According to the CIA, bin Laden was born in 1955 in Jeddah, Saudi Arabia. He was one of fifty-three children of Mohamed bin Laden, an illiterate bricklayer from Yemen. Bin Laden's mother was Syrian, one of Mohamed's four wives. According to family legend, Mohamed bin Laden was laying brick for one of King Abdul-Azziz's royal palaces when he suggested a way for the king

*Because she is still undercover, Mary's last name is not used here.

to get around more easily in his wheel chair. The king, who proclaimed Saudi Arabia an Islamic monarchy in 1932, helped Mohamed get started in construction and steered contracts his way.

After fighting against the Soviets in Afghanistan in 1979, Osama bin Laden formed al Qaeda, meaning "the base," in 1988. It was a loose-knit group of terrorist organizations and cells. In 1991, bin Laden relocated to Sudan. Algeria, Saudi Arabia, and Yemen accused him of supporting subversive groups, and in 1994 the Saudis stripped him of his citizenship. In May 1996, under Saudi and U.S. pressure, Sudan expelled him, and he returned to Afghanistan. A few months later, the Taliban, a fundamentalist Islamic group, gained control of some areas of the country and offered him protection. After his father died, bin Laden inherited an estimated $100 million. However, most of the money to fund al Qaeda came from wealthy Moslems who believed in his cause.

Just as Adolf Hitler had blamed the Jews for the economic problems of Germany after World War I, bin Laden blamed the United States for sins against Moslems, which included sending thousands of troops to Saudi Arabia. By not adopting his corrupted version of Islam, the U.S. was the infidel.

Aware of his financing of terrorism, the CIA's Khartoum station in the early 1990s conducted surveillance of bin Laden. Bin Laden's henchmen even tried to assassinate J. Cofer Black, the head of the station, but the CIA learned about the plot and foiled it.

"Bin Laden was one of many of our targets, including Carlos the Jackal," Black, fifty-two, told me. "We got Carlos in August 1994. I could have had bin Laden for a song in Khartoum." Back then, bin Laden "did contracting, building apartments and roads," Black said. "Bin Laden was like a soft Saudi, with no callouses on his hands. He was almost feminine, but very charismatic. Bin

Laden had $300 million when he left the Sudan. He said, 'Money talks.' People who joined him had no hope."[139]

In 1996, bin Laden called for holy war against "Americans occupying the land of the two holy places"—the Moslem shrines at Mecca and Medina. Winston P. Wiley, the chief of the CIA's Counterterrorism Center, proposed a bin Laden station based in an office building in Tysons Corner, a commercial section of McLean.

"He's a bad guy," Wiley told David Cohen, then the chief of the DO. "We should have a stack of reports on him."

After bin Laden's organization detonated two truck bombs that killed 224 people, including twelve Americans, at U.S. embassies in Kenya and Tanzania on August 7, 1998, Tenet publicly proclaimed bin Laden the greatest threat to the U.S. That month, bin Laden issued a *fatwa*, or religious decree under Islamic law, telling Moslems it was their duty to kill Americans and their "allies, civilians and military . . . in any country in which it is possible to do it." In return he promised his followers an honored place in paradise. In a December 1998 interview, bin Laden said acquisition of weapons of mass destruction was a "religious duty." He noted: "How we use them is up to us."

In 1999, Black became chief of the Counterterrorism Center, and bin Laden became his main target. Black's rimless glasses and studious appearance suggested a college professor. But his approach was more like a boxer, fitting nicely with Tenet's desire to make the agency more aggressive. Unlike his predecessors, Tenet was not content to issue written estimates and intelligence memos to policymakers, hoping they would read them. He peppered them with calls.

"If he felt there was a need, Tenet would call cabinet-level officials personally to make sure that they had seen or been briefed on the latest intelligence nugget," Snider said.

"He is not big on process," said Joan A. Dempsey, who was Tenet's chief of staff when he became DCI. "He does not like structures, boards, committees, or papers." Instead, "He responds to oral information. He is totally focused. He wants to know what decisions he can make on questions he has posed, and he wants to know how things can get done. He is very intuitive. He understands what policymakers need."[140]

Some—including former Senator David Boren—thought Tenet had become obsessed with bin Laden. In meetings at the NSC, Tenet pounded his fists on the table, saying it was not enough to gather intelligence on bin Laden. The only way to wipe out the threat was to decimate the Taliban that harbored him.

By 1999 the Counterterrorism Center had issued seven hundred reports to policymakers on bin Laden's operations. Tenet ordered even more focus on him, and the number of reports increased to nine hundred in the first nine months of 2000. But on October 12 of that year bin Laden struck again. In Aden, Yemen, a small boat laden with explosives blew up alongside the USS *Cole*, killing seventeen U.S. sailors. Later a recruitment video showed bin Laden praising the bombers.

In contrast to the CIA, which spied overseas, the FBI, which focused on domestic law enforcement, was not nearly as alert to the threat. The FBI foiled an attempt by al Qaeda to blow up the Holland and Lincoln tunnels, the United Nations, and the FBI's New York Field Office. The bureau also determined that al Qaeda had connections through Al Kifah Refugee Center in Brooklyn to some of those convicted in the 1993 attack on the World Trade Center. But under Louis Freeh's leadership, the FBI tended to treat each incident as a separate case, instead of recognizing the larger threat and mounting an effort against the entire al Qaeda organization, as the bureau did with the Ku Klux Klan and organized crime.

Freeh, a former New York field agent, had a vendetta against headquarters and slashed its staff. In doing so, he cut back on the ability of the FBI to disseminate and pursue intelligence leads. Freeh had no use for technology, either. In fact, the first thing he did when he became director in 1993 was to banish the computer from his office. He did not use e-mail. As a result of Freeh's aversion to technology, the bureau was paper-based and inundated with information that it could not assimilate, much less analyze. Shockingly, the FBI was still grinding along with 386 and 486 personal computers unsuitable even as donations to charity. The bureau's computer system was so flawed that memos sent to agents never arrived, and there was no way for the sender to know if a memo had been received. To store a single document on the FBI's Automated Case Support system required twelve separate computer commands. On these green-screened terminals, the FBI could search for the word "flight" or the word "schools"—retrieving millions of documents each time—but not for "flight schools."

The CIA, in contrast, had been able to perform searches for "flight schools" on its computers since 1958, but it was still suffering from neglect both by Congress and by DCIs who wanted to subvert it. Tenet, who avidly sent e-mail by Lotus Notes, recognized the importance of technology, and he recognized the need for HUMINT. He tried to strike a balance between being a cheerleader for the CIA and fixing it, between empathizing with the troops and making needed changes.

"At the end of the day, the men and women of U.S. intelligence—not satellites or sensors or high speed computers—are our most precious asset," Tenet would say. It was the opposite of Deutch's approach, symbolized by his quote in the *New York Times Magazine* comparing CIA employees unfavorably with the military.

"Tenet restored a sense of pride," Joanne Isham said.

At the same time, Tenet did not put up with employees who did not measure up, and he made it clear he would not tolerate lack of cooperation, either within or without the agency.

"Early on the Counterterrorism Center was not liked by any division," said Jack Devine, the former acting deputy director for operations. "It was a turf battle. The center and division chiefs were at each other's throats. This changed as the centers took root. George recognized that if you really want to get the job done you have to do it together."

"George doesn't want excuses about lack of cooperation," said John O. Brennan, who was his chief of staff and became deputy executive director.[141]

While Tenet had a clear vision of where he wanted the agency to be, it would take time for the DCI to put his own people in place, to put his stamp on the agency, and to alter the culture of the DO, known for its parochial mind set. While the CIA had shifted its focus away from Russia, it was not focused enough on counterterrorism. Like an ocean liner, the CIA changed course slowly. That was illustrated by two highly embarrassing failures early on under Tenet's watch. The first, on May 8, 1998, was the CIA's failure to warn that India was about to conduct a nuclear weapon test. The new Indian government had campaigned on a promise that it would develop a nuclear program. While the Indians learned through previous cooperation with the U.S. how to conceal preparations for a test, with the proper focus, the CIA, with the National Imagery and Mapping Agency (NIMA), should have been able to penetrate the deception.

The second mistake—the erroneous bombing of the Chinese embassy in Belgrade on May 7, 1999—was far more egregious. Every American diplomat in Belgrade knew the address of the Chinese embassy. Yet a CIA contract employee gave the Pentagon the Chinese embassy as the address of the Yugoslav Federal Directorate of Supply and Procurement, an arms agency and military target.

In both cases Tenet moved quickly to admit mistakes and get out the facts. Unlike Casey, Tenet was comfortable with oversight, just as William Colby had been. The way to handle delicate issues in public testimony was simple. CIA officers were instructed, "If you feel uncomfortable talking about a subject because of its sensitivity, tell them," according to Stanley M. Moskowitz, Tenet's chief of congressional affairs.[142]

Rather than stiffing lawmakers, Tenet was constantly on the phone with them, informing them of the latest developments and schmoozing them, just as he kept his Intelligence Advisory Group informed. By building relationships, he inoculated himself against unfounded criticism. The longer remedial action was delayed, the more the issue would fester, with members of Congress leaking bits of information and the media yelping about the agency's failings. Tenet dealt with negative news by jumping on the issue and dealing with it.

"There's no secret to this," Tenet would say about his good relations with Congress. "You just have to be straight."

Because the Indian matter involved not just the CIA but the National Reconnaissance Office (NRO), Tenet asked an outsider, retired U.S. Navy Admiral David Jeremiah, a former vice chairman of the Joint Chiefs of Staff, to investigate and issue a report. In the Chinese embassy case, he asked Britt Snider, the CIA's inspector general, to investigate.

"George called me in and wanted me to investigate and report back in three weeks," Snider said. "This was an extremely unusual task for us. Ordinarily it took us months to do a report, but I pulled twelve or fifteen people off other investigations, and we met the DCI's deadline."[143]

Snider found that the agency contract employee had identified the building that was bombed by using an old city map of Belgrade. Believing that he could identify the street number of a Serb military building on one street by comparing it with a building number known to him on a parallel street, he managed to identify instead the new Chinese Embassy, which was not shown at all on the map he was using. A subsequent review of the target identified by the U.S. military did not reveal the mistake, despite the fact that those reviews were specifically intended to identify, and avoid damage to, buildings like embassies and hospitals.

Tenet fired the employee responsible and gave oral warnings or issued letters of reprimand to six others. As a result, they were not eligible for promotions or financial awards for a year. He also praised an analyst from another agency who was assigned to the CIA and, based on his knowledge of Belgrade, had repeatedly questioned the target location. Tenet made sure each member of the intelligence committees got a copy of Snider's report.

As for the Indian failure, less than a month after the test, Jeremiah held a news conference reporting his findings. In contrast, under Louis Freeh, nine separate FBI and Justice Department investigations were conducted over the course of a decade into an accidental FBI shooting at Ruby Ridge in Idaho. While the investigations were pending, Freeh promoted Larry A. Potts, one of the FBI officials in charge of the engagement at Ruby Ridge, to be deputy FBI director.[144]

Jeremiah said that the CIA, in a classic case of mirror imaging, thought the hard-line Bharatiya Janata Party, which came to power a month before the Indian tests, would "behave as we have" and avoid a confrontation over nuclear tests. Thus, increased coverage that would have detected preparations for the tests was not ordered. The fact that Frank Wisner Jr., then the U.S. ambassador to India, showed top Indian officials photographs from spy satellites that detected preparations for tests in 1995 did not help. The photos gave the Indians clues on how they could conceal cables and wires running into the shaft where they conducted tests. In addition, the CIA did not have agents on the inside who might have reported on the preparations for the tests. Finally, there was not enough coordination among the CIA, National Imagery and Mapping Agency, and other agencies that were part of the intelligence community. In part, the decreased satellite and analyst coverage was due to budget cuts. NIMA had only one analyst on duty looking at images of Indian test facilities.

"There is no getting around the fact that we did not predict these particular Indian nuclear tests," Tenet told reporters after briefing members of the Senate Select Committee on Intelligence about the failure. "We did not get it right, period. We have a professional responsibility to stand up, acknowledge that, and learn from it," he said.

In theory, as DCI, Tenet was in charge of the intelligence community and thus could give orders to NIMA and the NRO. In practice, beyond the CIA, he had little real control over the fourteen agencies that comprised the intelligence community. Trying to get them to cooperate was like trying to get a consensus between the litigants in divorce court. It was the one part of his job that bored Tenet. In May 1998, Tenet appointed Joan Dempsey, his chief of staff, deputy DCI for community management. He hoped Dempsey, like Judge Judy, would resolve the spats.

Dempsey, forty-seven, was a naval reserve officer who became deputy assistant secretary of Defense for intelligence and security before coming to the CIA. She had also been director of the Military Intelligence Production Center. In her new job, Dempsey, a calm, confident woman, was in charge of the intelligence community. Besides the CIA, the members ranged from NSA, NIMA, the FBI, and the NRO to the State, Treasury and Energy departments, and the Coast Guard, within the new Homeland Security Department.

When I met with Dempsey in her office on the sixth floor of CIA headquarters, the chiefs of two of the intelligence community agencies had just left. They had been fighting over which one would run a new collection capability, and Dempsey had been trying to negotiate a settlement.

"They literally almost came to blows," she said. "Sometimes it's like Middle East diplomacy," she confided. "They value our perspective, but I can't tell them what to do. With the two agencies who were in before, we did work out a solution. Things are better than before 9/11 and a lot better than five years ago. But the DCI should have more control."

Tenet tried to foster more cooperation by letting the chiefs of the other agencies in on some of the CIA's more sensitive projects. That made them open up about their own activities and fostered trust. But while their budgets were part of the $40 billion annual intelligence budget that Tenet was in charge of, how the money was spent was up to each agency. A total of 85 percent of it went through the Defense Department.

For years, commissions and committees had studied the problem. It was no surprise that most concluded that one person—the

DCI—should hold the purse strings. But the many vested interests in the military and in Congress blocked any change.

"The community is still very competitive," John Gannon said. "The management of the community is almost nonexistent. In practice, there is no director of Central Intelligence."

Besides being dysfunctional, the intelligence community had been starved for funds. After she took over management of the intelligence community, Tenet told Dempsey, "I need you to get me more money."

"How much money? What for?" she asked.

"More HUMINT, analytical, overhead," Tenet said. Everything needed rebuilding.

While the Clinton administration gave her a cold shoulder, through Tenet, she was able to get Newt Gingrich, the House speaker, behind the effort. Soon, the CIA and the intelligence community began receiving supplemental appropriations—$260 million for fiscal 1998 and $1.8 billion for fiscal 1999, bringing the total in 1999 to $29 billion.

Supplementals, however, were good for one year. The CIA received only about $4 billion of the total allocated to the intelligence community. Supplementals were no way to rebuild an organization.

17

—

When it came to bin Laden, Tenet was not content to convey warnings. He wanted bin Laden and his cohorts killed. That was the only way to deal with al Qaeda. But Clinton, a master of spin, tended to look no further than the next day's headlines.

After the attack on American embassies in Africa, Clinton ordered a cruise missile attack in August 1998 on an al Qaeda paramilitary training camp in Khost, Afghanistan, and on the al-Shifa pharmaceutical plant in Khartoum, Sudan's capital. The plant was believed to be making VX, a clear liquid so lethal that a fraction of a drop on the skin can kill a person by disrupting the nervous system. Bin Laden was thought to be behind its production.

Whether the pharmaceutical factory was, in fact, making biological weapons quickly became an issue. An agent had collected a soil sample at the al-Shifa plant containing Empta, a chemical used in making VX nerve gas. But later investigation raised questions about whether the agent had been sloppy and had allowed the sample to be contaminated.

"Today we have struck back," Clinton said after the missile attacks.

If the statement was risible, it diverted public attention from Clinton's televised admission three days earlier that he had misled the American people about his relationship with White House intern Monica S. Lewinsky. Even if bin Laden had been killed, such an attack could never inflict real damage on al Qaeda.

"The Clinton people couldn't seem to decide what to do," James Simon said. "They had fifth or sixth thoughts about almost everything."

Tenet did not like controversy, and he was loyal to the presidents who appointed him. If Clinton—and initially Bush—were not ready to wage all-out war on al Qaeda, Tenet would have to accept it, just as he accepted the role of helping to negotiate peace in the Middle East. Both sides in the conflict liked and trusted Tenet, and Clinton asked the DCI to serve as mediator. Tenet acted as a broker in negotiations that produced an accord in 1998 at the Wye River Plantation in Maryland and helped forge a cease fire between the Israelis and the Palestinians in 2001.

Major General Giora Eiland, chief of the Israeli Army's planning division and one of the negotiators, told reporters that Tenet was probably the only person in the world who could have brought the two sides together.

The Palestinians were just as effusive in their praise of Tenet. "Neither the Palestinians nor the Israelis want to look bad in front of this gentleman," Saeb Erekat, a senior Palestinian negotiator, said of the DCI.

But the cease-fires were ephemeral, and Tenet's role as a policy player undermined the CIA's image as an impartial purveyor of intelligence. Clinton was looking for a quick fix, and Tenet went along. However, Tenet drew the line when, in November 1998, Clinton seemed to be moving toward pardoning the Israeli spy Jonathan Jay Pollard. As a research specialist with the Naval Investigative Service, Pollard, thirty-one, had stolen over a thousand classified documents and gave them to Israel. While he tried to portray himself as a savior of Israel and the U.S., Pollard received from the Israelis cash and gifts equal to his after-tax salary and his wife's.[145] At the White House, Tenet told Clinton he did not think he could set foot again in the agency if the president pardoned Pollard. Clinton backed off.

In contrast to Clinton, George W. Bush understood how important intelligence was, and he came into office with a desire to put more money into it. Eventually he phased out Tenet's role in Middle East peace talks.

George Bush's approach to life dovetailed with Tenet's: Both were very focused, both prized action over words, both were highly patriotic. Accepting the Ellis Island Medal of Honor on November 6, 1997, Tenet described how his Greek mother had fled southern Albania on a British submarine to escape Communism, never to see her family again.

"She was my hero," he said.

Tenet's Greek immigrant father "taught me to value hard work, to honor this great country, and to take nothing for granted," Tenet said. "Nowhere in the world could the son of an immigrant stand before you as the director of Central Intelligence. This is simply the greatest country on the face of the earth."

Like Tenet, Bush was an emotional man, tearing up when speaking of the sacrifices of American troops fighting to defend freedom. While Bush was a product of Andover, Yale, and Harvard, he harbored resentments against the East Coast elite. Like

Harry Truman, who was from Independence, Missouri, and never graduated from college, Bush thought of himself as a humble man from Crawford, Texas, which he considered home.

Similarly, Tenet thought of himself as having blue-collar roots. He once worked as a busboy in his father's diner and was not impressed by fancy academic credentials. In 1999, when speaking at his high school alma mater, Benjamin N. Cardoza in Queens, Tenet told the students: "Many of you will go on to college and you will run into people who went to fancy prep schools and who appear to have a higher quality education than you do. They don't."

If Tenet could be blunt at times, so could Bush. Neither man was given to pretense or "hand-wringing," the phrase Bush applied contemptuously to those who endlessly worried about taking decisive action. With Tenet, there was no meandering academic analysis, just straight talk.

"He wasn't puffed up or pompous," Vice President Dick Cheney said of Tenet. "The president clearly likes that."

Bush and Tenet had one more trait in common: They were both baseball fans. Growing up, Bush dreamed not about being president but about being Willie Mays. He later acquired an interest in the Texas Rangers. When Tenet was in New York seeing his mother in Queens or attending to CIA business, he tried to take in a Yankees game whenever he could.

Although Tenet occasionally slept over at Camp David when attending meetings there, he and Bush were not personal friends. "He can like you, but that's not what he judges you on," Tenet said. "Instead, it's, 'Are you doing your job? Are you delivering what you're supposed to be delivering?' " With Bush, "What you see is what you get," Tenet said. "He's not prepackaged. He tells you what he thinks. He's direct, and he's blunt."

"George knows his brief, has great personal charm and recall, and doesn't play games with presidents," Simon said. "If you are Bush, you want Joe Friday, not Richelieu. You already have your Richelieus. George laid out the facts and wouldn't intrude."

On September 2, 2000, the CIA gave Bush, while he was running against Al Gore, his first briefing in Crawford. Harry Truman had begun the custom in 1952 of giving presidential candidates CIA briefings on world developments.

"If what you give me is useful, you're in," Bush told Jami Miscik, when she went to Texas to start the postelection briefings. A former executive assistant to Tenet, Miscik became deputy director for intelligence.[146]

A week before Bush's inauguration Tenet and Pavitt met with him, filling him in on covert action and clandestine operations throughout the world. In any given year, the CIA undertook about a hundred covert action programs. The vast majority were covert propaganda or drug interdictions or eradications. The fact that the CIA tracked drug smugglers flying over Peru was a covert action. Similarly, at the request of some countries, the CIA provided weapons, vehicles, training, and data bases for checking on travelers going through customs. The funding for these activities was covert because the countries did not want their own people to know the United States was helping.

By executive orders going back to the Ford administration, assassinations were banned. But the executive orders didn't define assassination. By definition, assassination is a killing for a political motive. As the CIA saw it, killing as part of an effort to arrest an individual, killing in retaliation for an attack, or killing as part of a military action was not assassination and thus was not banned.

Moreover, a president could always rescind the order and permit assassinations. In that case, the danger was that other countries would feel emboldened to retaliate.

At their briefing of Bush, Tenet and Pavitt warned that bin Laden was an immediate threat, and Tenet said that bin Laden was definitely coming after the U.S. again. They briefed Bush on the previous efforts to capture him. With Clinton's authorization, the CIA in 1999 began training six Pakistani commandoes to corner bin Laden in Afghanistan. The operation was stopped after a military coup in Pakistan. The CIA also recruited thirty Afghan agents to track him, but he moved so often they never could pinpoint his location in time for a missile attack. Clinton's findings had not authorized killing bin Laden outright. Instead, he could have been arrested and killed if he posed a threat to those who sought to capture him.

The CIA had 110 lawyers, including fifty assigned to the DO. One of their functions, according to John A. Rizzo, the agency's senior deputy general counsel, was seeing that a covert action conformed with the finding the agency submitted to the president to sign.[147]

Bush thought the Clinton's administration's response to bin Laden only confirmed that the U.S. would do little to go after him. In effect, tossing cruise missiles into tents was like waving a red handkerchief in front of a bull, goading him to attack again. Condoleeza Rice, Bush's national security advisor, called it "feckless."

Pavitt and Tenet reviewed other threats with Bush: proliferation of weapons of mass destruction and the rise of Chinese military power. They cited a December 2000 CIA estimate warning of more sophisticated terrorist tactics and a growing threat of missile attacks by rogue states.

"Between now and 2015, terrorist tactics will become increasingly sophisticated and designed to achieve mass casualties," the estimate stated. It said North Korea had one and possibly two nuclear weapons and could have "a few to several" intercontinental ballistic missiles deployed by 2005. In fact, going back to the early 1990s, the CIA had obtained the help of the Russian SVR intelligence service in placing sensors in North Korea that successfully detected North Korean efforts to reprocess plutonium that could be used as fuel in nuclear bombs, violating international agreements. In 1992, the CIA created a Nonproliferation Center to focus on the growing problem of proliferation of weapons of mass destruction, a trend fueled by the demise of the Soviet Union.

Tenet appreciated Bush's focus and understanding of the role of intelligence.

"The great thing is, you bring him a problem and he wants to know what the solution is," Tenet said. "He puts a premium on action and movement. He doesn't waste a lot of time. He understands the way the world works and how our business works in this world. It's all about what we're getting done and what we're accomplishing. He holds us to high standards, and that's all you can ask for."

By the middle of January 2001, Bush had decided to ask Tenet to stay on as DCI, making Tenet the first CIA director in twenty-eight years to stay on after the White House switched parties.

"I think his word is considered good in this town, which is high praise," Representative Porter J. Goss, a former CIA case officer who headed the House Permanent Select Committee on Intelligence, said of Tenet, then forty-seven, after being told of Bush's decision to retain him.

"We got lucky," said Senator Bob Kerrey, formerly the top

Democrat on the Senate Select Committee on Intelligence. "George is an extraordinary manager."

When Tenet returned to the CIA from his breakfast with Boren at 9:50 A.M. on September 11 he convened a meeting first in his office and then in the CIA's Incident Management Center. The center was a small conference room on the first floor of head-quarters with two 42-inch plasma video screens on one wall. It was next to a larger Security Command Center. Staffed around the clock, the command center had seven consoles where dis-patches monitored alarms and watched forty-two color digital screens with views of the CIA complex inside and out. When an alarm came in, the dispatchers could zero in and see, for example, whether an intruder was trying to scale a fence or whether a deer was the offender.

In 1977 three Marine officers got drunk in Georgetown and decided to prove their manhood by climbing over the CIA's fence. Well past midnight, they parked their car along George Washing-ton Memorial Parkway and made a run for the fence near the side entrance. Alarms went off, pinpointing the exact location of the intrusion. By the time armed security guards reached the area, one of the Marines was already inside. The guards drew their guns and stopped him. With the help of Fairfax County police, they caught the other two running back to their car. The CIA reported the incident to Quantico Marine base, where the officers were assigned. Each got two weeks in the brig.

A little over a month before 9/11 a fire in a CIA elevator shaft sent black smoke billowing through parts of the CIA's original building, forcing an evacuation of both buildings. The fire started at 5:45 P.M. on August 6, 2001, when a workman at the top of an elevator shaft dropped a welder, which ignited wood left from the building's construction at the bottom of the shaft. The fire brought sixty firefighters to the CIA's complex.

Buzzy Krongard was dismayed when he found that plans for an evacuation of headquarters were spotty, and some fire alarms did not work. No one had been told if they should store classified material first before leaving, and no clear-cut plan existed for assembly at offsite locations so that the CIA's work could continue.

After the fire Krongard initiated regular fire drills and equipped key CIA officials with tiny walkie-talkies. If cell phones went out, they could still communicate. Exiting safely, Krongard decreed, was more important than storing classified material. He had the CIA's computer network reprogrammed so that, if necessary, a warning to evacuate would flash on all computer screens.

The fire turned out to be fortuitous. After issuing orders in the Incident Management Center on September 11, Tenet decided to evacuate the CIA. A fourth hijacked plane was over Pennsylvania and believed heading toward Washington, probably to hit the Capitol. There were reports of additional aircraft having been hijacked. The CIA could be the next target.

Following procedures laid out by Krongard after the fire, Tenet and other top officials met at another location on the CIA campus. As the chief of the Counterterrorism Center, Cofer Black insisted that the eight people assigned to the center's Global Response Center remain on the job on the sixth floor. They monitored the latest intelligence on terrorism. The job was critical. If they were killed, so be it.

By now, the Counterterrorism Center had grown to 340 people, compared with twenty when it was started in 1986. The personnel included more than a dozen FBI agents detailed to the CIA. The center knew a great deal about al Qaeda, and agents had penetrated the organization, but not at high levels. For his inner circle, bin Laden recruited fanatics he had known for decades. Most had family connections to him or to other high-level leaders of al Qaeda. While twenty-year-old American John Philip Walker Lindh joined the Taliban and met bin Laden several times, he learned few secrets. The fact that no one turned in bin Laden, even after the U.S. government offered rewards that began at $5 million and eventually zoomed to $25 million, demonstrated how loyal his organization was.

"He has a small council," said Charles E. Allen, who once served as a deputy director of the Counterterrorism Center and served for several years as the National Intelligence Officer for counterterrorism. "It's highly compartmented. His key lieutenants carried out the plot." At the same time, Allen said, al Qaeda was patient. "They take a year to two years to execute," Allen said. "They won't be tied to artificial deadlines."

In their temporary meeting place on the CIA campus, CIA officers resorted to using grease pens on white board to post the latest developments. An officer from the Counterterrorism Center brought Tenet a list of passengers who were on the plane that crashed into the Pentagon. Pointing to two names, he said he recognized them as al Qaeda members the CIA had been tracking.

Tenet had no time to dwell on how many times he had issued warnings about al Qaeda. He had to appear strong. "When you're in the middle of anything like this, you're leading an organization, and everybody is looking at your face," he told me.

Within an hour of the attacks, commentators began referring to the "intelligence failure." Tenet bristled every time he heard the term. It was true that ever since the CIA had been formed in response to the attack on Pearl Harbor, its purpose had been to thwart such an assault. Clearly, it had failed in that mission. But "intelligence failure" implied that the CIA was capable of knowing everything before it happened, and that when it didn't—like a jet engine that quits over the Atlantic—it had failed.

"Intelligence is imperfect," Cofer Black, the chief of the Counterterrorism Center, said. "We knew another attack would occur. We thought it would happen overseas. George said in 1998 we are at war. We did everything possible with what we had. We work with what they give us."

"We never claimed we could protect the U.S. from every attack," said former assistant DCI for administration Simon. "That's impossible."

Tenet told his people there would be no excuses. "We were working hard to stop al Qaeda. What we did well or didn't do well we don't tell people," he said. "We do not point fingers at other people, because it's your turn in the barrel in another two minutes in this town. Do not focus on the grenades being lobbed at us. Let me deal with that. You do your job. We are going to move forward and prove our worth."

For months, Black and his people had been preparing a plan to work with the military to topple the Taliban who harbored al Qaeda and to go after bin Laden. Tenet and Black recognized that there was a limit to how much intelligence alone could accomplish. The only way to protect the U.S. was to go on the offensive.

"We have to run them down like dogs," Black told Tenet. "When we get them, they will have flies walking across their eyeballs."[148]

By 1 P.M., Tenet was back in his office, polishing an action plan to present to Bush. At the same time, he issued orders to obtain intelligence on the attack, including from other security services.

For three days after the attacks, Allen, who coordinated satellite coverage, slept on an air mattress in his office. His job was to focus the satellites on targets selected by Tenet and Bush. Each day thousands of requests poured into the CIA from the intelligence community for satellite surveillance and intercepts. Only a fraction could be accommodated.

Besides HUMINT, the CIA and NSA used eavesdropping satellites, orbiting the earth from about twenty-two thousand miles up, to listen in on radio transmissions, cell phones, or walkie-talkies. CIA and NSA officials were furious when bin Laden and his key lieutenants stopped using a satellite phone in 1998, following what NSA Director Michael V. Hayden has referred to as "press reports of our intercepts." In congressional testimony in October 2002, Hayden described the compromise as a "setback of inestimable consequences."

The press report Hayden had in mind has never been identified publicly. When asked, NSA declined to comment. But a CIA official told me the source of the compromise is believed to be an article in the *Washington Post* on August 17, 1998, ten days after al Qaeda bombed American embassies in Kenya and Tanzania. The article paraphrased Vincent Cannistraro, who had been chief of operations at the Counterterrorism Center in the late 1980s, as claiming that he was "aware of intercepted electronic communications among bin Laden associates in the aftermath of the embassy bombings in which they take credit for the attacks and exchange warm congratulations."

In a subsequent letter to the editor, Cannistraro, without denying that he had made the claim, said his own statement was untrue. "I do not have current access to intelligence-collection techniques, nor am I aware of the specific nature of any intelligence information the U.S. intelligence community has on bin Laden's alleged responsibility," Cannistraro wrote.[149]

Within days of the publication of Cannistraro's claim, bin Laden and his people stopped using the phone. Based on other intelligence pinpointing bin Laden's location, the U.S. launched the August 20 cruise missile strike on the training camp where he was that day. Regardless of the strike, intelligence officials believe bin Laden would have continued to use the phone if the intercepts had not been compromised.

Two days before Cannistraro's claim was published, a Knight-Ridder story that appeared in nine local papers quoted Cannistraro extensively on the bombings. It said that "U.S. intelligence officials" said "an exhaustive review of electronic intercepts of traffic on bin Laden's communications network has uncovered some evidence that bin Laden helped plan the attacks, along with some congratulatory messages after the August 7 bombings in Nairobi and Dar es Salaam."

Because that statement appeared in papers such as the *New Orleans Times-Picayune* and the *Dayton Daily News,* the CIA did not consider it as significant a compromise. An on-the-record comment in the *Washington Post* by a former CIA counterterrorism official was an entirely different matter. Once the comments appeared, subsequent press stories speculated about whether NSA was intercepting bin Laden's communications. Because those stories were not as specific or credible and appeared days after bin Laden stopped using the phone, they were not considered as significant as the original story.

Cannistraro's public statements years earlier that the CIA was a "dinosaur" and more recently that it was a bureaucratic "mush factory" had not endeared him to his former colleagues at the agency. But the intelligence community never fingered him for compromising the bin Laden intercepts because any SIGINT information is highly classified and because intelligence officials as a rule do not want to call even more attention to the fact that NSA intercepts communications of terrorists. In addition, no one is eager to single out for criticism a powerful and normally responsible media outlet like the *Washington Post*.

Cannistraro recently told me he had no comment on the matter beyond his letter to the editor.

Two months after the embassy bombings top CIA operatives began meeting daily to work on the bin Laden problem under the direction of David Carey, then the executive director. After September 11, Tenet took charge of the daily bin Laden meeting. It was held in his office and began anywhere from 5 to 6 P.M. With tongue in cheek, Tenet called it the "Small Group."

Meanwhile, CIA managers called in Gilman Louie. Suddenly, they could not get enough of In-Q-Tel's wares.

"Prior to 9/11, some at the agency were receptive, but most said, 'We're busy,' " Louie said. "We were considered an interesting concept. We had to prove that we were of value. After 9/11, they said, 'Show me everything you have.' "[150]

Beyond programs, In-Q-Tel began seeking such technology as smaller batteries and advanced geospatial positioning systems. More than a year after 9/11, the CIA was using thirty programs or other technology supplied by In-Q-Tel.

"Especially after 9/11, they came to realize what In-Q-Tel could do for them," John McMahon said.

As with his statements warning that bin Laden posed the greatest threat to the U.S., Tenet's support of In-Q-Tel, despite tremendous skepticism, had proved uncannily farsighted. The Pentagon and other agencies began looking into setting up their own In-Q-Tel's. Now everyone wanted to claim credit for the idea. Everyone, that is, except for John Deutch, who dismissed In-Q-Tel as "silly."

18

On the morning of September 12, Tenet's CIA security guards picked him up at his home and drove him to the White House. On the way, he read his copy of the President's Daily Brief (PDB), the TOP SECRET/CODEWORD digest of the latest intelligence. Tenet had seen a draft at ten the previous night. Revisions had been added to the PDB until 3 A.M. Additional material was often sent by courier. On the trip over, Tenet's own briefer filled in gaps.

Until President Ford took office, presidents read the PDB but were not briefed in person. The face-to-face briefing served not only to convey information more fully but also to pick up any questions the president had.

At 8 A.M. Tenet and Mike, the regular CIA briefer, met with Bush in the Oval Office and gave him the PDB. The PDB ran ten to twelve pages with five to six items. Another twelve pages contained full reports from case officers, the DI, or from NSA. Images from NIMA were also included.

"We say, 'Here is what we know. Here are the gaps. Here is

what we extrapolated from that and why,'" said Jami Miscik, the head of the Directorate of Intelligence (DI), which oversaw the preparation of the PDB. "Our mission is to inform the policy-makers. We help them think through the ramifications of possible actions."

Before 9/11, the briefing lasted from fifteen to twenty-five minutes. After 9/11 it sometimes lasted an hour, followed by a briefing by FBI Director Mueller. Usually, National Security Advisor Condoleeza Rice sat in. Besides Bush, the CIA provided daily briefings to thirty other key policymakers, including Defense Secretary Donald H. Rumsfeld and Secretary of State Colin L. Powell.

Bush and the others asked questions that the briefers funneled back to the CIA. In August 2001, Bush asked for more information on bin Laden's possible interest in attacking the U.S. The CIA put together an historical analysis of his previous attacks. The analysis mentioned an al Qaeda plot to take over an airliner and demand the release of Sheik Omar Abdel Rahman, who is serving a life sentence for plotting to blow up New York landmarks in 1993.

"Bush reads the PDB and asks questions," said Mike, the regular briefer. "Or he and George Tenet have a policy discussion. George has experience in intelligence and foreign policy and provides context."

"The Bush people listen," said Simon. "If you said something in the Clinton White House, you would have a breach if you disagreed with their policy position. Bush made it clear it was our job to tell him, and it was his job to decide."

On the morning of September 12, the PDB cited reports tying the attacks to bin Laden, including one from Kandahar saying the plot had been in the works for two years. Several reports cited

Ayman Zawahiri, the Egyptian doctor who was the second-ranking member of al Qaeda, as having played a role in the 9/11 attacks.

Tenet promised Bush he would present him with a plan for covert action. The CIA had been working with the Northern Alliance in Afghanistan for years, doling out millions in exchange for intelligence. The plan developed by Cofer Black and Pavitt would make use of these assets and tribal leaders in the south of Afghanistan. Being inseparable from al Qaeda, the Taliban had to go. Tenet warned Bush that the plan would be expensive. To get up to speed, the agency might need as much as an additional $1 billion—about half the cost of a B-2 stealth bomber.

Walking through the corridors of the CIA, Tenet turned to John McLaughlin, the deputy DCI.

"These bastards don't know what they started," he said.[151]

As chief of the DO, Pavitt issued another electronic cable to all stations. The agency, he said, was developing "an unprecedented new covert action program" intended to "wreak havoc" upon the sponsors and supporters of radical Islamic terrorism. Pavitt asked officers to come up with "novel, untested ways" to do the job.

Later that day Tenet marshaled the troops in the Bubble.

"The important thing for us now is to do our job," he said. "To run to ground a vicious foe—one without heart or pity . . . the terrorists behind these atrocities—and those who give them shelter and support—must never know rest, ease, or comfort. The last word," Tenet said, "must not be theirs."

The following day, at 9:30 A.M., Tenet and Black met with Bush and the NSC in the White House Situation Room. Tenet presented the president with a plan to track down bin Laden, topple the Taliban in Afghanistan, and confront global terrorism. The plan called for CIA paramilitary teams and U.S. Special Forces to hunt down the terrorists and kill them if necessary. The CIA would support and pay off the Northern Alliance to fight the Taliban, who harbored bin Laden and al Qaeda. And the agency would use its full complement of techniques—from human spying and interception of communications to satellite and reconnaissance plane surveillance—to find terrorists all over the world.

Black warned that Americans would die.

"That's war," Bush said. "That's what we're here to win."[152]

"Bush is focused," Black later told me. "He is a leader. He follows up. He holds you accountable. Two weeks later, he asks what you did to follow up on his questions or orders. He knows what is at stake. He assumes we are ten feet tall until we prove otherwise." Black said, "After 9/11, the gloves came off."[153]

Tenet gave a more detailed presentation of the covert action plan at Camp David on Saturday morning, September 15. He distributed a packet labeled "Going to War." The words recalled his statement in May 1997 to the Senate Appropriations Committee: "I think we are already at war." This time it was for real.

The packet featured a photo of bin Laden inside a red circle with a slash over his face. The CIA plan called for an attack on the network's financial support and a ferocious effort to track down bin Laden's supporters. In that effort, the CIA would enlist the help of eighty countries and would use friendly Arab intelligence services—those of Jordan, Egypt, and Morocco, in particular. The CIA would subsidize them with funds for training and equipment.

Tenet wanted broad authority to conduct the CIA's war, one that would allow use of deadly force as part of the U.S. effort at self-defense and thus would not require him to seek approval for each action. He presented it as a modification of Reagan's 1986 intelligence finding, the one that gave Dewey Clarridge authority to apprehend Fawaz Younis on board a yacht in the Mediterranean.

Bush thanked Tenet for his presentation. He said he would think about his proposals and those of his other advisors and would come back to them with decisions by Monday. Back at the agency, Tenet made it clear that foot-dragging would not be tolerated.

"There can be no bureaucratic impediments to success," Tenet said in a memo to top CIA officials on September 17. "All the rules have changed. There must be an absolute and full sharing of information, ideas, and capabilities." Having helplessly watched the CIA disintegrate to serial meetings under John Deutch, Tenet said, "We do not have time to hold meetings to fix problems—fix them quickly and smartly. Each person must assume an unprecedented degree of personal responsibility."

Tenet said the CIA should employ the same approach in dealings with law enforcement, military, civilian and other intelligence agencies. "Whatever systemic problems existed in any of these relationships must be identified and solved now," he said. "There must be an absolute seamlessness in our approach to waging this war—and we must lead."

"For days afterward, we had a feeling of, 'Dammit, why did this happen?' " Pavitt said. " 'Could we have stopped it?' This was as significant as the attack on Pearl Harbor. We had a lot of arrogance before 9/11, and that was wrong. You can't do it all alone."

By September 17, Bush had decided to grant all of Tenet's requests, including an extra $1 billion. Bush wanted the CIA to be first on the ground, preparing the way for the military with both intelligence officers and paramilitary officers.

The events of 9/11 "fundamentally changed the way the president looked at the world," said McLaughlin, who periodically briefed Bush and attended most of the meetings with the president to plan a counterattack. "I'm convinced he wakes up every morn-

ing thinking about how to prevent anything like that from hap-
pening again."

On Tuesday, September 25, Tenet reported to the NSC that
a paramilitary team from the CIA's Special Activities Division was
poised to enter Afghanistan. Formerly called the Military Support
Program, the Special Activities Division was a direct descendant of
the OSS. Over the years it had atrophied and now consisted of
only fifty officers. But, like the rest of the CIA, it leveraged its
work, recruiting agents to conduct operations.

Whether the CIA should have a paramilitary capability or
should leave the job to the Defense Department has always been
an issue. The intelligence purists argued that participating in military action undercut the CIA's role as an impartial purveyor of
intelligence; the military could do the job on its own. Tenet
believed that, because the CIA could operate undercover, it was
uniquely equipped to infiltrate a country. Normally, it could deploy faster than Special Forces. Besides, Tenet felt, actively engaging in operations, rather than passively gathering intelligence, gave
the CIA more clout, both literally and symbolically.

"There is a tradition that we turn on a dime faster than anybody
else," Tenet said. "We get on the ground fast. When you integrate
CIA paramilitary with Special Forces it's a very powerful tool. It
doesn't apply to every scenario," Tenet said, "but it sure does work."

Miscik, the deputy director in charge of the DI, had set up a
team of analysts whose job was to put themselves in bin Laden's
shoes and mind. The team listed his likely targets—airports, harbors, railroads, dams, tunnels, bridges, sports stadiums, military
centers, federal offices, Hollywood and Wall Street—and concluded that bin Laden would revisit locations al Qaeda had targeted
in the past.

"The U.S. will never set boots on the ground," bin Laden thought, according to the team, meaning America would lob missiles into tents but would not risk losing lives in a war.

Bin Laden was wrong. On September 27 a CIA officer named Gary led ten paramilitary officers into Afghanistan in a Russian-made Mi-17 helicopter owned by the CIA. Gary had spent twenty years undercover in Kabul, Tehran, Islamabad, and Dubai. After thirty-two years with the agency, he was just about to retire when Cofer Black asked him to stay on and lead a paramilitary team code-named JAWBREAKER. Not only was he the right leader for the job, he spoke Pashto and Dari, Afghanistan's principal languages.

"Find al Qaeda and kill them," Black said. "I want bin Laden's head in a box."

Gary took with him $3 million in nonsequential $100 bills that he carried in a large steel suitcase. Along with case officers who spoke Pashto and other local languages, Gary met with Northern Alliance leaders already recruited by the agency. He would place bundles of cash in front of them and ask for their help in preparing the way for U.S. Special Forces. He wanted the positions of enemy forces and intelligence on their communications, arms, and structure. Village elders could be bought for $5,000; warlords could be bought for $50,000 to $100,000.

By the end of September, the U.S. had amassed twenty-eight thousand sailors and troops and more than three hundred warplanes and two dozen warships in the Indian Ocean and Red Sea for an attack on the Taliban. On October 7, the bombing, aided by the British, began on Kabul, the capital and largest city in Afghanistan. Bombers, fighter planes, and Tomahawk cruise missiles pounded the airfields and other strongholds.

In prosecuting the war, the Predator, a CIA unmanned aircraft, was critical. It allowed the troops and U.S. Special Forces on the ground to view targets remotely in real time. The CIA developed the aircraft despite opposition from the Pentagon and Congress.

"The Predator represented out-of-the-box thinking," said Gene Poteat. "Originally the military did not like the idea."[154]

"When George asked for money for more Predators so we could build more than one or two, key staffers in Congress acted like he was trying simply to pump up his budget," Simon said.

In hunting terrorists the CIA also operated the Gnat, a twenty-four-foot-long unmanned plane that was equipped with radar called Lynx. Made by General Atomics, the plane could detect objects as small as four inches—about what a satellite could see—at a distance of up to sixteen miles, day or night, rain or shine. It relayed still photos or videos via satellite to remote locations. The Gnat flew quietly at four or five miles above the earth. It could stay aloft for forty-eight hours without refueling.

The Predator, also made by General Atomics, was twenty-seven feet long. It flew about as high as the Gnat and could stay in the air for forty hours at a time. Like the Gnat, it could hunt for small bands of fugitives, spot tire tracks and footprints, and detect objects as small as four inches. It had the horsepower and top speed of a motorbike. By day or night, the plane took full-motion video. Using radar, it took still images in cloudy weather.

Not content with aerial reconnaissance, Tenet had the Predator equipped with Hellfire antitank missiles for use by the CIA. In Afghanistan, the Predator's missiles destroyed enemy targets and killed Mohammad Atef, bin Laden's military commander, who was indicted in the 1998 embassy bombings and the 9/11 attacks. The Air Force operated the unmanned Predators.

By December 7, it was almost all over. The Taliban had abandoned Kandahar, their last stronghold, where the CIA had helped create a force of three thousand fighters. The CIA had spent $70 million on getting the Northern Alliance and tribal leaders to work for the agency. Much of the money went for equipment, light weapons, four-wheel-drive vehicles, and communication devices like satellite phones. Working in the shadows, the CIA had broken the enemy's spine.

In mid-December, U.S. and Afghan troops surrounded a giant cave complex in the eastern Afghan region of Tora Bora, where a radio transmission was believed to have come from bin Laden. The CIA had obtained maps of the caves from Russia, whose GRU, the military intelligence service, had compiled them during the Soviets' ten-year occupation of Afghanistan.

U.S. warplanes blanketed the area with bombs, but the U.S. relied largely on local Afghan forces on the ground. Hundreds of al Qaeda suspects escaped across the border to Pakistan. Bin Laden was believed to be among them.

On December 13, the Bush administration released a videotape of bin Laden chatting with followers. Recovered in Afghanistan, the videotape showed he had had prior knowledge of the attacks. Bin Laden gloated over the deaths.

"We calculated in advance the number of casualties" that would result when two airliners crashed into the World Trade Center, he said. "I was the most optimistic of all" in predicting how many would be killed, he said. On the morning of the attacks, bin Laden turned on a short wave radio to hear the news. His followers, he said, were "overjoyed when the first plane hit the World Trade Center, so I said to them, 'Be patient.'" Chuckling, he said that most of the hijackers recruited for the "martyrdom operation" had not been aware until the last minute that they were going to their deaths.

After days of reports by Northern Alliance commanders that an American intelligence officer had been killed, Tenet decided to confirm that Johnny "Mike" Spann, a CIA officer, had been gunned down on November 26. The fact that Spann was the first U.S. combat casualty of the war underscored that the CIA was back in the game, no longer an abject, risk-averse agency.

A former Marine, Spann was from Winfield, Alabama, and joined the agency in 1999. He had two daughters, Allison, nine, and Emily, four, from his first marriage. He met his second wife, Shannon, a pretty, slim woman with light brown hair, when they were trainees at the CIA. They had an infant son.

A paramilitary officer, Spann was killed when Taliban and al Qaeda revolted at a prison fortress outside the northern Afghan city of Mazar-e Sharif. Spann, thirty-two, had been questioning prisoners.

Before leaving Washington for Afghanistan Spann wrote a note to a CIA colleague: "I don't mean to sound dramatic, I'm sure this will be a piece of cake, but if anything happens to me, I want you to be the one to tell Shannon. I don't want her to hear it from someone she doesn't know." Shannon told journalist and author Edward Klein about the note for a piece in *Parade*.

The CIA sent a "grief team" of five, including the colleague Spann had designated, to tell Shannon the tragic news in southern California, where she was visiting her family for Thanksgiving. When Shannon told her children, Allison began crying.

"Who's going to teach Jake the daddy stuff?" Allison asked, referring to her baby brother.[155]

Like Shannon, Spann was a devout Christian and would read the Bible before going to sleep at night. He kept a journal, which was blown up when an air strike hit his vehicle near the prison fortress where he was killed. Spann's team leader managed to retrieve a few scraps of the journal and give them to Shannon.

"One thing has troubled me," he wrote to Shannon. "I'm not afraid of dying, but I have had a terrible fear of not being with you and our son . . . I think about holding you and touching you. I also think about holding that round boy of ours . . . It would be cool to have a slow dance with you to *Always and Forever*."

19

BEFORE 9/11 THE word *patriotism* was almost archaic, used mostly by aging veterans of World War II. President Johnson's dissembling about the war in Vietnam, the CIA and FBI abuses portrayed in the Church Committee hearings, and the cover-ups by President Nixon during Watergate turned Americans against their own government. That changed after two airplanes hit the World Trade Center, one hit the Pentagon, and a fourth plane hurtled into a Pennsylvania field.

E-mails poured into the CIA from the public. "God bless you, and I wish you great success in capturing Osama bin Laden and destroying all terrorist cells," said one from Canada. "You can do it. You are the best. If you ever decide to hire people with Canadian citizenship, please put me on your list."

"Thank you for being there for us," said one from the U.S. "We never hear the good that you do, and that is probably the way it should be. Just know that my prayers go out to you, our silent soldiers."

"Please do everything you can to get these guys," another

e-mail said. "I speak for everyone I know when I say we believe in you, but we're scared to death. May God direct you to these guys and give you the strength to shut them down."

A man signed over his $600 tax rebate check. "Buy bullets," his note said. After the death of Mike Spann, people sent in checks for his family.[156]

The CIA experienced a 40-percent surge in applications. A year later, the number had almost doubled, reaching two thousand to three thousand a week. CIA recruitment booths at colleges were swamped. Suddenly, it was cool to work for the shadowy agency.

Many of the applicants were people with established careers who wanted to help their country. Some were lawyers and investment bankers who were willing to take pay cuts of up to $100,000 a year or more to work for the CIA, where the starting salary was $40,000 to $60,000.

The patriotic fervor called to mind the early days of the agency. Back then, recalled Rolfe Kingsley, a wealthy Texas oilman who took a job with the CIA became incensed when his boss turned down his proposal to provide $3,000 a month—about $22,000 in today's terms—to support an anti-Communist cell in Europe.[157]

"I'll pay for it myself," the man stormed until his boss relented and agreed to support the project.

"We've always gotten people who want to make a difference, but now it's people who specifically want to contribute to the war against terrorism," said Robert A. Rebelo, the chief of the CIA Recruitment Center.

Like many CIA operations, the center is housed in a secure building in northern Virginia with no sign to mark it. As at headquarters, identification cards must be swiped at turnstiles to enter or leave. Rebelo, who spent much of his career in counternarcotics, displayed the agency's latest recruitment ads.

"Intelligence Secretary," said the headline on one ad. "Why work for a company when you can serve a nation?" A full-page ad in *Newsweek* said, "Your heritage is Arab-American. Your citizenship is all-American." The ad continued, "Patriotism. Freedom. Love of nation. If these words describe your values and beliefs, the Central Intelligence Agency would like to add a few more. Rewarding career. Outstanding opportunity. Worthwhile endeavor." Other ads specifically sought case officers ("The Ultimate International Career"), analysts, open source officers, language instructors, scientists, and engineers.

Applicants were directed to the CIA's Web site—www.cia.gov— or to a post office address box in Reston, Virginia. If they sounded promising, candidates were interviewed by two or three officers. In interviews for the DO, officers tried to determine if applicants had street smarts.

"We might try to see what sort of story an applicant comes up with when faced with a question about his or her identity," Rebelo said.[158]

If they passed that hurdle, they took psychological tests designed to weed out people who were impulsive. They underwent background checks and took a polygraph test. The process could take six months or more.

"We're looking for good judgment, people with a sense of self and a strong moral compass," said Martin C. Petersen, a former associate deputy director over the DI who was director of human resources. "If you work in a grey area, you better have some values that you believe in or you're going to run into problems. Some of the strengths we're looking for can also be weaknesses. You want people who take risks, but you are probably going to get some who push it too far. We try to weed out the cowboys."[159]

The entire training of a DO officer takes a year, including

paramilitary training at Camp Peary and Fort Bragg in North Carolina. Language training—the CIA teaches twenty languages—may take another year or two. It takes up to four years for a DO officer to be fully prepared to begin recruiting agents. Because of that, the CIA welcomed back retired operatives who wanted to help.

"I could not stop retirees who wanted to come back," Pavitt said. "They wanted to get back into the fight."

Twenty-five percent of new hires were minorities, but the CIA needed more Arabs, Pakistanis, and Iranians, who were not considered minorities. In a three-year period, the CIA tripled the number of Arabic speakers, but it needed more of them as well. Nationally, only about six hundred students were enrolled in Pashto, Dari, Farsi, or Uzbek courses. That meant the CIA had to train speakers in those languages from scratch.

Along with a torrent of applications the CIA got the usual nut cases. In one letter an applicant said, "I wanted to go to Korea, but I was suicidal. I wanted to go to Vietnam and die fighting for my country." He added, "I want to run a major rock band for the CIA. The CIA controls the rock business. I am in prison. Can you get me out of here?"

The letter bore stamps showing it had been screened by the Monroe Correctional Center in Monroe, Washington.

One morning Petersen and Frans Bax, the dean of CIA University, greeted twenty-six new CIA analysts in the CIA's main lobby. The analysts had completed what is called "CIA 101," a general course of a week. They were about to begin a six-month training program at the Sherman Kent School for Intelligence Analysis. Established by Tenet in 1999 and named for the founder of CIA intelligence analysis, the school was part of CIA University, which the CIA created in 2000. Overall, two-thirds of new analysts had graduate degrees. Some had doctorates in economics or physics; others worked for other federal agencies.

Along the left wall of the lobby was a statue of former OSS director William J. Donovan. On the wall was a biblical inscription from John 8:32, "And ye shall know the truth and the truth shall make you free."

Carved into the right wall were seventy-nine stars flanked by an American flag on the left and a flag with the seal of the CIA on the right. Each star represented a CIA officer who lost his or her life in the service of the agency. Beneath the memorial stars was a glass case that displayed a book listing the years when the officers died. In some cases the names of the officers were listed—Richard Welch, for example, who was killed by terrorists in Athens in December 1975, and Frank A. Darling and Lansing H. Bennett, who were killed at the CIA entrance in January 1993. Slightly less than half the names were not listed because the officers were operating undercover and their affiliation has never come out.

Once a year, the CIA holds a ceremony in front of the stars for the surviving families. Some leave flowers, either anonymously or with names and photos of deceased loved ones.

Standing in front of the stars, Petersen pointed out to the analysts—sixteen men, including one black man and ten women—that there was more than one star for every year of the agency's existence.

"Those stars commemorate the men and women of this agency who gave their lives in service to our nation," he said. "There are analysts on that wall. And those men and women walked through the same doors you walked through and strode across the seal on which you now stand," Petersen said, referring to the CIA's seal imbedded in the grey and white Georgia marble floor. Petersen noted that thirty-five of those who died were not listed in the book below the stars.

"We labor in the shadows," he said.

Originally, Bax said, CIA analysts were confined to Langley. Over the years that gradually changed. Back in the 1980s, Bax said, he was a counterterrorism analyst based in Lebanon and Jordan. "I knew Bob Ames, who was killed in a bombing of the embassy in Lebanon," he said. "I knew Bill Buckley, who was kidnapped by Hezbolah. He was tortured and died. I knew Lansing Bennett," one of the two men gunned down by terrorist Aimal Kasi at the Route 123 entrance to the CIA in 1993.[160]

Bax mentioned the permanent memorial Tenet had just dedicated to the two CIA officers Kasi had slain. It consisted of a Dakota mahogany granite wall and two teak benches at the Route 123 entrance. The wall was inscribed, "In Remembrance of Ultimate Dedication to Mission Shown by Officers of the Central Intelligence Agency Whose Lives Have Been Taken or Forever Changed by Events at Home and Abroad."

Petersen held up a loose-leaf book with a blue cover and the presidential seal on it.

"This is what the building is all about," he said, displaying the President's Daily Brief. "Everything here—the case officers in the field, the analysts at their desks, the support people and the clerical people, the collection gadgets—are all geared to produce this slim binder six days a week, fifty-two weeks a year, for the most important and powerful man in the world and a handful of his closest advisers."

In 1766 George Washington wrote, "There is nothing more necessary than good intelligence . . ." If anything, Petersen said, it was truer today.

"When we get it wrong, American lives are lost. When we get

it right and do not communicate it properly, the consequences are the same," he said.

There were lessons to be learned from 9/11, Petersen told the analysts.

"Some day, God forbid, your very best may not be good enough," he said. "If that happens, then you have to critique your own performance, draw the right lessons, and rededicate yourself to the mission, even as waves of criticism—the merited and the unmerited—break over you. We do not have the option of quitting our post, of walking away, or even answering back. There will be late dinners, missed events. There will be times when it will be hard to read a newspaper or watch the news, perhaps because what they have to say is incorrect, sometimes because what they have to say is too true."

The CIA, he said, tries to make the world a little safer. It is committed to the truth.

"We are a secret intelligence organization in a democracy, and we often work in grey areas," he said. "We are an organization chartered by our government to break the laws of other governments. This puts a heavy obligation on us to be honest and ethical in all our dealings with one another, with the consumers of our services, and with the people of the United States."[161]

Sitting around a conference table on the first floor of CIA headquarters, the twenty-six new analysts related in turn why they came to the agency. They were well-dressed, proud-looking, expectant.

"I was in the DIA specializing in the Middle East," one woman said. "I could see from the reports what was really going on. Going to the CIA will give me a broader perspective."

"My parents were from the counterculture," a woman said. "I

was always interested in the Middle East. When I first mentioned the CIA as a place to work, they were against it. I read up on it and I told my parents more about it. They decided it was a good idea."

"I had a childhood dream of being a spy," a woman said, "but I wound up as a statistician at the Bureau of the Census. I can't tell you what I went through on September 11. It galvanized me and I decided to apply to the CIA."

"I worked on the Hill for nineteen years," a man said. "I had policy disagreements over Iran. At the CIA I can present analysis impartially."

"When my classmates in elementary school were dreaming of being ballerinas I was dreaming of working for the CIA," a woman said. "In my senior year in college I stumbled over the CIA recruiting booth."

"I've always wanted to serve my country," a man said. Another said, "I wanted to give something back."

"My father works here as a carpenter," another man said. "He put three kids through college with no loans. He lived in poverty to do it. Where else in the world can the son of a carpenter send out a résumé and get a job like this one where one can make a difference?"

Stephanie Glakas-Tenet, shown with her husband, George Tenet, helped CIA families encountering personal difficulties.

As executive director, A. B. "Buzzy" Krongard, a former investment banker and a black belt in karate, ran the CIA on a daily basis.

All photos are courtesy of the CIA.

As deputy director for operaions, James L. Pavitt was the nation's spymaster and in overall charge of the Counterterrorism Center.

Dr. Donald M. Kerr, the deputy director for Science and Technology, oversaw everything from the Predator unmanned plane to bugging devices.

As deputy DCI for community management, Joan A. Dempsey tried to coordinate the squabbling intelligence community.

William J. Casey established the Counterterrorism Center.

William H. Webster restored the CIA's credibility with Congress and the public.

Robert M. Gates, left, shown with former DCI George H. W. Bush, found William J. Casey was able to speak with him when Casey was hospitalized.

After Aldrich H. Ames was arrested, R. James Woolsey came uner fire for not dealing aggressively enough with the aftermath.

Under John M. Deutch, the CIA became politically correct and risk averse.

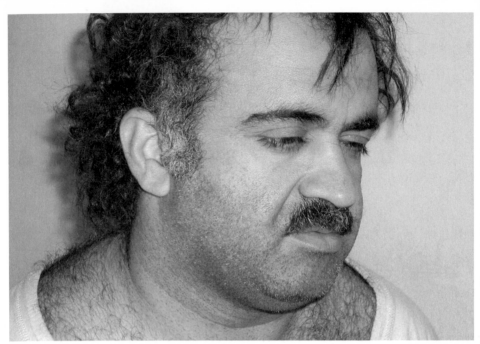

Khalid Shaikh Mohammed, Osama bin Laden's operational chief, was captured because of information based on CIA intelligence.

Deputy DCI John E. McLaughlin, shown with George Tenet at the White House, warned six months before 9/11 that "the potential for unwelcome surprise is greater than at any time since the end of the Second World War."

Under George Tenet, shown meeting at Camp David with President Bush, National Security Advisor Condoleeza Rice, and Chief of Staff Andrew H. Card Jr., the CIA was focused, aggressive, and not afraid to take risks.

President Bush, shown with George Tenet, told CIA employees, "I trust you, and I need you."

20

On june 6, 2002, FBI Special Agent Coleen M. Rowley arrived at a Senate Judiciary Committee hearing room with a blue fanny pack strapped beneath her suit jacket. She wore large glasses and no makeup. In her testimony, Rowley, the Minneapolis Field Office's legal counsel, described the circumstances that led her to write a thirteen-page, single-spaced letter to FBI Director Mueller. Written the previous month, the letter poured out her frustration at the lack of headquarters support for an application the field office had made in August 2001 to search the computer of Zacarias Moussaoui, who would later be charged in the attacks of September 11.

The month before her testimony, stories had begun coming out about a memo Kenneth Williams, a Phoenix agent, had written to headquarters on July 10, 2001. In that memo, Williams suggested that the FBI look into Middle Eastern men who were enrolled in flight-training schools. Headquarters ignored the suggestion.

The media reports and testimony were just the start of a crescendo of criticism of both the FBI and the CIA. The condemnation reached its climax in the fall of 2002, when a joint inquiry of the House and Senate intelligence committees held hearings on the failures of September 11 and issued a series of so-called staff statements laying out missed opportunities—things that could have been done either to detect the plots or to keep potential hijackers out of the country.

"Connecting the dots" became the phrase of choice to describe what the intelligence and law enforcement communities should have been doing before 9/11, so that roughly three thousand people would not have died. To generations brought up on TV and computers it all sounded so simple. Americans were used to watching crimes unfold live on television. Computers and the Internet were thought to hold the answer to almost any question. If only the Phoenix memo, the Minneapolis matter, and thousands of other dots had been connected, the country would have been safe.

Yet in the real world, things are not simple. Moving a cursor around a PC screen will not uncover the kind of carefully compartmented scheme hatched by bin Laden and a few of the top people in his organization. The problem was not one of connecting the dots, as with Pearl Harbor, but one of "lack of actionable information in the first place," as Jack Devine, the CIA's former acting deputy director of operations, put it.[162]

"I don't think there were any dots to connect," said Mike, who briefed Bush.

Still, the hearings and media reports revealed fundamental flaws in the system for protecting America from terrorism. While none of the information uncovered before September 11 by itself would have stopped the plots, even if connected by the most powerful computers in the world, bringing it all together and analyzing it properly would likely have led to more aggressive investigations.

Whether those investigations would have stopped the plots can only be speculated upon. Whether such investigations are necessary to uncover future plots is a certainty.

The most glaring missed signal did not surface until hearings by the Joint Inquiry in the fall of 2002. It turned out that two years before, the CIA had developed information that, in January 2000, two of the hijackers, Khalid al-Midhar and Nawaf al-Hazmi, were going to attend a meeting of terrorists believed to be associated with bin Laden in Kuala Lampur, Malaysia. The CIA arranged to have surveillance conducted on them. By January 5, 2000, the CIA had passed a copy of al-Midhar's passport with a copy of his U.S. visa to the FBI. In an e-mail to the FBI that month, according to CIA records, an officer assigned to the CIA's Counterterrorism Center referred to the fact that the CIA had briefed the FBI about the surveillance. He said the pair engaged in suspicious activity, using public phones and cyber cafes exclusively, while not engaging in any business or tourist pursuits. But there was no evidence of an impending attack.

By March the CIA learned that al-Hazmi had entered the country at Los Angeles International Airport on January 15, 2000. While the agency did not know al-Midhar had accompanied al-Hazmi, the CIA could have assumed he did. They often traveled together. However, the CIA failed to place either man on a watch list to ensure that they would not enter the United States.

Because of the increasing number of threats of major attacks, Tenet had ordered a review of Counterterrorism Center files. In the course of reviewing the files, an FBI analyst assigned to the Counterterrorism Center on August 21, 2001 realized that both men had entered the U.S. at the same time. Two days after this discovery, the CIA sent a message marked "immediate" to the FBI and other relevant agencies recommending that the two men be placed on a watch list. But, since they were already in the country, it was too late.

On August 29 an FBI agent in the New York field office, which was responsible for overseas terrorism investigations, pleaded with headquarters to approve a criminal investigation so that the full resources of his squad could be used to find al-Midhar. Attorneys at the National Security Law Unit at headquarters gave the agent incorrect legal advice, saying that, because the source of the information about the terrorist was intelligence from the CIA, the FBI could not open a criminal investigation to find them. In fact, the FBI used CIA information to begin criminal investigations all the time. The incorrect advice was but one illustration of how artificial barriers, either real or imagined, hobbled FBI counterterrorism investigations. In response to the rejection of his request, the New York agent pursuing al-Midhar e-mailed back to headquarters that someday "someone will die [and] the public will not understand why we were not more effective and throwing every resource at certain problems."

On September 11, al-Midhar and al-Hazmi boarded American Flight 77, which took off from Washington's Dulles Airport en route to Los Angeles and crashed into the Pentagon at 9:40 A.M., killing 189 people. After the attacks, the New York agent pursuing al-Midhar learned that he was one of the hijackers. The agent informed his supervisor, who reassured him, "We did everything by the book."

Beyond the kindergarten-like impediments to sharing information, the FBI's counterterrorist effort was hampered by lack of technology, analysis, and manpower. In contrast, the CIA had been in the forefront of the fight against al Qaeda. On February 2, 2000, Tenet told the Senate Select Committee on Intelligence that bin

Laden posed the greatest terrorist threat to the U.S. and was trying to develop biological and chemical weapons.

"Everything we have learned recently confirms our conviction that he wants to strike further blows against America. Despite some well-publicized disruptions, we believe he could still strike without additional warning," Tenet said.

In a December 4, 1998, memo Tenet told his deputies, "We must now enter a new phase in our effort against bin Laden. We are at war . . . I want no resources or people spared in this effort, whether inside the CIA or the [intelligence] community."

The following year Tenet traveled to Israel to warn intelligence officials there about bin Laden.

"Israel knew little of the bin Laden threat," Stan Moskowitz, a former station chief in Israel, said.

Going back to its founding in 1986, the Counterterrorism Center had rolled up seventy terrorists. They included Ramzi Ahmed Yousef, the convicted mastermind of the first World Trade Center bombing, who at the time was staying at a safe house in Pakistan financed by bin Laden and an associate, Wali Amin Shah, who plotted to blow up twelve U.S. airliners and assassinate the pope. The center also was responsible for tracking Aimal Kasi, who, while not part of an organization, engaged in terrorism when he murdered the two CIA employees outside the main gate in 1993.

Since 1998, working with other governments, the CIA had rolled up more than two dozen terrorists. About half were members of al Qaeda. At least a dozen attacks planned to happen during celebrations of the millennium at the end of 1999 were stopped after the CIA identified thirty-six terrorists who were then arrested around the world. When the CIA began picking up signs of new attacks on the U.S. beginning around March 2001, the agency worked with twenty other intelligence services to detain terrorists who might be involved.

Despite the successes, Tenet told the Senate intelligence committee, "I must be frank in saying that this has only succeeded in buying time against an increasingly dangerous threat."

In contrast, the FBI never saw the overall picture and never warned forcefully of the threat. Yet an assessment by the CIA director hardly should have been necessary. Anyone who read the newspapers or watched television knew of al Qaeda's previous attacks and threats. Sheik Omar Abdel Rahman, the radical Islamic leader who was convicted of plotting to bomb the United Nations, the FBI's New York Field Office, and the Holland and Lincoln tunnels, urged followers to "break and destroy the morale of the enemies of Allah" by attacking their "high world buildings . . . and the buildings in which they gather their leaders." Ramzi Yousef, the mastermind of the 1993 plot on the World Trade Center, told FBI agents after his arrest as they flew in a helicopter over Manhattan that the World Trade Center would not "still be standing if I had enough money." In 1995, a terrorist based in the Philippines threatened to fly a plane loaded with chemical weapons into the CIA at Langley and to blow up twelve U.S. airliners. All these plots were linked to bin Laden, and all were made public.

In retrospect, no one took the threats seriously enough. Certainly, American arrogance played a role. How could people with unpronounceable names living in caves threaten American technology and power? But al Qaeda had an appreciation of America's vulnerabilities. The FAA allowed knives up to four inches long to be taken on airplanes. Without any difficulty, the hijackers could pack knives and box cutters that they would use to threaten passengers and crew. Thanks to lax regulation and the airlines' shortsighted fixation on cost cutting, airline security had long been a joke.

Hijacking airplanes and plunging to one's death is not high tech. But the hijackers were as sophisticated as KGB officers in concealing their activities. They took phony names and communicated on the Internet from public libraries. They used couriers and codes imbedded in graphics to convey messages. They listed Mail Boxes outlets as home addresses and transferred money through an ancient secret system called *hawala*, which relies on trust to move sums around the world. As the FBI delved into their backgrounds, it found that all the hijackers were in the U.S. lawfully. They blended into America and ate at Pizza Hut. They did not own computers.

To finance the plot, the hijackers used at least $500,000 funneled by Mustafa Ahmed al-Hawsawi, believed to be al Qaeda's finance chief. At least $325,000 of the money was disbursed through ATMs, money orders, and credit cards, and the rest in cash. Al Qaeda operatives hatched the plot in Germany, with connections in France, Britain, Spain, the Netherlands, Italy, Bosnia, and the Czech Republic.

Most important, to avoid detection, each group or cell targeting a plane isolated itself from the others. As specified in an al Qaeda training manual, the hijackers themselves generally did not go to mosques or see other Moslems. Some of them even drank alcohol, which was forbidden by Islam.

"Those terrorists knew a lot more about our world than we knew about theirs," Gannon said.

In the months before 9/11, the CIA received and distributed reports on hundreds of terrorist threats. When read with the benefit of hindsight, they all sounded ominous. Yet none of them pin-pointed the plot that finally unfolded; most were third-hand accounts that were not credible. For example, a 1998 report about a plot to crash a bomb-laden plane into the World Trade Center originated with a police chief in the Caribbean. The chief said he had heard from Islamic militants in his country that Libyan officials were planning the attack on behalf of Iraq. The CIA considered such an attack highly unlikely but distributed the report anyway. Nevertheless, the headline over one story said: U.S. FAILED TO ACT ON WARNINGS IN '98 OF A PLANE ATTACK.

An August 1998 report said a group of unidentified Arabs planned to fly an explosives-laden plane from a foreign county into the World Trade Center. In November 1998, a report said an Islamic extremist group in Turkey was considering crashing an airplane into the tomb of a Turkish leader. In January 1995, police in the Philippines raided an apartment in Manila and found materials suggesting a plot to crash a hijacked plane into CIA headquarters.

The Joint Inquiry reviewed 650,000 documents and conducted six hundred interviews. The CIA provided fifteen employees to help the staff and gave the committee a 327-linear-foot chronology of 2,600 terrorist incidents and threats from 1993 to 2000. None of the reports constituted what is called actionable intelligence. Hijacking airplanes, like bombing buildings, was nothing new. Without specifics of a plot, it would have been impossible to take action that would thwart a future attack. In fact, none of the threatened attacks occurred.

"We had threats to malls, threats to power plants, threats of assassinations; across the board we had threats coming in every day," said Dale Watson, who was in charge of counterterrorism at the FBI.

In general, it is easier for a terrorist group to conceal its activities than a government. Because of that, and because of the removal of the constraints imposed by the cold war, the proliferation of weapons of mass destruction, and the emergence of volatile regimes like Iraq and Iran, "the potential for unwelcome surprise is greater than at any time since the end of the Second World War," McLaughlin, the CIA's deputy director, warned in a speech at Princeton University in March 2001, six months before 9/11.

"We suffered a drain in personnel and funds for ten years after the cold war was over, but things were in many ways more threatening after the cold war, both from terrorists and from technology and proliferation," Allen said. "Non-state actors can acquire weapons of mass destruction," he said. "It's a certainty that they will use them."

Over the years, Tenet had sent to the Hill reports of most serious threats and had warned that bin Laden was the biggest terrorist threat, but members of the Joint Inquiry took to TV and pretended they were shocked to learn of the threats. When the Joint Inquiry finally held its hearings in the fall of 2002, the testimony by the staff director, Eleanor Hill, turned out to be far more balanced and factual than comments by some panel members would have suggested. Hill was a former assistant U.S. attorney and Pentagon inspector general who had overseen hearings conducted by Senator Sam Nunn, known for his professionally run investigations. Most recently, Hill had been a partner with King & Spalding, a prestigious Atlanta law firm.

Hill said that prior to September 11, the "U.S. intelligence and law enforcement communities were fighting a war against terrorism without the benefit of what some would call their most potent weapon in that effort: an alert and committed American public." She emphasized that no one could say whether the plots would have been averted even if the FBI and CIA had pursued every lead flawlessly.

"A lot of things could have been done better," Eleanor Hill said. "But the direct fault lies with the terrorists who perpetrated these acts."[163]

Cofer Black declined an offer from the panel to testify behind a screen.

"The American public needs to see my face," he said. "I want to look the American people in the eye."

In his testimony before the Joint Inquiry, Cofer Black described CIA counterterrorism operatives and analysts as "the finest Americans this country can produce. They are highly professional, smart, hard-working, brave, and have an unbelievable work ethic— working fourteen- to eighteen-hour days, seven days a week, month after month."

Among the senators, only Senator Pat Roberts, a Republican from Kansas, defended the CIA, saying his committee had produced a report full of "gotcha charges" meant to grab headlines. He read from a briefing book prepared by the panel staff to help frame questions posed to witnesses. Roberts highlighted a passage that said, "Mr. Black will probably dissemble" on certain points. Raising his voice, Roberts looked at Black and said, "You're almost on trial, sir!" He added, "I have to apologize . . . for the committee."

In a slow, deep voice, Black answered, "Senator, you really made my day . . . I work for the American people," he said. "I'm a big boy. Things happen. People die. But dissemble, no. This is like living a nightmare."

Hill issued a statement saying the briefing materials contained a "poor choice of words" because of "an editing error." Back at Langley, the joke was that everyone had worried that Black, known for his candor, would say too much, not too little.

Apparently, the congressional staffer who thought Black would lie had become obsessed with what amounted to an accounting dispute between the agency and the committee over how many people were assigned to counterterrorism. Convinced that the agency was trying to fudge numbers, the staffer decided that Black was part of the conspiracy.

For months, the media and Congress had lambasted the CIA over its failings. Senator Bob Graham, the Florida Democrat who was chairman of the Joint Inquiry, used words like "inexcusable" and "outrageous" to describe the agency's lapses. But when Tenet finally had a chance to testify publicly in October 2002, Graham tried to limit the DCI's prepared statement to ten minutes. As Tenet endeavored to plow ahead Graham kept cutting him off.

"Mr. Tenet, twenty-one minutes, now," Graham said at one point.

"Well, sir, I just have to say I have been waiting a year," Tenet responded.

After other members sided with Tenet, Graham allowed him to continue. The DCI pointed out that in the past decade Congress had cut the CIA's budget 18 percent after inflation was taken into account, and that the number of employees had declined as a result by 16 percent. Covert officers had been cut by 25 percent.

Worldwide, the CIA had sixteen-thousand employees, plus thousands of contract employees, figures that began climbing as Congress began flooding the agency with money after 9/11. Just over half the CIA's employees worked at headquarters. Fifteen percent worked overseas, and the rest worked in some twenty-four unmarked CIA offices scattered throughout Washington, or in domestic stations in cities like New York and San Francisco.

In the months leading up to the hearings, another committee member, Senator Richard C. Shelby, a Republican from Alabama,

repeatedly called for Tenet's resignation. Many at Langley attributed his antipathy to an April 1999 incident, when Shelby complained that he had not been seated on the dais for a ceremony
renaming CIA headquarters for George H. W. Bush. Representative Rob Portman, a Republican from Ohio who sponsored the
legislation naming the building, was seated on stage. But Shelby
denied his nose was out of joint.

Obtusely, Shelby would lament that he could find no one in
the intelligence community who knew about the plots of 9/11 and
had failed to issue a warning. "It would be nice to find a smoking
gun," Shelby said wistfully. "But absent that, we're looking for
problems that need to be solved."

21

If much of the criticism was unfair, it helped create an even greater sense of urgency within the agency.

"Every day we live with the fact that we did not uncover the plot," Executive Director Buzzy Krongard said. "We took it harder than other people. You're always frustrated because you want that piece of the mosaic that will give you all the answers. This is a business built on frustration, not mathematics."[164]

"There was anger, chagrin, humiliation," said former assistant DCI for administration James Simon. "But mainly anger."

By the summer of 2002, Tenet had increased the staff of the Counterterrorism Center from 340 to 1,500. That did not include officers working on the problem in stations in almost every country. Located on the first floor of the new building, the Counterterrorism Center consumed acres of space, including components that focused on subjects like weapons of mass destruction spread throughout headquarters. The center looked like an insurance office, with endless cubicles and computers. CIA officers each had three office computers connected to a keyboard and a monitor:

one computer for sensitive compartmented information, one for information classified secret, and one for nonclassified material.

Each day, some 2,500 classified electronic communications streamed into the Counterterrorism Center from stations throughout the world, from other foreign intelligence services, and from interrogators interviewing prisoners at the Guantanamo Bay detention facility. The center produced five hundred terrorist reports a month, many of which were distributed to eighty other government agencies. The center produced a color-coded chart for Bush. It showed which al Qaeda operatives had been captured or killed and which ones remained at large. The center held a video conference with the National Security Council three times a day.

Besides DO officers and DI analysts, Tenet assigned scientists and engineers from the Directorate of Science & Technology (DS&T) to support the Counterterrorism Center.

Ironically, on the morning of September 11, Kirk Lippold, the commanding officer of the USS *Cole*, had breakfast with Donald M. Kerr, a physicist who was chief of the DS&T, and others at the CIA. When he was in charge of the FBI Laboratory, Kerr worked closely with Lippold on the Cole case. From 1979 to 1985, Kerr was director of the Los Alamos National Laboratory.

After 9/11, government labs sent volunteers to work with the agency for six to ten weeks to help answer questions about nuclear, biological, and chemical weapons systems and about explosive devices that could be used by terrorists.

As chief of the DS&T, Kerr's job was to rebuild the directorate, returning it to the days when it was on the cutting edge of technology in support of intelligence operations. Among other projects, the DS&T was developing sensors to detect biological weapons.

"If you detect the pathogen when it has arrived, I've lost," Kerr said. "I want to get it when there is intent to acquire biological weapons—when the material to make the weapons is being delivered. We have to detect and interdict."[165]

The DS&T was also developing miniaturized systems to support clandestine operations and collection platforms for the future.

"One of our highest priorities is geolocation of Osama and Mullah Omar and those close to them," Kerr said. "There have been times when we felt we have been close to his supply chain, his communications. We target anything we can. We are up against an adversary who has some understanding of the tools and techniques that the U.S. employs and who is trying to avoid detection and understands how hard it is to find any one person anywhere in the world."

"We have a fair amount of intelligence on where bin Laden might be," McLaughlin said in June 2003. "He is in remote areas that are very hard to penetrate. I doubt that he's very comfortable where he is. He does not have much access to the outside world or to his organization. No one here will ever give up until he's found."

In seeking to penetrate al Qaeda, the CIA made extensive use of bugging devices provided by Kerr's DS&T. The CIA targeted mosques where al Qaeda operatives would pray and also hatch terrorist plots. Besides recruiting agents and intercepting communications, the CIA made extensive use of information gathered by foreign security services. When the CIA had difficulty with a foreign service, President Bush would occasionally place a call to the leader of its country.

"We said, 'If you have information but don't give it to us and we find out you had it, we will show you no mercy,'" said Simon. "We started getting information."

Lack of cooperation with other government agencies was no

longer accepted. Pavitt began attending meetings of FBI special agents in charge. "As Americans, we have to make sure the FBI succeeds," Tenet would say.

The CIA overcame its aversion to allowing undercover officers to participate in law enforcement court proceedings.

"It's okay to testify in a trial," Pavitt said. "There used to be a mind set that we can't do that."

Nor was the CIA's self-protective attitude tolerated. Under Tenet, James Angleton and his paranoid theories were a bad memory. The coddling that allowed Aldrich Ames to continue as an employee was now condemned.

"Angleton was arrogant and probably crazy," Pavitt told me. "Rick Ames was passing out at dinner parties. That was outrageous."

In pushing the agency to be more aggressive, Tenet struck the right balance between taking what he called "creative risks" and engaging in foolish or illegal activities. Like most modern CIA officials, he considered Robert Baer, a former CIA officer who wrote the best-selling *See No Evil,* a cowboy who did not quite understand how the CIA fit into a democratic society.

In his book, Baer railed that the CIA, at the behest of Anthony Lake, Clinton's national security advisor, forbade him to support Iraqi opposition leaders and Kurds who came up with a plan to topple Saddam Hussein in January 1995. As Baer described the plan on NPR, "Within two days of my arrival in northern Iraq, a former Sunni officer, a major general, came to me and said that he was in touch with a group of military officers preparing to overthrow Saddam Hussein, and they wanted U.S. backing. They eventually told me the details—how they were going to do it. They were going to box Hussein in his compound long enough to send an armored unit of twelve tanks to the compound and force Saddam to resign."

In another version given to the World Media Association, Baer said the plot required inducing Saddam Hussein to "come up north to Tikrit by causing a diversion in Baghdad, a diversion in the north, in Mosul and Kirkuk, at which time, when Hussein was in his compound, they were going to box him in and level the compound. Don't ask me the difference between assassination and leveling Saddam in his house, but anyhow . . ."

Learning from the CIA that Baer was supporting a plot to depose Saddam Hussein, Lake discussed it with Tenet, who was then on his staff at the NSC. Like the agency, they were horrified that a CIA officer was apparently freelancing a coup. About the same time, Lake learned of an intercept suggesting that Baer, under the name Robert Pope, planned an assassination of Hussein. As a result of his concerns and Tenet's, the CIA brought in the FBI to investigate. Meanwhile, Ahmad Chalabi, the head of the Iraqi opposition group involved in the proposed plot, was saying publicly that America supported the plan to topple Saddam Hussein. Lake sent a message through the CIA and Baer to Chalabi and his Iraqi National Congress saying the plan had been compromised, and the U.S. could not support it. In doing so, Lake was acutely aware of how the U.S. had pulled the rug out from the Kurds who wanted to go after Hussein during the Persian Gulf War and how they had subsequently been massacred.

"I did not want America to be blamed again for supporting a plan to topple Saddam and then backing out," Lake told me. Beyond that, Lake thought Baer's plan made the CIA's debacle at the Bay of Pigs "look good."[166]

Lake learned about the plot thirty-six hours before it was to unfold. No one had given Baer the go-ahead. In fact, Baer complained to the World Media Association that after he had proposed the plan to headquarters, "Not a word out of Washington. I sent three or four messages and said, 'Do you want to continue with this or don't you?' So I went back to the Iraqis, the Kurds, and the general, and I said, 'Guys, as far as I know, it's okay. I wouldn't call this a green light. It's a yellow light, maybe. But it's your country. If you want to kill Saddam, go ahead. It's fine with me." Baer recognized that at that point, "I was left on my own."

Contrary to these statements, Baer denounced Lake and the CIA in his book for having engaged in a "massive betrayal" of Chalabi and General Wafic Sammarai, who had devised the proposed plot.[167] Baer quoted Chalabi as saying, "Lake could not have picked a worse time to pull out . . . I'm afraid that at the end of the day it's going to be our blood on the floor rather than Saddam's."

Indeed, the plan was compromised. Saddam had 150 members of Chalabi's group executed. As Baer told NPR, the last thing he knew, the "courier between me and the military group inside was arrested by one of the Kurdish groups and the whole thing fell apart."

Meanwhile, the FBI investigated Baer to see if he had violated the executive order banning assassination. He could have been prosecuted under a federal law banning murder-for-hire. The FBI's investigation arose when NSA intercepted a letter Chalabi, who had left Jordan after being accused of defrauding a bank, had forged stating that the NSC supported a plan to kill Saddam Hussein. Chalabi had let Iranians see the letter so they would help him against Hussein. If Chalabi was behind the letter, it was another reason not to work with him, but Baer didn't see it that way. In the end, no charges were brought against Baer, who remained out-raged that the FBI would investigate him.[168]

So what if no presidential finding had authorized Baer's support of a coup or assassination plan? Baer figured that he had general authorization to conduct such an operation, because he had been instructed to set up a base in northern Iraq.

"The one chance that I know about we could have gotten rid of Saddam Hussein, the CIA people end up charged with a capital crime?" Baer huffed. Despite his own admission that he never got the go-ahead, Baer claimed the White House "pulled the plug" without "warning or decent explanation."

Too idiotic even for a TV drama, the plan to topple Hussein bore a striking resemblance to some of the CIA's proposed plots in the early days to assassinate Fidel Castro, when the agency wanted to contaminate a box of Castro's favorite cigars with bot-ulinum toxin or place an exploding seashell at Castro's customary skin-diving spot.

"There was universal agreement at the CIA that Baer's plan would not work," Gannon said.

Having left just after Tenet took over, Baer was right that the CIA he knew was risk averse. It was a time, as Tenet's former chief of staff Joan Dempsey put it, when everyone outside the agency wanted "politically correct case officers." Baer was talented, brave, and a genuinely nice guy. But Baer was wrong in thinking that the plot would work and that he could support it without proper authorization. He was also wrong in thinking that the White House had no business interfering in an endeavor that he alone thought was practicable. Like Dewey Clarridge and William Casey, Baer was a throwback to the days when the CIA thought only it knew what was best for America and that the people's elected representatives were nuisances, if not adversaries.

Perhaps most disturbing, when I asked Baer for comment, he said he simply reported the plan to the CIA and did not endorse it. Baer—who spent more than a year promoting his book by excoriating Tony Lake and the NSC for torpedoing the plan— told me he was not "bitter or indignant." In an e-mail he said, "For a start, I was never confident [General Wafic] Sammarai's plan would work. I could only go by what Sammarai told me. Obviously, it needed a lot of looking into."[169]

Informed of Baer's comment, Lake said incredulously, "This was something that we brought to the attention of President Clinton, the secretaries of Defense and State, and the CIA director because it looked as if it was proceeding. And now he says he didn't know if it would work?"

"Baer was a courageous officer who needed to be closely supervised," said Frank Anderson, who was chief of the Near East Division until 1994. "What Baer didn't appreciate was he was wrong on almost every issue, but his courage made up for it."[170]

"We can do risk-taking without being cowboys," said John Brennan, Buzzy Krongard's deputy and Tenet's former chief of staff.

While Tenet changed the self-protective culture of the CIA and made it clear that cowboys were not wanted, two holdovers from earlier days remained: Even at the highest levels, CIA officials continued to see defectors like Vitaly Yurchenko as difficult, spoiled brats—an attitude that sometimes became self-fulfilling. And while the agency was far more open than before, excessive secrecy remained. Asked how many employees he supervised, the chief of the CIA's history staff, which prepares useful public studies, said he could not say. When pushed, he finally said it was a "handful," as if specifying "four" or "six" would jeopardize a top-secret program.

After the CIA let Dana Priest of the *Washington Post* attend a recruitment session, a CIA officer e-mailed Pavitt saying it was "outrageous" and "shameful" to have allowed a reporter to cover it. For my book *Inside the CIA*, I had attended a similar session ten years earlier. Somehow, the agency survived.

While the CIA has released millions of pages under the Freedom of Information Act and the provisions of a presidential order, even material revealed by presidents in their autobiographies or made public in congressional hearings is still redacted, according to Charles A. Briggs, the former CIA inspector general who now declassifies CIA material.

That the CIA has a training facility at Camp Peary, which has been publicly identified as an agency site for decades, was still classified, as was the CIA's use of the *Glomar Explorer* to raise a sunken Soviet submarine in 1974.

Tenet decided to make public the intelligence community's budget for fiscal 1998, but in subsequent years he bowed to those who said listing the figure would let the enemy know intelligence capabilities, or might lead to further public exposure of expenditures. Thus, although press accounts invariably pinpointed the correct figure, the total annual budget of the intelligence community remained classified. One could argue that, if the budget and its broad components were public and open to debate, Congress might not have been so willing to scrimp on intelligence programs.

"Not putting out the total budget is ridiculous," Snider said. "You can't tell anything from the bottom line. There were absurd debates about it."

"Many of the CIA's seemingly idiotic activities in the past occurred because of excessive and unnecessary secrecy," said Gene Poteat, the former DS&T officer.

"We need as much as ever to protect sources and methods and people undercover," John Gannon, the former chief of the DI, said, "but in today's information environment, we also need, more than ever, to promote transparency where sensitive sources and methods are not involved. To classify gross budget figures and aggregate employee numbers is silly. There is still a pervasive culture of secrecy at CIA that needlessly complicates congressional oversight, that conceals poor management practices, that blurs dysfunctional community relationships, that erodes trust with other U.S. government agencies, and that hampers the efforts of community analysts to interact with outside experts," Gannon said. "This is a heavy price to pay."

22

—————

Having ramped up its efforts after 9/11, the CIA began seeing results. By the middle of 2002 the CIA had rolled up three thousand terrorists in a hundred countries. Usually a foreign service made the arrest based on CIA information. It became so common that Pavitt stopped telling Tenet about each success. In other cases, the individual was sent to another country and held or prosecuted. The process was called rendering.

If an arrest took place in the U.S., a cover story was developed so that it appeared the FBI or Customs Service had arrested the suspects without receiving any inside information from the CIA. Planned attacks on U.S. embassies in Italy, France, Yemen, and Albania, and on other U.S. facilities in Turkey and Saudi Arabia were thwarted.

"Bush wanted us to find and get these guys," Simon said. "No matter what else he was dealing with, Bush would say, 'Attack, attack, attack.' That was critical. After 9/11, we were busting ass."

The Counterterrorism Center formed a task force of a hundred undercover operatives, analysts, and technicians to pursue Abu Zubaydah, a key bin Laden deputy. For six weeks, in a former large conference room, they worked around the clock reviewing thousands of agent reports, intercepts, and spy satellite photos. The task force pinpointed the Saudi-born terrorist in a villa near Faisalabad, Pakistan.

On March 27, 2002, CIA, FBI, and Pakistani intelligence agents closed in on his villa and captured him. Over speaker phones in a conference room at the Counterterrorism Center, Tenet and task force members heard the raid as it occurred. Abu Zubaydah was wounded in the groin and survived. The CIA seized ten thousand documents and translated and analyzed them. The terrorist soon began singing to the FBI and CIA about other planned plots.

In September 2002, the Counterterrorism Center, working with the Pakistanis and FBI, captured Ramzi Binalshibh, a key operative in the September 11 plot. In an interview on Qatar-based Al Jazeera television, the thirty-year-old Yemeni had said that he was meant to be the twentieth hijacker. He was disappointed that he failed to obtain a visa. Instead, he funneled money to the hijackers.

Symbolizing the agency's new approach to terrorism, in November 2002, a CIA-operated Predator armed with Hellfire missiles killed Abu Ali al-Harethi, an al Qaeda operative in Yemen. He was one of the top dozen Qaeda figures in the world. The strike killed five associates as well as they traveled by car in northwestern Yemen.

Yemeni officials had given the CIA permission to operate the aircraft in their air space but did not want the fact publicized. When news of the strike leaked, they were furious. Back when FBI agents went to Yemen to investigate the bombing of the *Cole,* they had been frustrated by the lack of cooperation. Yemen's help now illustrated how profoundly relations with Arab countries had changed since 9/11. The fact that al Qaeda often ended up killing more Moslems than Americans in countries like Saudi Arabia only played into American hands, galvanizing Arab countries to help in the war on terror.

From its earliest days the CIA had engaged in extensive covert propaganda. In the Italian national election of 1948, for example, besides delivering $3.5 million in cash, the CIA distributed campaign leaflets and posters backing candidates opposed to Communist candidates. The Soviets spent even more money to back the Communist candidates, who lost. During the cold war the CIA printed books for distribution in the Soviet Union or planted articles favorable to the United States or American ideals in countries where the media were anti-American.

"All we had to do was tell the truth about the Soviets," former DCI Gates said.

During the Vietnam War, a former CIA officer said, the agency paid off journalists to write from the American perspective. "We would present anything that made the Soviets or North Vietnamese look bad," he said. "It was not necessarily untrue. The Soviets did that all the time. Truth is generally thought to be a better weapon [in propaganda efforts]. In a lot of places, you can't get anything in the paper that is pro-American. Everything was pro-Soviet, so they only knew that side."

After 9/11, the new challenge was radical Islamists and an Arab world where the media were anti-American. Tenet wanted to counteract that slant. The U.S. openly funded Voice of America and Radio Sawa ("together" in Arabic), a station that beamed Western and Arab pop music and a sprinkling of objective news to the

Middle East. But those stations gained acceptance in a limited number of countries like Jordan.

In 1977, after the Church Committee hearings revealed that the CIA had eleven officers working under journalistic cover provided by fifteen American news organizations, the CIA adopted a regulation prohibiting hiring journalists working for American news organizations. The regulation also banned using American clergy or Peace Corps workers as agents. Of course, journalists were free to volunteer tips to the CIA, a practice that was usually part of a trade of information. The regulation allowed the DCI to waive the prohibition in rare cases when the national security was said to be at stake.

"We have had a few waivers when there was no other way to obtain the information," John Rizzo, the CIA's senior deputy general counsel, said.

Under the regulation, non-U.S. journalists and clerics were fair game. Thus, the CIA was free to put Islamic academics and journalists, as well as mullahs, on the payroll to convey a more moderate message and even to support the U.S. in the war on terror, and it did so. In Islam, as in many other religions, anyone can call himself a religious leader. So, besides paying mullahs, the CIA created fake mullahs—recruited agents who would proclaim themselves clerics and take a more moderate position about nonbelievers. Their statements were not inconsistent with the teachings of the Koran, which, like the Bible, was a largely benign document.

The CIA's use of Islamic leaders was not without precedent: During the Iranian hostage crisis the CIA paid mullahs to issue a *fatwa* stating that taking hostages was against Islam.

"We are taking over radio stations and supporting clerics," a CIA source said. "It's back to propaganda. We are creating moderate Muslims."

In seizing key al Qaeda operatives in countries like Pakistan, the CIA, usually working with the FBI, pinpointed the locations of the terrorists and informed the local security service. As an example, the Inter-Services Intelligence Directorate of the Pakistan Military (ISI) might make the arrests. However, aware that the Taliban had penetrated the ISI in the past, the CIA and FBI staked out the neighborhood where arrests were to take place, often wearing disguises. Sometimes, the local arresting officers included CIA assets, as happened with the capture of Abu Zubaydah.

"You can't take the risk that they will get away like in the movies," a former CIA official said.

The agency interrogated captured terrorists at Guantanamo Bay and at secret locations throughout the world, such as Bagram Air Force Base, an American installation in Afghanistan. Some press reports claimed that if prisoners did not cooperate, the CIA forced them to kneel for hours or turned them over to Arab countries, where they would be tortured. The CIA fueled the reports, hoping to instill fear. But, while CIA psychologists suggested ways to manipulate the prisoners, and prisoners might be deprived of sleep, the CIA had found that torture was not needed and, in any case, it produced bad information. Simply offering them tea and sympathy was often enough to get al Qaeda members to talk. Often the Stockholm Syndrome took over. Most al Qaeda members cooperated after a day or two. If not, they might be turned over to intelligence services in Egypt, Morocco, or Jordan where rough techniques could be used. The idea was not to obtain information but to turn them over to countries that had an interest in incarcerating them.

"You start by getting him talking to you," David Manners, the former station chief in Jordan, said. "You start with items you already know about. That shows him you know a lot. His defenses diminish. Then you ask about items you don't know about. Beating a guy up doesn't work. He will tell you anything to stop the pain. We never used such tactics."[171]

The biggest catch, Khalid Shaikh Mohammed, thirty-seven, began cooperating three days after his capture. Mohammed was bin Laden's operational chief and third in command after Ayman Zawahiri. He was the architect of the 9/11 plot and was involved in the bombing in Bali where 180 people were killed, the fire-bombing of a synagogue in Tunisia, and the attempted dirty bomb attack on America by Jose Padilla, who was in U.S. custody.

The CIA first became interested in Mohammed in 1995 because of his role in a Phillippines-based plan hatched by his nephew, Ramzi Yousef, to blow up as many as a dozen airplanes as they crossed the Pacific. Mohammed would meet associates in karaoke bars and go-go clubs and hold meetings at four-star hotels.

In an interview with Al Jazeera television on the first anniversary of the 9/11 attacks, Mohammed said planning the plot began in 1999. "The attacks were designed to produce as many deaths as possible and havoc, and to be a big slap for America on American soil," he said proudly.

In early 1996, the CIA had traced Mohammed to Qatar, where he was working for the Qatar Water department. A CIA agent took a job with the department so he could obtain Mohammed's fingerprints and make a positive identification. Aware that the Qatar government might compromise a plan to seize him, the Clinton NSC tried to arrange to fly Mohammed out secretly. But the CIA said it lacked sufficient resources.

"The CIA's paramilitary force had been dismantled," said Michael Battles, a former Army Ranger who joined the CIA in the

Special Activities Division. "What we were doing was considered unseemly," he said.[172]

Since the CIA would not help, the NSC asked the Pentagon to devise a plan to seize Mohammed. The plan entailed sending helicopters into Qatar, but the NSC feared that country would think it was being attacked by Bahrain, triggering a war. So the CIA wound up asking the Qatar government for help with an FBI arrest of Mohammed. The result was that Mohammed was tipped and got away.

Mohammed was almost arrested four more times. Each time he escaped or did not show up as expected. Finally, intercepts and information developed months earlier after the arrest of Ramzi Binalshibh, a former roommate of hijacker Mohamed Atta, allowed the CIA to trace Mohammed to the Westridge district of Rawalpindi in Pakistani. When he took a plane to Islamabad on February 28, ISI officers followed him. At 3 A.M. on March 1, 2003, ISI and the CIA closed in on Mohammed, who was sleeping in a white T-shirt in a spacious two-story villa. Besides snatching him, the CIA also got Mustafa Ahmed al-Hawsawi, who allegedly oversaw the hijacking plot's finances through bank accounts in the United Arab Emirates.

Tenet had been following the developments all day. At 11:30 P.M. a CIA operations officer called him at home.

"We got him," he said.

This was, as Tenet said later, a "big deal." Tenet sped to headquarters. From the Counterterrorism Center he called the station chief in Pakistan and congratulated him on a job well done.

Mohammed told the CIA about a range of planned attacks— on U.S. convoys in Afghanistan, nightclubs in Dubai, targets in Turkey, and an Israeli embassy in the Middle East. Within a few months the transcripts of his interrogations were four feet high.

The CIA shipped his computers, telephone records, and other seized evidence under armed guard to Langley. The material disclosed plans, operatives, and sources of financing.

The arrest was a turning point in the war on terror. It showed that Bush meant what he had said at Barksdale Air Force Base on September 11, 2001, "Make no mistake: The United States will hunt down and punish those responsible for these cowardly acts."

Senator Richard Shelby, Tenet's severest critic, was nowhere to be seen on TV.

By 2003, about half of al Qaeda's senior leadership had been captured or killed. At least a hundred known plots had been disrupted. Many more had been nipped in the bud, with the planners under arrest. More than $100 million in terrorist assets had been seized. The lack of another attack on U.S. soil for an extended period was the clearest sign of victory.

"The good news is that it takes al Qaeda time to change their attack plans," Cofer Black said. "They wish to be successful. They have operational rules. It took them five years to plan the East Africa embassy bombings. We have disrupted them and changed the nature of their targets, such as airplanes. Their plans are out of date now. They have to change targets to keep ahead." Meanwhile, al Qaeda's losses have been "catastrophic," Black said.

After 9/11, "Everything was ratcheted up," Pavitt said. "The American spy service has never done a better job than it is doing now." But he said, "We have to be agile. We have to improve our language capability. We are at war with global terrorism. We have to stay the course and rebuild our infrastructure." No matter how good the CIA was, "The fact is, they are going to hit us again," Pavitt warned. "But I want every one of those sons of bitches looking over his shoulder."

On any given day, the Daily Threat Matrix listed as many as

a hundred threats, ranging from possible attacks on embassies to biological attacks on U.S. cities. Ironically, having attacked the CIA and FBI for not publicizing threats that were not considered specific or credible enough before 9/11, the media and many members of the public now attacked them for publicizing threats that didn't materialize. Having endured scathing criticism, Tenet and the FBI's Robert Mueller never again wanted to find themselves sitting on information that, however vague or useless, could later be misinterpreted as forewarning an actual attack.

Both responsible for the security of the country, both subject to urgent calls in the middle of the night, Tenet and Mueller became soul mates. Mueller was a graduate of Princeton and the University of Virginia Law School. After serving as U.S. Attorney in Boston and San Francisco and becoming assistant attorney general in charge of the Justice Department's Criminal Division, he returned to private practice with the prestigious Boston firm of Hale and Dorr. With $1.7 million in assets and $4 million in his wife's trust fund, Mueller did not need the money. He left the law firm in May 1995 to prosecute homicide cases for the U.S. Attorney's office in Washington, where he began working on knifings, batterings, and shootings. He answered the phone, "Mueller, Homicide."

Like Tenet, Mueller had an aversion to talking to the press. He associated it with calling attention to himself and being boastful. In three years on the job in San Francisco, he had given two press conferences. He told aides that when he had something to say, he would say it. His interest was in looking forward, not backward. Reputations are based on what people do, not what they say. After Mueller became FBI director in September 2001, he overcame that distaste and met regularly with the reporters who covered the FBI.

With far more experience in Washington than Mueller, Tenet

became his mentor, guiding him in how to respond to attacks, fair or unfair. For Mueller, the nadir was when the *Wall Street Journal,* in an editorial, called for his resignation over the failures of 9/11, even though Mueller had become FBI director one week before the attacks. It was, said Democratic Senator Patrick J. Leahy of Vermont, "a parody of Washington scapegoating."

Besides giving advice, Tenet provided the bureau with CIA analysts who could connect the dots. When I asked Mueller about Tenet's help, he was briefly speechless with emotion. Their biggest secret was that every three weeks, they socialized with their wives, Stephanie and Anne, at DeCarlo's, an unremarkable neighborhood restaurant in Washington's Spring Valley section.[173] Mueller originally frequented the Italian restaurant, which served skimpy portions of linguine but was located about halfway between their homes. The other diners left the two couples alone as FBI agents and CIA security officers hovered discreetly.

Even as Tenet and Mueller broke bread together, some FBI counterterrorism agents were miffed that the CIA insisted on debriefing al Qaeda operatives first and, only after a few weeks, let the FBI in on the interrogations. When Mohammed was arrested, the CIA shut out the FBI entirely, dismaying agents who were steeped in his background and operations. But Tenet said having the CIA conduct the debriefings allowed for a more focused approach.

"It's a matter of how we maximize the psychology of the team we have doing this," the DCI said. "Everybody asks questions, sees the product, and gets to ask follow-up questions. No one is being shut out. This is about how we maximize our leverage."

For all of Tenet's efforts to turn around the agency, it remained a bureaucracy, with some individuals still excessively cautious or territorial.

"Pavitt and Tenet can say, 'Be more aggressive,' but you still have some at headquarters and in the field who evaluate what they will do based on their own career ambitions," said Chris Eades, a former CIA officer who was assigned to the agency's Counterterrorism Center. "Some are afraid that if they try to recruit a sensitive source in a European country, for example, and they are rebuffed and a foreign government creates a flap about it, it will be a blemish on their careers and hinder their advancement. That kind of preoccupation with careerism inhibits the out-of-the-box operational risk-taking that is necessary to prevent future attacks."[174]

Still, there was no comparison with the way the CIA operated before Tenet took the helm, particularly after the events of 9/11. Bush's support was critical.

"One week after 9/11, Bush came to the CIA," Tenet recalled. "He said, 'I trust you, and I need you.' It doesn't often happen that way in Washington, D.C. The president could have easily cut us off at the knees. Instead, he came to us and said, 'I have enormous confidence in the men and women of this organization. I know what your work has been like.' If you don't think that made a difference in everything that has happened since," Tenet said, "you don't understand the relationship between the CIA and the president. It gave us peace of mind so we could do our jobs. Our boss was at our back. There isn't enough money in the world to tell you what that meant."

Based in part on advice from Tenet and Mueller, Bush vetoed a plan, pushed by people like former NSA director William Odom, to create a domestic counterterrorism agency similar to the British MI5. The plan scared almost everyone who had actually been involved in investigating terrorism. A domestic spy agency would have meant a return to the years when the FBI, under J. Edgar Hoover, investigated citizens simply for subscribing to leftist publications or speaking out against the government. It was all done in the name of intelligence gathering, an amorphous standard that could be used to justify investigating and compiling files on anyone perceived to be different. In the process, the FBI—often with the approval of presidents—not only violated Americans' rights under the Constitution, it also lost sight of what it was supposed to be uncovering. Because Hoover confused political dissent with spying, the FBI did a poor job of investigating the real threat at the time: espionage.

Once the FBI got hold of a case, it invariably did a first class job. What made the FBI effective and kept it from engaging in the abuses of the Hoover years was that, under the supervision of the Justice Department, it focused on violations of criminal laws. If that standard for undertaking investigations were removed, investigators would lose their compass, straying into extraneous matters such as political beliefs and associations and forgetting what their real target was.[175]

The beauty of J. Edgar Hoover's creation was that it could bring the leverage of law enforcement to bear on people to get them to talk, threatening them with prosecution if they didn't cooperate. According to spy catcher John Martin, who dealt extensively with MI5 for twenty-five years, "MI5 looks with a bit of envy at our system, where we have a law enforcement organization that also gathers intelligence. Because it has no law enforcement powers, MI5 has the usual problems with sharing intelligence information leading to arrests and prosecutions."

Instead of adopting the MI5 idea, to make the counterterrorism effort more seamless, Bush approved physically combining a component of the FBI's Counterterrorism Division with a component of the CIA's Counterterrorism Center and a new Terrorist Threat Integration Center, reporting to the DCI. Temporarily they were housed at the CIA. Eventually, they will move to a renovated office building in McLean. If he were still alive, Hoover—who ordered his agents not to talk to the CIA—would have gone into cardiac arrest.

Three years before 9/11, John Gannon, then chairman of the National Intelligence Council, a community-wide body that develops midterm and long-term intelligence estimates, warned in a speech at the Hoover Institution that bin Laden was working on biological weapons. He said a system was needed to warn first responders of impending attacks. Only after 9/11 did the U.S. develop such a system through the intelligence community's Terrorist Threat Integration Center, the FBI, and the Homeland Security Department.

Like department store detectives, the Homeland Security Department worked with potential targets like power generating plants to improve their security and also warn them and the rest of the country of threats. The Terrorist Threat Integration Center was like the store's security center, monitoring potential threats—most of which were forwarded by the CIA—and distributing them to the Homeland Security Department, the FBI, and local police. On the outside of the store, the FBI and police investigated plots and arrested those involved.

"Did we do everything we should have before 9/11? No," Charles Allen said. "Are we doing everything possible now? Yes. Almost every day Islamic fundamentalists are put in detention because of our information."[176]

"Everything changed after 9/11," McLaughlin said.

In the end, it required a commitment by the entire U.S. government to change the way business was done.

When he spoke to employees in the Bubble back on September 12, Tenet quoted Winston Churchill as saying that after the attack on Pearl Harbor many thought Americans were soft and "would never stand bloodletting," but Churchill concluded otherwise. Churchill recalled a remark by Sir Edward Grey, a British foreign minister, more than thirty years earlier. Grey said that the United States was like a "gigantic boiler. Once the fire is lighted under it, there is no limit to the power it can generate."

23

For years, Tenet had complained to Clinton's National Security Council about the allocation of satellite resources over Iraq. Clearly Saddam Hussein had not disarmed, which was a condition of the cease-fire after the Persian Gulf War of 1991. Not only had he not accounted for known stocks of chemical and biological weapons, he was trying to hide a budding nuclear program by constructing buildings within buildings, concealing power lines and water pipes to hide a building's purpose, suppressing emissions, and moving equipment at night or burying it underground.

The sole fact that Hussein eventually forced out United Nations weapons inspectors demonstrated that he was not abiding by his agreement to disarm. But Clinton, sensitive to charges of not supporting the military, insisted that spy satellites focus primarily on military targets, instead of tracking Hussein's program to develop weapons of mass destruction. The president wanted to protect U.S. planes that the Iraqis were trying to shoot down in "no-fly" zones, the areas of southern and northern Iraq where Hussein's planes were prohibited from flying. The restriction had been imposed to keep Iraq from attacking opposition Kurdish and Shiite Muslim groups from the air.

"The no-fly effort made tracking Iraq's weapons of mass destruction difficult indeed," Simon said. "The Clinton administration told the military to take no, repeat no, chances of losing a pilot. So every effort was subordinated to that goal. The consequence was years of indifferent coverage of Iraqi WMD. We all knew that sooner or later, this would be the issue, and we would never make up for the lost opportunities. We needed more SIGINT and IMINT from satellites to do the job with confidence. There was outrage throughout the intelligence community at an administration that seemed not to be able to set clear priorities."

After Bush became president, he approved Tenet's proposal to reallocate satellite coverage to track Iraq's weapons program. As evidence of Hussein's deception poured in, Bush came to realize that he had to confront him. As presented by the CIA, the evidence began with the last report of the UN weapons inspectors in October 1999. It catalogued massive amounts of chemical and biological weapons that the Iraqis had had in the past and had not accounted for. The attacks of 9/11 reinforced the president's conclusion. After being crucified by members of Congress and the media for not doing enough to prevent 9/11, he was not going to sit by and let Hussein continue to acquire weapons of mass destruction that he could use to blackmail the U.S. The Iraqi dictator would either disarm or face the consequences.

In contrast, when the CIA warned Bush's father about Saddam Hussein's intention to invade Kuwait, he did nothing. From intercepted communications, the CIA learned back on July 19, 1990 that Hussein had ordered two elite Republican Guard divisions to the Kuwaiti border. Two days earlier Hussein had denounced Kuwait, which was slant-drilling for oil under Iraqi soil. Hussein claimed Kuwait's government was not legitimate.

"Kuwait was slant-drilling, but that's no excuse for going to war," William Webster, who was DCI at the time, said.[177]

In 1953, Walter Bedell Smith, the DCI, established a warning center the job of which was to sound the alarm to avoid another Pearl Harbor. By the late 1970s the CIA had created the position of National Warning Officer. Having read the intercepts indicating the Iraqis were on the move, Charles E. Allen, who held that post in 1990, requested more satellite coverage over Iraq. On July 21 the satellites detected the first movements of Republican Guards. On July 23 a large logistic buildup was observed. Intercepts revealed that civilian resources were being diverted to support the military buildup, suggesting that the preparations were neither a bluff nor an exercise.[178]

Allen issued a "warning of war" memo to policymakers on July 25. It rated the chances of a military incursion at 60 percent. But the State Department discounted the warning, advising the White House to trust in Hussein's assurance that he had no intention of taking military action. Meanwhile, Saddam called in April Glaspie, the U.S. ambassador to Iraq, to discuss the price of oil and ask what the U.S. would do if he went into Kuwait. According to an Iraqi government transcript, she said that the standing instruction, reaffirmed by then-Secretary of State James Baker, was "we have no opinion on the Arab-Arab conflicts, like your border disagreement with Kuwait." Six months after the release of the transcript, Glaspie, in testimony before the Senate Foreign Relations Committee, said it did not include her statement to Hussein that "we would insist on settlements being made in a nonviolent manner, not by threats, not by intimidation, and certainly not by aggression."

Up to that point, neither she nor the State Department had claimed the transcript was inaccurate. Regardless of Glaspie's actual statements, the State Department was sending mixed messages about what the American response might be if Iraq invaded Kuwait.

By 6:45 A.M. on August 1, satellites detected Iraqi armored and mechanized infantry brigades and artillery battalions arrayed in attack formation within 1.3 miles of the Kuwait border. Allen called officials of Bush's NSC and gave them a final warning. Many did not seem convinced, Allen said. Besides listening to the State Department, they were persuaded by Middle East leaders and the Soviets that Hussein would not attack Kuwait. Thus, the warning went unheaded. By eight that evening the invasion had begun, setting into motion a chain of events that would culminate by February 27, 1991 in Iraq's defeat by American and allied forces.

What George H. W. Bush would have done if the White House had taken Allen's warning seriously is open to question.

"I don't know if it would have done any good to warn him," Webster said. "Saddam Hussein was right that we were not focused on him."

In contrast to his father, George W. Bush wanted an action plan to deal with Saddam Hussein and his weapons of mass destruction program. After years of *de facto* rule, Hussein in 1979 had taken the title of president of Iraq, a country of twenty-three million. Hussein quickly established a police state modeled after the Soviet Union, whose former leader, Josef Stalin, was his hero. One of Hussein's early acts was to videotape a session of his Ba'ath Party's congress, during which he personally ordered several members executed. As Hussein seemed to be laughing at some private joke, the video showed guards leading the officials out. The video ended with scenes of the men being executed in the courtyard. The message Hussein conveyed to the Arab press was that they had been killed for *thinking* about overthrowing him.

To enforce his will, Hussein established a web of security services and informants. The government tortured officials and then sent them back to their jobs. It urged children to inform on their parents. It handed out bonuses to Ba'ath Party loyalists for arranging demonstrations in support of Hussein. It concocted phony statistics to show Hussein how many millions had signed up to fight against Israel, when only a handful had signed up. The CIA judged Hussein to be a brutal murderer, but not crazy.

Knowing Hussein as a murderous thug trying to develop a nuclear weapon (the Israelis had already bombed Iraq's nuclear reactor at Osirak), the Reagan administration nevertheless backed him with intelligence, economic aid, and covert supplies of munitions against Iran.

In 1990 Hussein had his puppet legislature name him president for life. After Hussein shut down United Nations weapons inspections in late 1998, Clinton authorized Operation Desert Fox, which entailed sending 650 bomber and missile sorties against one hundred Iraqi targets during a seventy-hour period. The Clinton team called this a "proportional response." It was the same approach that led to the U.S. defeat in the Vietnam War. President Johnson called Vietnam a "war of attrition" and measured success by tallying enemy body counts and asking the CIA if the enemy was demoralized. It was like going into a boxing match with one arm tied behind your back and measuring success by the number of punches thrown. Obvious as it seems, if a war was worth fighting, it had to be to win. Johnson had no clear idea of how the Vietnam War would be won. In dealing with Hussein, Clinton repeated Johnson's mistakes.

"Under Clinton, the White House wanted to appear to be doing something without doing something. It was a joke," said Manners, the former CIA station chief in Jordan.

When Operation Desert Fox did not convince Hussein to allow weapons inspections, Clinton turned a blind eye while Hussein continued his efforts to develop weapons of mass destruction. Like Clinton's efforts against bin Laden, the strikes gave Clinton good sound bites, while confirming that the U.S. was afraid to take decisive, effective action to protect itself, even against a dictator who had tried to assassinate former President George H. W. Bush as he toured Kuwait in 1993.

In contrast, almost a year before the second U.S. invasion of Iraq, Tenet presented Bush with a plan that would make unique use of intelligence and CIA paramilitary operatives, working with U.S. Special Operations forces, to help defeat Iraq and remove Hussein from power. No longer would the CIA fool around with cockamamie covert action plans, such as the early efforts to assassinate Fidel Castro or Ahmad Chalabi's plan to overthrow Saddam Hussein in 1995. Since then, another $20-million CIA effort to overthrow Hussein in 1996 had come to nothing. Tenet told Bush that covert action had a 10- to 20-percent chance of success. Only military action could be counted on to work.

"Covert action against Saddam cannot guarantee that he will be killed," Donald Kerr, the head of the DS&T, said as the plans were being hatched. "We want certainty."[179]

In an April 4, 2002, interview, Bush told British journalist Trevor McDonald that he had made up his mind that Hussein "needs to go." Bush said that "the worst thing that could happen would be to allow a nation like Iraq, run by Saddam Hussein, to develop weapons of mass destruction and then team up with terrorist organizations so they can blackmail the world. I'm not going to let that happen." Asked how he was going to achieve that, Bush said, "Wait and see."

In preparation for a military strike, Bush approved a finding directing the CIA to identify targets, intensify intelligence gathering on the ground, work with Special Forces, and solidify relations with possible future leaders of Iraq.

Meanwhile, the agency reported on North Korea's threatening actions and its violation of an agreement with the Clinton administration not to produce nuclear weapons. North Korean scientists who worked on the weapons program had defected and were helping the CIA, which concluded that North Korea did not pose the kind of threat represented by Saddam Hussein. Unlike North Korea, Iraq posed a direct threat to the U.S. because Hussein had invaded Kuwait, which, together with Iraq, accounted for a major chunk of the world's oil supply, and because he had used weapons of mass destruction. Between 1983 and 1988, Hussein had ordered the use of mustard gas, which blisters or burns exposed skin, eyes, lungs, and mucous membranes, and nerve agents that cause convulsions and death, against the Kurds and Iranians in his own country, killing an estimated 20,000 people. Not only was he developing more chemical and biological weapons, he was intent on developing nuclear weapons. In the new world, when such weapons could wipe out millions of people, there was no margin for error. As Tenet saw it, the fact that North Korea already had such weapons only confirmed the need to take action before it was too late to do anything about it.

Tenet created a special task force that would use all the agency's tools to pinpoint targets in Iraq, learn the enemy's capabilities and weaknesses, manipulate Iraqi forces, and preserve oil fields once the invasion began. At the same time, Tenet presented Bush with intelligence demonstrating that Iraq had weapons of mass destruction, particularly VX, mustard gas, and sarin. Besides making use of intelligence from defectors, agents, and satellites, the CIA had tracked shipments of material that likely would be used to make chemical weapons. By placing electronic beacons in the shipments concealed within pieces of wood used for crates, the CIA could often track the material. The CIA used the same methods to track cocaine shipments so the people picking them up could be arrested. In some cases, in shipments to Iraq, the CIA substituted inert chemicals or blocks of concrete. The agency also rigged communications equipment and computers being shipped to Iraq so they would eventually stop working or would communicate with the CIA.

To protect sources of information, some of the evidence of Hussein's weapons of mass destruction program could not be revealed publicly. Even after the war, many human sources were afraid that their role would come out. Moreover, once an invasion began, the military would have to move quickly to dismantle any known weapons of mass destruction. If they were revealed beforehand, the Iraqis could move them elsewhere. Thus, the CIA played a cat-and-mouse game, revealing just enough to be convincing without tipping its hand.

The full classified report on Hussein's weapons program was four inches thick, while the CIA's public report amounted to only a few dozen pages. But the public version made it clear that Saddam Hussein had not disarmed, as required by twelve years of United Nations resolutions. Like the CIA, the Iraqis had intercepted the communications of UN weapons inspectors, so they knew their future plans. Long before the inspectors arrived at a suspected weapons site the Iraqis removed anything suspicious.

Colin Powell spent four evenings at CIA headquarters reviewing the evidence with Tenet. Ordering in pizza, they selected examples of intercepted calls and satellite photos to present to the UN. The CIA took the unprecedented step of declassifying intercepted Iraqi calls made on nonsecure phones to demonstrate how the Iraqis concealed weapons of mass destruction before UN weapons inspectors arrived. Calls made on encrypted lines were not disclosed.

On February 5, Tenet sat behind Powell as the secretary of State presented the case to the UN. He displayed images from U.S. spy satellites that had caught apparent "housecleaning" efforts at close to thirty suspected sites for making biological or chemical weapons. Just before inspectors arrived, decontamination vehicles that would be used if anything went wrong were moved. Powell played intercepts of Republican Guard officers instructing Iraqi soldiers not to refer to "nerve agents" and to hide "forbidden ammo." A "modified vehicle," according to another intercepted conversation, "should not be seen" when the weapons inspectors arrived.

While Powell did not claim Iraq had nuclear weapons, he said it had been working actively to acquire them and had two of the three necessary ingredients: a bomb design and a cadre of nuclear scientists. He said Hussein was working on obtaining the last requirement, sufficient fissile material to create a nuclear explosion.

Powell cited human sources reporting that the Iraqi military distributed rocket launchers and warheads filled with biological agents in western Iraq. He said defectors and current sources described mobile biological weapons factories in trucks or rail cars that were moved around the country to escape detection. He pointed out that Iraq had refused to permit U-2 surveillance flights over Iraq and had prevented inspectors from having unfettered access to Iraqi scientists, not to mention kicking out UN weapons inspectors in 1998. Hussein warned scientists that they faced execution if they cooperated with inspectors, Powell said. And Powell pointed out that Iraq had failed to account for known weapons produced in the past, including an estimated 25,000 liters of anthrax and between 100 and 500 tons of other chemical weapons agents. When given a chance to declare the material, Hussein failed to do so. The concealment and deception led to a simple question: Why would anyone go to so much trouble to hide something unless they had something to hide?

Generations brought up on television expected the evidence to unfold before their eyes. Without seeing a video of a murder or hearing a confession, they were skeptical that a defendant was guilty. But when the object was to protect rather than to convict, a smoking gun in the form of a videotape was not necessary. That was the job of intelligence, to collect information that might form a pattern leading to a reasonable conclusion. When the dots were connected, it appeared clear that the CIA had amassed convincing intelligence revealing that Iraq was concealing a weapons of mass destruction program.

Led by France, which had been covertly supplying Hussein with missiles and tanks for years, members of the Security Council refused to accept that Saddam Hussein had not disarmed, and it condemned the U.S. for planning an invasion without the endorsement of yet another UN resolution. In the same way, the U.S., France, and Great Britain had ignored the fact that Adolf Hitler was building up Germany's military in clear violation of the Treaty of Versailles. The result was World War II, in which an estimated fifty-five million soldiers and civilians lost their lives. Many more millions were left crippled, homeless, and impoverished. The U.S. military alone lost 291,557 in World War II, about the same number of coalition troops deployed for Operation Iraqi Freedom.

By the time Bush decided to proceed with the attack, CIA and Pentagon paramilitary forces had wired the country. Satellites, effective as they were, could not pinpoint targets as well as sensors on the ground could. Since Saddam Hussein often placed military components and armaments next to schools, hospitals, mosques, and residences, it was important to locate targets with tremendous precision. The CIA and paramilitary placed sensors that could determine what was in facilities and also where those facilities could be hit so that surrounding structures and residential neighborhoods would remain unscathed. The sensors might be hidden in fake rocks.

Most of the sensors collected Measurement and Signature Intelligence. In the early days, the CIA used one form of MASINT—telemetry—to track Soviet missiles. Now MASINT, developed in highly classified programs, could detect, identify, and track the unique physical signatures and scope of anything in the world except images and sound, which were collected though IMINT and SIGINT. MASINT used radar, laser, optical, infrared, acoustic, nuclear, radiation detection, and seismic systems, as well as gas, liquid, and solid materials sampling systems. The sensors could detect motion based on vibration, magnetic properties, reflected energy, and emitted energy from nuclear, chemical, or biological devices. They could see through walls and detect chemicals in smokestack emissions or soil. When placed on the ocean floor, they could even detect submarines passing above. A form of MASINT called hyperspectral imaging used several infrared spectral bands to identify solid materials, such as crops and camouflage, and the chemical composition of gases, including poisonous gases laid down on a battlefield.[180]

An example of the capabilities of sensors was displayed in 1997 when the Pathfinder spacecraft's wheeled robotic vehicle moved about the surface of Mars and reported back to Earth on the mineral and chemical composition of the planet's surface. A central MASINT office within the Defense Intelligence Agency coordinated MASINT development and deployment within the intelligence community, reporting to Tenet through the director of the DIA.

Besides using sensors, the CIA, through NSA, tried to track the communications of Hussein, his two sons, Qusay and Uday, and other Iraqi leaders. Uday, Hussein's eldest son, tortured young girls who would not submit to his demands. He would have them suspended by the backs of their knees from a beam, then club them mercilessly as many as fifty times. When he saw pretty women on the street or young girls in a school, he would order his bodyguards to deliver them to him so he could rape them. As the head of the Iraqi Olympic Committee, he ordered beatings of soccer players who had lost games until their backs were bloody. In contrast to Uday, who was considered unstable, Qusay, Hussein's younger son, was simply ruthless. Qusay ran the special security forces and would order mass shootings to instill fear.

While he enjoyed Cuban cigars and Johnny Walker Blue Label on the rocks, Saddam Hussein spent most of his time hiding, never staying at the same place more than one or two nights. He used doubles as well.

In trying to track Hussein, his sons, and other Iraqi leaders, small aircraft and satellites homed in on cell phone and satellite phones. In Buck Rogers style, the CIA plotted the location of the phones and relayed the coordinates quickly so the areas could be bombed.

The CIA planted tiny video cameras to look for Iraqi leaders and to monitor the position of troops and suspected facilities for the production of weapons of mass destruction, beaming the images to Langley in real time through satellites. Agents attached electronic beacons to the undersides of cars that might be used by Hussein. They dragged radar-imaging sensors across the ground to look for hidden underground bunkers and storage facilities.

Working with the military, the CIA developed propaganda leaflets warning the Iraqi military not to use weapons of mass destruction and instructing them on how to surrender.

"Don't let the destiny of Saddam's regime become your destiny," said one leaflet.

Before the CIA had become "healthy," as Pavitt put, he would agonize over leasing a plane. Now, with money pouring in from Congress, he hardly thought twice about it.

Nine months before the U.S. invasion, the CIA had paramilitary officers on the ground—the CIA's force had grown to 150 out of 1,400 DO officers—who sabotaged Iraqi military equipment. Agents let the CIA know that Iraqis would welcome the U.S. once they thought Saddam Hussein was gone. They kept the CIA informed on which segments of the loyal Republican Guard and security forces would fight to defend themselves. The agents predicted the greatest resistance would come from the Fedayeen Saddam, fierce but untrained irregulars. The agents agreed to discourage use of chemical weapons. In return, the CIA paid them and identified buildings where they could hide and not be targeted.

"A lot of the CIA's role was pre-emptive, persuading Iraqi forces not to follow orders," said former deputy DCI Richard Kerr.[181]

The CIA and U.S. Special Forces also paid Iraqi guards who protected oil wells to continue to guard the facilities, to snip wires to explosive devices, and to shut down the wells after the war began. Hours before the Iraq invasion the CIA coordinated with U.S. Special Forces skilled at setting explosives. They killed leaders, blasted missile sites, and took out units that might sabotage dams or bridges. To win the propaganda war, the CIA, with offers of cash, arranged for mullahs to issue *fatwas* urging Iraqis not to resist the Americans.

Most important, the CIA developed agents who could report on Hussein's whereabouts. In the end, to pinpoint a human target, nothing was as reliable as an agent. From his swearing in as DCI in July 1997, rebuilding HUMINT had been Tenet's top priority.

"This business is becoming very high tech," he told employees in the Bubble in May 1998. "But, no matter how technical it becomes, our job is—and always will be—the same: We are in the spy business. We steal secrets, recruit agents. We do it better than anybody else, and this will not change."

To communicate with agents, the CIA issued devices ranging from satellite phones concealed in rifles to laptop computers that sent and received encrypted documents. The programs were secreted on hard drives in innocuous games or graphics. At prearranged times when satellites passed overhead, the agents aimed the computers out a window and the secret messages were sent or received.

The agency even used secret writing, a technique that dated to biblical days. In the CIA version, agents wrote over innocuous letters to their aunts or mothers through a second piece of paper impregnated with chemicals, much as carbon paper was used. The writing would show up when placed under a special light.

Normally, Tenet left the agency at 7 or 8 P.M., then often

attended functions like receptions for visiting officials from MI6 or Mossad. Even when he went to the beach for vacation, the CIA plugged him into meetings with Bush by secure teleconferencing. He usually got five to six hours of sleep a night. Now he got by on even less. He even stopped going to his favorite Greek restaurant, which served an outstanding moussaka and succulent stuffed grape leaves with egg-lemon sauce.

"Tenet was energized by problems, uncertainties, and challenges," Gannon said. "He performed best in an environment of crisis. In a rare moment of tranquility, you'd almost feel you had to make one up for him."[182]

In the middle of the war preparations, Lloyd Grove, who wrote the *Washington Post*'s "Reliable Source" column, reported that the CIA had been hand-delivering glossy postcards to neighbors around headquarters urging them to report "anything unusual or suspicious associated with your community and/or the headquarters."

After his item appeared, Grove wrote, "CIA spokesman Bill Harlow sounded a tad grumpy when we told him that dozens of alert readers had pointed out that the CIA's mail drop was a violation of federal law."

It seems that Title 18, Section 1725 of the U.S. Code made it a crime, punishable by a fine, to place mail without postage affixed in mailboxes used by the U.S. Postal Service. In other words, the U.S. Postal Service wanted to preserve its monopoly.

"I'll look into it and get back to you—after the war," Harlow told Grove after being informed of the law. "When we persisted," Grove wrote, "he groused: 'No, no, no, no. I've got all kinds of important issues to deal with—al Qaeda and Iraq. We'll get to the postal regulations when we can.'"

24

On Wednesday, March 19, 2003, the CIA received information from an Iraqi agent that Saddam Hussein and his two sons would be at a compound in Baghdad called Dora Farms that night. With blue lights flashing on his security detail's SUV, Tenet sped to the Pentagon to discuss the intelligence with Rumsfeld and General Richard B. Myers, the chairman of the Joint Chiefs of Staff.

General Tommy R. Franks got the same heads-up from CIA officers in the field. Just in case Bush ordered a strike, Franks sent two F-117A stealth fighter-bombers aloft. By 3:40 P.M., Tenet, Rumsfeld, Myers, Powell, Cheney, Rice, and White House Chief of Staff Card had convened in the Oval Office to discuss the risks of the operation. Tenet brought with him CIA officers who briefed the president on the reliability of the Iraqi agent.

As they discussed the plan, more details came in from the Iraqi agent.

"You're meeting with the president in the Oval Office with seniors, and you're getting more agent information while you're in the meeting," Tenet said. "Not bad for government work."

Bush had already given Franks orders to proceed with the invasion at a time of his own choosing. Now the question was whether to speed up the plans. The debate centered on the veracity of the information and the propaganda value to Saddam Hussein if the tip proved wrong.

"Bush asked hard questions," Pavitt said.[183]

"I was hesitant at first, to be frank with you," Bush told NBC anchor Tom Brokaw, "because I was worried that the first pictures coming out of Iraq would be a wounded grandchild of Saddam Hussein . . . that the first images of the American attack would be death to young children."

By 7:15 P.M., Bush decided it was worth the risk. The day before, after playing cat-and-mouse with UN weapons inspectors for months, Hussein defiantly had rejected Bush's ultimatum that he leave the country within forty-eight hours. Calling that Hussein's final mistake, the president said, "Go."

At 9:33 P.M.—5:33 A.M. Baghdad time—two satellite-guided one-ton bombs hit the Dora Farms bunker. Warships and submarines in the Persian Gulf and Red Sea fired thirty Tomahawk cruise missiles at the compound as well. Forty-five minutes later, Bush addressed the nation from the Oval Office. "On my orders, coalition forces have begun striking selected targets of military importance," he said.

"The president listens," Tenet said. "He acquires data. He is always interested in competing views, but then he decides. He doesn't get paralyzed. When we're good, we go."

Like most Americans, Tenet had friends and members of his family who were against the war. "Going to war is a pretty serious decision for anybody to take," he said. "The reason this is a great country is people can express those views."

With Rumsfeld's prodding, General Franks had conceived a brilliant, flexible plan using the Army, Navy, Marines, Air Force, and special forces in parallel, to quickly overrun Iraq. The idea was to stay a step ahead of Hussein and overcome his defenses before he could issue instructions or figure out his next move. The plan depended heavily on intelligence and technology that had not existed or was just being developed in the first Gulf War.

In Desert Storm, only 20 percent of air-to-ground fighters could deliver a laser-guided bomb. In Operation Iraqi Freedom, all fighters possessed that capability. In Desert Storm, it took up to two days to photograph a target, confirm its coordinates, plan the mission, and transmit the information to the bomber crew. In the more recent conflict, with near-real-time imaging, photos and coordinates of targets were e-mailed. With the CIA's Predator drone aircraft and other reconnaissance techniques, commanders could view the battlefield and communicate with each other in ways never before experienced in the history of war.

The plan employed just half the number of troops from coalition countries—the U.S., Great Britain, Australia, Denmark, and Poland—as had been used in the first Gulf War, when 550,000 soldiers were deployed to achieve the more limited objective of expelling Iraq from Kuwait.

This time, CIA intelligence started and ended the war. Saddam Hussein, sixty-five, escaped the first bombing, but the ability to target Hussein was a triumph for Tenet's policy of resurrecting HUMINT. Pavitt felt Hussein's inner circle never recovered from the blow.

On Monday, April 7, the CIA received a tip from others on the ground pinpointing the location of Hussein in another of his compounds, this one in Baghdad's Mansur neighborhood. A B-1B bomber, flying over western Iraq after an in-flight refueling, received an urgent order. Twelve minutes after receiving the coordinates by e-mail the bomber unleashed two satellite-guided one-ton bombs that pierced the building's roof, followed three seconds later by two more bombs equipped with delays, which allowed the massive explosives to penetrate deep into the target before exploding. All that was left was a crater forty-five feet deep.

After the strike, the regime melted away. The Ba'ath Party enforcers, who had been stationed on street corners, were nowhere in sight. Official minders did not show up to chaperone foreign journalists. State TV went off the air, and command and control communications ceased. Information Minister Mohammed Saeed al-Shahaf, whose pronouncements on the success of the Iraqi forces provided the only humor of the war, had disappeared. If Hussein was alive, the CIA decided, he clearly was not functioning.

In similar fashion, after allied bombs killed Ali Hassan al-Majid, known as "Chemical Ali," resistance in Basra ceased. Chemical Ali was Hussein's half brother and part of his inner circle. He was known for his ruthlessness. He once encountered police checking the IDs of a crowd of Iraqis in Basra's Saad Square. "No IDs? Just shoot them all," he said, and he watched in satisfaction as the police killed all six hundred people.

After Mohammed Odeh al-Rehaief, a thirty-two-year-old Iraqi lawyer, told the Marines the location of twenty-year-old Jessica Lynch, an army supply clerk, the CIA provided intelligence so Special Operations forces could rescue her more easily. The CIA had an agent photograph the route to her room in Saddam Hospital in Nasiriyah where she was imprisoned. At the time she was under guard.

"Jessica Lynch," a soldier called to her as she tried to hide under a sheet in her hospital room, "we're United States soldiers and we're here to protect you and take you home."

Lynch, a onetime Miss Congeniality winner at the county fair beauty pageant in Palestine, West Virginia, shot back: "I'm an American soldier, too."

"The military took action on what we said," Pavitt told me. "The bad news is, they'll want us for the next war," he joked.[184]

In the end, the tyranny upon which the regime was built was its undoing. Having seen colleagues executed for giving Hussein bad news, commanders were loath to tell him the Americans were wiping out Iraqi forces. Soldiers whose motivation to fight was based on fear posed little threat. Since commands came only from Hussein, his personal secretary Abid Homad Mahmud, his son Qusay, or his cousin Ali Hassan Tikriti, Americans' ability to wipe out military communications meant that Hussein's forces were paralyzed. Citizens who had been intimidated into turning out to cheer on Hussein's birthday were only too happy to see him go.

"Totalitarian regimes tend to be good at terror but tend to be incompetent in most everything else," formal assistant director James Simon said.

On Wednesday, April 9, after a series of increasingly aggressive armed reconnaissance missions through nearly every quarter of Baghdad, Iraqis in Firdos Square were the first to visibly defy the regime. As TV cameras recorded the scene and Tenet watched from his desk, an Iraqi took a sledgehammer to a towering bronze statue of Saddam Hussein. Others pounded the statue with the soles of their shoes, a profound sign of disrespect in the Arab world. That gave other Iraqis, who had lived in fear of Saddam Hussein, the courage to follow their lead and begin trying to tear down the statue.

In the past the CIA had instigated such defiance. In fomenting the agency's 1953 coup in Iran, a journalist who was a CIA agent led a crowd toward parliament, inciting people to set fire to the offices of a newspaper owned by left-wing Mohamed Mossadegh's foreign minister, according to the CIA's secret history of the operation, TOAJAX. Other CIA agents posed as Communists who then criticized the religious leaders, turning them against Mossadegh.

In Baghdad, there was no need for CIA intervention. "They took charge of their own destiny," Tenet said. "It was the natural reaction of people."

A Marine tank recovery vehicle eventually toppled the statue of Hussein, and a young boy sat on its head as Iraqis dragged it away. The episode demonstrated that the Iraqis had been liberated. After three weeks, the war, for all practical purposes, was over. As Cheney had said, it would take weeks, not months, to topple Hussein. But the rapidity of the victory and the low number of American casualties—139 up to that point—surprised even the agency.

On March 26, Pavitt sent a two-page electronic cable to all stations. "The commitment of the CIA to this war is unprecedented," Pavitt said. In a cable at the end of the war, he said, "It was one team, one fight."

Overjoyed Iraqis welcomed the Americans. "Thank you, Mr. Bush. Thank you, Mr. Bush. Mr. Bush Okay!" an Iraqi said over and over on television. "Human Shields Go Home," a homemade sign said. Women asked American soldiers to kiss their babies. Iraqis danced in the streets.

The critics had questioned whether the U.S. could win the war with so few troops, whether the Iraqis would support the Americans, whether the war would lead to hundreds of thousands of casualties, whether Iraq would attack Israel, and whether going to war would lead to immediate terrorist attacks on the U.S. When the objections proved wrong, the critics then questioned whether Iraqis—whose homeland was known as the cradle of civilization—could govern themselves democratically. Since diplomacy had not worked, the critics blamed Bush.

"I'm saddened that the president failed so miserably at diplomacy that we are now forced to war," Senate Minority Leader Thomas A. Daschle, a Democrat from South Dakota, said. "Saddened that we have to give up one life because this president couldn't create the kind of diplomatic effort that was so critical for our country."

Yet, diplomacy had as much chance of working with Saddam Hussein as it had with Hitler. Like Bush, British Prime Minister Tony Blair had risked his political career on the decision to go to war. Acutely aware of how Neville Chamberlain, the British prime minister at the start of World War II, had naively appeased Hitler, Blair drew a line in the sand, later revealing that he had been prepared to quit his position if Parliament failed to support him.

While going into Iraq may have appeared to well-intentioned people who opposed the war to be a preemptive strike, it was a continuation of the Persian Gulf War, when the U.S. agreed to a cease fire only on condition that Saddam Hussein disarm. In contrast, the U.S. under Clinton had used force in Bosnia, Haiti, and Kosovo without going to the UN first. No one complained. Nor did anyone seem to mind that Hussein was sending his planes into the no-fly zones and firing on U.S. planes protecting those zones hundreds of times a year.

As in Afghanistan, just before American victory, the critics and pessimists declared the U.S. to be stuck in a "quagmire." When victory was achieved, they said the fight had been too easy and compared American forces to bullies crushing a feeble foe. Remarkably, even after Operation Iraqi Freedom had proven successful, the critics ignored not only conservatives' concerns about protecting American security but liberals' concerns about protecting human rights.

When asked if Iraqis were better off after the war than under Hussein, who had ordered the execution of an estimated three hundred thousand of his countrymen, Democratic presidential hopeful Howard Dean said, "We don't know that yet." In making such statements, Dean and other critics brushed aside the fact that the liberation of Iraq meant that Iraqis would no longer undergo torture by having electric prods attached to their genitals or by being given acid baths, having holes drilled into their ankles and skulls, being left naked in refrigerators for days, having their tongues cut out and their ears cut off, or by being forced to watch their wives and sisters being gang raped.

"I have absolutely no regret about my vote on this war [opposing it]," said Nancy Pelosi, the Democratic House minority leader from California. "The same questions remain: The cost in human lives, the cost to our budget, probably $100 billion. We could have probably brought down that statue for a lot less. The cost to our economy. But the most important question at this time, now that we're toward the end of it, is: What is the cost to the war on terrorism?"

Even as Pelosi spoke, the CIA was interrogating Khalid Shaikh Mohammed, bin Laden's third in command, and rolling up dozens of al Qaeda operatives as a result. Among them was Walid Ba'Attash, one of bin Laden's top lieutenants who was believed to have played a crucial role in the bombing of the USS *Cole* and the attacks of 9/11. Less than a week later, the CIA and Pakistani authorities stopped an al Qaeda plot to fly an explosives-laden plane into the U.S. consulate in Karachi, arresting two al Qaeda members who had had roles in the September 11 plot and the bombing of the USS *Cole.*

Based on information from the CIA's interrogation of Mohammed, the FBI secretly arrested Iyman Faris, an Ohio truck driver, for plotting with al Qaeda to bring down New York's Brooklyn Bridge by cutting its suspension cables while launching a simultaneous unspecified attack on Washington. Faris, a Kashmiri-born naturalized American citizen, met with bin Laden and transported cash, cell phones, and other supplies for al Qaeda. After performing surveillance of the bridge, Faris determined that New York City Police security at the bridge was too tight and that trying to sever the bridge cables with blowtorches was not feasible. He sent a coded e-mail message to al Qaeda saying, "The weather is too hot."

After his arrest, Faris agreed to plead guilty to providing material support to a terrorist organization. The arrest demonstrated both the success of the CIA's war on terror and the impact of increased domestic security.

Contrary to the critics' dire warnings, the CIA could do two things at once: prosecute the war on terror and prepare the way for a spectacular victory in Iraq. Suggesting that the U.S. should win the war on terror before taking on Saddam Hussein—as Senator Bob Graham did in announcing his bid for the Democratic presidential nomination—was like saying the FBI should wipe out the Mafia before it tackled kidnappings and corporate fraud perpetrated by Enron and WorldCom.

If Pelosi trivialized the American success by saying the statue of Saddam Hussein could have been toppled for far less, the Iraqis who showed journalists prisons where Saddam Hussein had tortured inmates by squeezing hot irons against their backs did not. In Baghdad, embedded journalist Bernard Jones of UPI reported that, after repeated assaults by Iraqis armed with rocks, chains, and lengths of rope, a statue of Hussein finally toppled onto three men. They suffered minor cuts and a few broken bones. When asked if it was worth it, one of the injured men—identified only as Durayd—replied, "For freedom from the statues, I'd give my life."

With the war over, the CIA worked with the military to find and identify weapons of mass destruction. They found two mobile biological weapons labs with equipment made as recently as 2002 and 2003, confirming what the CIA had learned from four people with knowledge of the labs. The chief source, an Iraqi scientist who had been involved in the weapons program and had fled the country, said he made slurry for producing anthrax in the labs. Anthrax is made from the slurry after fermentation and drying.

From the outside, the labs looked like standard trucks on the highway. Inside, they were fitted with an array of tanks, fermentors, air compressors, and water chillers that, most scientific experts said, could only have been designed to produce biological weapons. As with other intelligence, the CIA worked closely with the British and other intelligence services, which concurred in the findings. Simply possessing the labs without declaring them was a violation of UN sanctions against Iraq.

Some media reports quoted mostly unnamed experts as saying the labs lacked equipment for steam sterilization, normally a prerequisite for biological production. But the CIA said steam treatment was not necessarily required or could be supplied by an additional unit such as existed on Iraqi decontamination trucks.

In all the questioning, no one came up with a logical explanation for why anyone would go to so much expense to turn vans into production facilities unless it was to conceal what was being made. Inspectors could have looked for the rest of their lives and never have found the mobile labs simply because they could be driven off to another location when the inspectors got near. Thus, there was no need to store vast quantities of weapons. With the labs, Hussein could create them overnight. In one weekend, the two labs could produce enough anthrax to kill more than fifty thousand people.

An Iraqi scientist told the CIA that the labs were part of Hussein's strategy of making chemical and biological weapons on demand. Besides the mobile labs, Hussein decentralized the weapons program by placing production equipment within commercial "dual use" facilities so it would not be discovered but could be used when needed, the scientist said.

As the hunt for weapons of mass destruction continued, Tenet was confident they would be found. Saddam "grew a clandestine program within an inspection regime," he said. "They may not have stored a lot of it because of the amount you can produce quicky in these mobile facilities. The document exploitation, the information from mid- to lower-level scientists, will develop a story that says everything we said at the UN was dead-on."

However, "There were a lot of dogs that didn't bark here," Tenet said. "There were a lot of scenarios that we were concerned about that didn't occur," such as use of chemical or biological weapons in combat. The reasons could range from incorrect intelligence to good use of intelligence and an effective military plan. "We need to ask ourselves why and learn from it," Tenet said.

In part, those answers would come from a panel of four former senior CIA officials chosen, at Rumsfeld's suggestion, months before the war started. The job of the panel, headed by former deputy DCI Richard Kerr, was to evaluate retrospectively what CIA and military intelligence got right and what they got wrong, with the purpose of improving intelligence and its use by policymakers. While it would take time to develop the answers, the panel prepared an initial report on how intelligence before the war compared with the known outcomes of the war—how much resistance was encountered, whether Iraq would attack Israel, what the reaction of the Arab street was, and whether terrorists would attack the United States.

On those issues, "There was some very sound analysis and some gaps, which is not surprising, particularly with the benefit of hindsight," Kerr said.

To assess why weapons of mass destruction were not used and how active Iraq's weapons of mass destruction program had been would require extensive review of Iraqi documents and interrogation of captured Iraqi scientists and leaders, most of whom were not talking because they feared being charged with war crimes. Close to fourteen hundred people were involved in the search, but they were hindered by what continued to be a hostile environment.

"Soldiers are still being killed," McLaughlin said. "People have to go out with armored escorts and be back before night. The Iraqis are still afraid. They are in shock. They are asking, 'Who will be with us a year from now?' "[185]

The initial failure to find weapons of mass destruction led to claims that the CIA had cooked the books to support the Bush administration's policy objectives.

"If we don't find these weapons of mass destruction, it will represent a serious intelligence failure, or else the manipulation of that intelligence to keep the American people in the dark," Senator Bob Graham said.

In making the charge, the Democratic presidential candidate

overlooked the fact that, in a February 1998 speech, Clinton had said that "Iraq still has stockpiles of chemical and biological munitions, a small force of Scud-type missiles, and the capacity to restart quickly its production program and build many, many more weapons."

The *Washington Post* quoted unnamed analysts as saying that the fact that Cheney and a senior aide visited the agency a number of times to question analysts created what they perceived as an environment of pressure for them to tailor their conclusions to the administration's policy.

Over the years the CIA has repeatedly come under pressure from administrations trying to marshal support for its policy positions. The best example was President Johnson's insistence that the CIA support his prosecution of the war in Vietnam. Despite that pressure, the CIA never wavered in its view that the war was predicated on faulty assumptions and that the North Vietnamese were far stronger than the administration was claiming publicly. It was the same message the antiwar protesters were trying to convey, only the CIA's reports were classified.

"The job of the CIA is to speak truth to power," said David Cohen, the former associate deputy director of the DI. "The analysts are always subject to tough questioning. They are grilled by the DCI. That should not be confused with pressure."

William Casey occasionally had tried to impose his right-wing views on analysts but soon learned that he could only so far. He could not push CIA analysts into saying something they did not want to say or felt they could not support. Overall, the CIA had continued to produce estimates that conflicted with Casey's views, demonstrating that ultimately he had little or no effect on the process. On the other hand, John McCone had had a hunch that the analysts were wrong when they said the Soviets would not send missiles to Cuba. Because of his questioning, the agency eventually pinpointed the missiles.

Given the subjective nature of analysis, some within the agency will always disagree with the final position. In the case of Iraq, some analysts were against the war, just as some State Department officials opposed it and resigned as a result. That did not mean that the CIA was trying to suppress views or had been politicized.

In reviewing CIA intelligence on Iraq and the agency's interaction with the administration, Richard Kerr told me the CIA encountered the same kind of "pressure" a reporter on a hot story might apply in asking a government official for a stronger quote. The reporter may argue that the facts warrant such a quote, while the official disagrees and sticks to his position.

In the case of Iraq, Kerr said administration officials had an obligation to delve into the facts and get involved in the process. Based on their own reading of the intelligence and their own worldview, they sometimes marshaled arguments to try to persuade the agency to say Hussein posed more of a threat than the agency was willing to conclude. They also asked why the CIA emphasized one fact or another. In the same vein, in questioning Tenet on the Hill, a senator might push for a particular answer because he feels it is the right one. While some analysts might interpret that as pressure, Kerr said no one tried to "direct" the CIA to change its opinions, nor did the agency do so.

"It was part of the normal give-and-take of the intelligence process," Kerr said.

When Cheney visited the CIA, McLaughlin would escort him into a conference room across the hall from the DCI's office. There, the vice president would spend three or four hours at a time with analysts. Besides the weapons of mass destruction issue, Cheney made such visits to look into three or four other issues that interested him, such as North Korea and China.

"He came out here a lot," McLaughlin told me. "The characterization Colin Powell gave was exactly right: He loves to dig into things. When he comes, he is polite and respectful. Most of the people I would bring in to talk to him were thankful he was here. We were saying, 'Thank you, God, for bringing us someone who is interested.' "[186]

McLaughlin said that every administration he has worked for, going back to President Nixon, has had a vital interest in CIA analysis.

"They will question how you arrived at your conclusions," McLaughlin said. "They will all start to read the raw intelligence because it's important to them. When they read something and it jars with our conclusions, they want to know why. This isn't patty-cake. This isn't Mr. Rogers's Neighborhood. People move planes, ships, men based on what we say. People risk their lives. So there is a lot at stake here."

McLaughlin said the professionals don't interpret honest, persistent questioning as pressure. "We're not here on Mount Olympus delivering revealed wisdom," McLaughlin said. "The truth is elusive. The questioning is normal interchange. There was no spinning of intelligence."

Anyone who knew Tenet and his reputation for integrity and outspokenness recognized that he would never tolerate any attempt to influence the CIA's conclusions. Those conclusions were presented publicly for all to examine and debate. When Powell cited the CIA's report that Hussein had been trying covertly to obtain high-specification aluminum tubes for enriching uranium, he acknowledged that there was a controversy about the tubes' possible uses. On the other hand, after discussing the issue in an October 2001 National Intelligence Estimate, the CIA never embraced a controversial British intelligence report that Iraq had begun trying to obtain uranium from Niger in 2001.

Because the CIA believed the intelligence behind it was too fragmentary, Tenet succeeded in cutting a reference to the British report in a presidential speech in October 2002, but a sixteen-word reference made it into Bush's State of the Union address on January 28, 2003. When Bush said, "The British governement has learned that Saddam Hussein recently sought significant quantities of uranium from Africa," the statement was technically true. However, because of continuing concerns by the CIA and the State Department's Bureau of Intelligence and Research about the soundness of the intelligence, Powell made no mention of Niger when presenting the case against Hussein at the UN eight days later. That same month, the CIA gave the International Atomic Energy Agency documents that backed up the British assertion, and the IAEA quickly concluded that they were forged or at least shaky. However, the British insisted that their report was not based on the documents and was true.

The reference was but a footnote to intelligence going back to 1991 demonstrating that Hussein had been working on a nuclear weapons program. In fact, he already had 550 metric tons of uranium. Yet Democratic presidential candidates and those who had opposed the war pounced on the reference in the State of the Union address as evidence that Bush was purposely fabricating intelligence to support going to war. During a slow news week in July, the charges surfaced again. This time, they were the lead story in papers across the country. A Democratic attack ad declared that "It's time to tell the truth" and ran a video clip of Bush's sentence omitting the critical words: "The British government has learned that . . ."

Tenet stepped up to the plate and said he took overall responsibility for the fact that when reviewing drafts of the president's speech his agency did not object more vigorously to citing the Niger report. Yet the fact remained that including the reference was an error, much like errors large and small that are corrected almost daily by the same papers that trumpeted what the *Wall Street Journal* called Bush's "non-lie" as the most important story of the day.

For all the politicking, the failure to find weapons of mass destruction understandably continued to create suspicion. Yet in the end, whether weapons of mass destruction were found, or whether Hussein relied on mobile labs to manufacture them overnight, became almost as relevent as whether a serial killer who reaches into the back seat of his car when an FBI agent orders him to keep his hands up actually has a handgun in the back. If the agent waits to find out, he may be shot dead. Regardless of what else was or was not found after the war, the question for policymakers before the war would have remained the same: Should Saddam Hussein be allowed to continue a weapons of mass destruction program?

While everyone at the CIA was convinced weapons of mass destruction would be found, McLaughlin told analysts, "We have to keep an open mind about it." When the intelligence committees decided to investigate the CIA's prewar conclusions on Iraq, Tenet volunteered to give them everything behind the CIA's assessments—a pile of classified reports more than six feet high.

Meanwhile, the CIA worked with the military to locate former Iraqi leaders. In a dramatic story that never came out, in late 2002, the agency suddenly withdrew a young case officer from Iraq when the CIA learned that the Iraqi Intelligence Service had discovered his identity and was casing his home for a possible kidnapping or assassination. The intelligence service, Mukhabarat, was the equivalent of the CIA and the FBI rolled into one. It was the agency that had tried to assassinate George H. W. Bush in Kuwait in 1993. As the head of operations for the Iraqi Intelligence Service, Hasan Izba Ubaydi would have been the one to order the action against the case officer.

After the war in late April 2003, the CIA lured Ubaydi to a meeting in Baghdad with the same case officer by tricking him into thinking the agency wanted to recruit him as a double agent. Ubaydi showed up for the meeting wearing a suit and tie and ridiculously large blue-blocker sunglasses. He confidently strode up to the case officer and shook his hand. As they spoke in Arabic, the case officer signaled to Navy SEALs, who seized his pursuer.

The CIA officer and the SEALs drove Ubaydi to a military facility in an open Humvee. Ubaydi pleaded for his dignity, asking his intended target to hide him as they drove. The U.S. never publicized his capture.

As the hunt for weapons of mass destruction dragged on, media stories and critics suggested the Bush administration had lied about the reasons for going to war, not only because no weapons of mass destruction had been found but because some al Qaeda captives told the CIA that bin Laden had rejected working jointly with Saddam Hussein. What the reports and critics failed to mention was that neither the CIA nor Bush had said the two were in league. What the CIA did say was that Hussein had allowed al Qaeda to operate in Iraq. In picking apart what the CIA did or did not say before the war, most of the media reports also failed to mention what in fact was found after the war.

In northeastern Iraq, the military found a terrorist training camp operated by Abu Musab al-Zarqawi, a bin Laden associate who allegedly masterminded the assassination of American diplomat Lawrence Foley in Amman in October 2002. While this section of Iraq was outside Hussein's control, it was under the control of one of his agents, who had allowed al-Zarqawi to train terrorists in the use of poisons and explosives at the camp. Debriefings of hundreds of al Qaeda members, including the operative sent to kill Foley, revealed extensive additional activity by al Qaeda within Iraq. This additional information linking Hussein with al Qaeda never leaked out and therefore never appeared in the media.

"It would be wrong to say there was complete separation between al Qaeda and Iraq," McLaughlin said. "Beyond that, by succeeding in Iraq, we denied important geographic space to people who threatened the U.S. with terrorism. It was one of several places where terrorists felt free to move and were not threatened."

Besides al Qaeda in Iraq, the military captured Mohammed Abbas, also known as Abu Abbas, who was the mastermind of the 1985 hijacking of the Italian cruise ship *Achille Lauro*. During that incident, a disabled American tourist was murdered and thrown overboard.

On the outskirts of Baghdad, a Marine unit found a terrorist training camp operated by the Palestine Liberation Organization. Documents showed that Iraq had sold weapons to the terrorist group as recently as January. Other troops found eight hundred black leather vests stuffed with explosives and ball bearings. Empty hangers suggested some of the lethal vests were already on the backs of would-be suicide bombers. As other countries like Syria and Iran saw the consequences of defying the U.S., they began to arrest al Qaeda members.

Going after Saddam Hussein was indeed part of the war on terror.

As Senator John F. Kerry, a Massachusetts Democrat and presidential contender, accused Bush of having "misled every one of us" about Hussein's weapons of mass destruction program, an Iraqi scientist led CIA officers to buried components needed to produce the only missing ingredient in making a nuclear bomb—fissile material. The scientist, Mahdi Obeidi, said he had buried the parts under a rosebush in his backyard twelve years earlier, on orders of Hussein's son Qusay. Obeidi, who headed Iraq's nuclear enrichment program in the early 1990s, said the components of a gas centrifuge system for enriching uranium, along with blueprints for building them, were to be hidden until Hussein could reconstitute his nuclear weapons program, perhaps when sanctions on Iraq were lifted. Experts said the buried cache would have allowed Hussein to cut years from reconstituting his nuclear weapons program.

The find demonstrated how crafty Hussein had been at hiding his weapons of mass destruction program, how determined he had been to maintain that capability, and how impossible it would have been for weapons inspectors ever to uncover the material. It was a vindication of both the CIA's intelligence and the common-sense approach to looking at life's problems: No one hides and obfuscates unless they have something to hide.

25

On MAY 13, 2003, al Qaeda operatives bombed residential com-
plexes in Riyadh, Saudi Arabia, killing thirty-four people, including
eight Americans and nine of the attackers themselves. It was a
reminder that al Qaeda was still a threat. Two days later I met
with Tenet for the second time. This time the interview, which
would last an hour and a half, took place in the DCI's office on
the fourth floor of the Eisenhower Executive Office Building—
previously the Old Executive Office Building—next to the White
House.

Because he had been meeting with Bush in the Oval Office.
Tenet arrived ten minutes late. He looked grimmer than the last
time I saw him, near the beginning of interviews at the CIA. He
looked slimmer as well.

On Tenet's desk was a framed photo of Stephanie and a CIA
mug, the kind that a shop on the first floor of the agency now
sells freely. Tenet took off his dark blue jacket and motioned for
me to sit on a sofa. He sat on a chair opposite me.

In our previous meeting at headquarters, we had bantered

about who had taught Bill Harlow to be such a good PR person. I suggested Tenet had taught him, or else Harlow's predecessor, Dennis Boxx. Jokingly, Harlow insisted he had taught himself.

This time, beyond a brief give-and-take about the merits of local Greek restaurants, there was no small talk. Tenet was like a laser beam, totally focused on the issues. He did not ingratiate himself. Nor did he inject himself into the interview more than was necessary. When he did refer to himself, he avoided the personal pronoun almost entirely. At the same time, Tenet was transparent as glass about his feelings. He spoke with passion about the events of 9/11 and his concept of risk-taking and leadership, honed by reading books by Jack Welch of GE and Louis Gerstner Jr. of IBM, along with Steven Pressfield's account of the Battle of Thermopylae.

In Pressfield's *Gate of Fire*, the fictional squire named Xeones described King Leonidas' leadership and bravery in battle. "I will tell his majesty what a king is," Xeones told King Xerxes. "A king does not abide within his tent while his men bleed and die upon the field," Xeones said. "A king does not dine while his men go hungry, nor sleep when they stand at watch upon the wall. A king does not command his men's loyalty through fear, nor purchase it with gold; he earns their love by the sweat of his own back and the pains he endures for their sake. That which comprises the hardest burden, a king lifts first and sets down last. A king does not require service of those he leads but provides it to them. He serves them, not they him."[187]

On the morning of the interview, a story in the *New York Times* said that Tenet had failed to fulfill a promise made to the Joint Inquiry nine months earlier: to turn over the names of CIA people who neglected to place Khalid al-Midhar and Nawaf Al-hazmi on a watch list after the two men had attended an al Qaeda meeting in January 2000. In fact, the Joint Inquiry already knew the names of everyone involved, but Senator Carl Levin, a Michigan Democrat, wanted Tenet, in effect, to brand particular employees as culprits. The problem, as Tenet explained it to the committee, was that the CIA at the time did not have a uniform system in place for putting terrorists on the list. Therefore, the failure was his.

"Senior leaders must take responsibility for those below them," Tenet told me. "It is not good leadership to take this person and throw him on the tarmac and say, 'He did it. Go torture him. Fire him.'" He said, "The leadership at the top cannot walk away from the bottom of the organization. If you didn't know there was a problem, somebody in your chain of command had to know. If there is a professional mistake, then you correct that. If someone is honestly doing his job to the best of his or her ability, and the system failed him in some way by not providing the tools or the standards, then the system has to be held accountable."[188]

As Tenet saw it, that approach was the only way to insure that the CIA did not return to the days when it was weak and scarcely relevant. In the early 1990s, "Everyone thought, we don't need the CIA any more," Tenet told me. "The Soviets were gone, the Russians were here. The world was about to break out in one harmonious whole. Well, it didn't happen that way. But decisions were made to reduce our workforce and pare down expenditures. In 2001, everyone woke up and said, 'Why aren't you perfect? Why don't you have continuous coverage of the world? Why aren't you omniscient?' Well, you're never going to be omniscient, and you're never going to have coverage of everything."

The CIA gives "the senior decision-makers a unilateral advantage that no other country has," Tenet said. "The question is: Do you want to pay for it and invest in it, or do you want to have hearings for the rest of our lives about why we didn't have this capability?"

Yet money was not enough. "This is unlike any other business in terms of what we ask people to do," Tenet said. "If you're not on the far edge of risk-taking to steal their secrets, using human beings or technology to get access to what's going to protect the country, you're not doing your job. When you take those risks things are going to go wrong. If the perception is, 'They're going to throw me overboard if a mistake is made,' then the men and women who work for you won't believe it when you say, 'We must take risks.'"

It was up to him, Tenet said, to accept responsibility when things didn't turn out right. "All the philosophy of taking risks is going to spatter on you," he said. "If that's going to bother you, then you're in the wrong job. If you think this is about protecting your image or yourself, you're finished. Forget it." Tenet said. "Nobody is perfect. But guys who have never run anything in their lives, who have never taken any risk in their lives, who have never managed a large workforce, will tell you how to suck eggs and how to do your job on a daily basis. If you listen to them, you're listening to the wrong people."

Tenet said he considered his constituencies to be "the men and women in the building and the president of the U.S., and a process on the Hill where you have to be honest with the American people through their representatives. If you care about anything else, you're not doing your job. That's the way it is."

What's important, Tenet said, is whether "you do your level best as a human being each day. Did you do something that you're proud of? If you are, that has to sustain you. Not what the *New York Times* or what the cable TV guy said. You have to go home and say, 'I think I did good for my country today.'"

Tenet said it is "really hard to screw up this job because you have terrific people. You never have to wonder if people are going to do the right thing—that they're going to work professionally and soundly ninety-five percent of the time. All you have to do is to provide the right kind of incentives and leadership and keep your eye on the ball and make sure you're changing with the times," he said.

The events of 9/11 left a deep emotional scar on the agency, Tenet said. "We were not perfect by any stretch of the imagination," he said. "But did we have a strategy, did we have a focus, were we relentlessly in pursuit of these people? You bet." Tenet added, "If there is one thing I wish I could convey to the American people and the families of the victims of 9/11, it's how much it means to us to make sure this never happens to another American family. But I can't guarantee that," he said. "I can't."

As for the war on terror, "We're going to have battles that we lose," Tenet said. "But we're winning more than we're losing. We have to have the fortitude to say, 'We're not going to get paralyzed because we lost a battle.' We're going to beat them with our smarts, with our intelligence, with our military, and with our values. And we will win this thing."

When Tenet returned to the agency, he passed by the stars representing CIA officers killed while serving their country. Since the death of Johnny "Mike" Spann, Helge P. Boes, 32, had died in Afghanistan. A Harvard Law School graduate, Boes decided after the attacks of 9/11 to give up the practice of law and join the agency. He said he wanted to serve his country. Boes' instructors called him a "case officer's case officer." It was one of the highest compliments in the agency. Boes volunteered to begin his overseas career in Afghanistan. He gathered intelligence during rocket, mortar, and machine gun attacks and directed an Afghan force against the Taliban. When he returned to Afghanistan for another mission, a grenade detonated prematurely in weapons training, killing him.

Tenet passed by the statue of William Donovan, a reminder of the agency's roots. For all the gaffes and abuses of the past, Donovan's "unusual experiment" had paid off. Through the most terrifying moments of the cold war, the CIA penetrated Soviet secrecy, warned of most threats, and allowed policymakers to orchestrate a measured response that eventually led to the collapse of the Soviet Union. While the CIA failed to uncover the plots of September 11, it scored a dazzling success in the war on terror and in the wars to rid the world of the Taliban and Saddam Hussein. Contrary to the John Deutch thesis, CIA officers were the best and the brightest, emblems of American ingenuity and determination. Their mantra—"Our failures are publicized, our successes are not"—happened to be true.

Under Tenet, the CIA was focused, aggressive, and effective, the negativism and self-doubt of the Deutch era a bitter memory. Once again, Donovan's "can-do" spirit infused the agency. The professionals, not the cowboys, were in charge. In crafting the effort against the Taliban and Iraq, Tenet adopted the OSS approach, combining covert intelligence-gathering and paramilitary operations with parallel military offensives. Unlike the military effort, the CIA's war was invisible.

As intelligence became even more critical in fighting wars, threats became more diverse, and weapons of mass destruction became more deadly and pervasive, the need for the CIA would become even greater. Intelligence was to security what the computer was to the information age: The need for it just kept growing. Congress appeared to agree, having upped the CIA's budget to close to $5 billion a year.

"We started out as babes feeling our way," said Rolfe Kingsley, who began with the OSS and became chief of the CIA's Soviet Division. "We had to learn the game. But we knew who the enemy was. Today, you have to find out who they are. The CIA has done a marvelous job of going after these disparate threats. They bene-fitted from the foundation which we laid, and they put it to good use. My hat is off to them."[189]

Five months before the war in Iraq, Tenet attended the funeral of Eloise Page, the executive secretary to Donovan who became the first female to head a major station. Tenet called her an "in-telligence pioneer." Three months before she died, Page, eighty-two, had told me that the risks of the job, the lack of recognition, and the demands of living undercover had all been worth it. "I love my country, and I loved doing it," she said.

"She represented the highest standards of the CIA," Jim Pavitt said at the service at Christ Church in Georgetown. "There was no spin."

At his confirmation hearings back in May 1997, Tenet had warned that the CIA must not be allowed to "wither." He pledged then to "create an intelligence culture that challenges conventional wisdom and encourages creative but responsible risk-taking."

From its earliest days, Tenet said, the "greatest successes of American intelligence have come at times when an intelligence officer was able to see what others could not, dare what others would not, and refuse to give up in the face of overwhelming odds."

Tenet, a son of Greek immigrants, had proven he was such an intelligence officer.

ACKNOWLEDGMENTS

My wife, Pamela Kessler, did so much to make this book a reality, beginning with her support of my desire to leave the *Washington Post* in 1985 and write books. Also a former *Washington Post* reporter, she informed my decisions with her wise counsel and pre-edited the manuscript. As author of *Undercover Washington: Touring the Sites Where Famous Spies Lived, Worked and Loved*, she is almost a spook herself.

My grown children, Rachel and Greg Kessler, were sources of pride, love, and encouragement. My stepson Mike Whitehead was a loyal and endearing supporter.

My late mother, Minuetta Kessler, taught me that nothing is impossible. A concert pianist and composer, she died at her home in Belmont, Massachusetts, at age eighty-eight, having completed her last work, an opera.

My agent, Robert Gottlieb, chairman of Trident Media Group, is always there when I need him, shaping the ideas for my books and providing brilliant direction.

I am lucky to have on my side Matthew Shear, vice president

and publisher of St. Martin's Press, and Charles Spicer, executive editor. So much goes into making a book, and they do it all superbly. As always, Charlie's editing was deft and incredibly insightful.

The CIA not only allowed me to interview fifty current officers, it actively encouraged former officers to talk with me as well. I was given tours of areas of the CIA never seen by the media. Providing that kind of unprecedented access and cooperation was a risk, but George Tenet recognized that the larger public interest was served by letting Americans know more about the agency. He has my gratitude. William Harlow, director of public affairs, was instrumental in that decision. He and his deputy, Mark Mansfield, made it happen.

I am indebted to former CIA officers who read portions of the manuscript to help spot errors. They are David Cohen, Jack Devine, William F. Donnelly, E. Peter Earnest, John C. Gannon, James Hirsch, S. Eugene Poteat, Lloyd Salvetti, Herbert F. Saunders, James M. Simon Jr., and Richard F. Stolz. John L. Martin, who formerly headed the Justice Department's counterespionage section, and his wife Carol also read the manuscript.

Edward Klein came up with the title for the book and was helpful in so many other ways as a friend and fellow author.

I am grateful to those who consented to interviews or helped in other ways. They include:

Charles E. Allen, Frank Anderson, Robert Baer, William M. Baker, Elizabeth Bancroft, Robert Barron, Michael Battles, Frans Bax, Stan Bedlington, Joseph Billy Jr., the late Richard M. Bissell Jr., J. Cofer Black, Robert M. Blitzer, Connie Boggs, Dennis R. Boxx, John O. Brennan, Charles A. Briggs, Janine Brookner, Dino A. Brugioni, Robert M. Bryant, Donald F. Burton, Duane R. Clarridge, David Cohen, the late William E. Colby, Alexandra Costa,

Tom Crispell, Ed Curran, Lloyd N. Cutler, Bill Danvers, Ruth David, Joan A. Dempsey, James V. De Sarno Jr., Jack Devine, William F. Donnelly, Chris Eades, E. Peter Earnest, John T. Elliff, Horace Z. Feldman, Benjamin R. Fischer, Debra Gaggiani-Tagg, John C. Gannon, Bradley Garrett, and Robert M. Gates.

Burton L. Gerber, Reuel Marc Gerecht, Mel Goodman, Richard F. Green, Douglas F. Groat, Howard Gutman, Samuel Halpern, William Harlow, the late Richard M. Helms, Toni L. Hiley, Eleanor Hill, R. Evans Hineman, James Hirsch, Frederick P. Hitz, the late Lawrence R. Houston, David P. Hunt, Joanne Isham, Donald F. B. Jameson, Paul Joyal, Oleg Kalugin, Donald M. Kerr, Richard J. Kerr, Rolfe Kingsley, Scott Koch, A. B. "Buzzy" Krongard, Anthony Lake, William Lofgren, William W. Loftin, Gilman Louie, the late Arthur C. Lundahl, David Manners, Mark Mansfield, Carol Martin, John L. Martin, Barry Mawn, Ken Maxwell, John E. McLaughlin, James McCullough, N. John McGaffin, Nancy D. McGregor, John N. McMahon, and Ken Millian.

Darrell W. Mills, Morton Mintz, Jami Miscik, Robert Lee Morris Jr., Dr. Stanley M. Moskowitz, Robert S. Mueller III, the late Eloise R. Page, James L. Pavitt, Martin C. Petersen, Charles Phalen, S. Eugene Poteat, Robert A. Rebelo, Paul J. Redmond Jr., Oliver B. "Buck" Revell, John A. Rizzo, the late Harry Rositzke, Lloyd Salvetti, Herbert F. Saunders, Representative Robert R. "Rob" Simmons, James M. Simon Jr., Jeffrey H. Smith, L. Britt Snider, Richard F. Stolz, Herbert Tate, John E. Taylor, George J. Tenet, Colin R. Thompson, Angus Thuermer, Robert Tucker, Admiral Stansfield Turner, John A. Turnicky, Gayle von Eckartsberg, Alan C. Wade, Robert B. Wade, Robert Bogdan Walewski, Mike Warner, William H. Webster, Albert D. "Bud" Wheelon, R. James Woolsey, and F. Mark Wyatt.

NOTES

PROLOGUE

1. Woodward, *Bush at War,* page 2; *New York Times*, December 17, 2002.
2. "Mike," October 24, 2002.

CHAPTER 1.

3. George J. Tenet, May 15, 2003.
4. Paul Joyal, February 3, 2003.
5. R. James Woolsey Jr., November 23, 2001.
6. L. Britt Snider, July 26, 2002.
7. R. James Woolsey Jr., November 23, 2001.
8. Ibid.
9. Ken Millian, January 31, 2003, as quoted in Kessler, *The Bureau,* pages 333–337.
10. Janine Brookner, July 18, 2002.
11. Maas, *Killer Spy,* page 210.
12. *Washington Post,* December 9, 1995, page 5.
13. Frederick P. Hitz, August 26, 2002.
14. CNN, *Cold War,* March 1998.
15. John N. McMahon, October 8, 2002.
16. Frederick P. Hitz, August 26, 2002.

CHAPTER 2.

17. Jack Devine, June 13, 2002.

18. James M. Simon Jr., January 18, 2003.

19. Herbert F. Saunders, February 10, 2003.

20. William Lofgren, February 22, 2003.

21. Representative Maxine Waters, statement to the House, October 7, 1998.

22. David Cohen, January 20, 2003, and William Lofgren, September 17, 2002.

23. Paul J. Redmond Jr., June 7, 2003.

24. William Lofgren, September 17, 2002.

25. *Washington Times,* June 4, 1993, page A5.

26. David Cohen, January 20, 2003.

27. Herbert F. Saunders, February 9, 2003.

28. Mel Goodman, April 19, 2002.

29. S. Eugene Poteat, August 30, 2002.

30. James M. Simon Jr., February 2, 2003.

31. Paul J. Redmond Jr., June 7, 2003.

32. Anthony Lake, February 21, 2003.

33. Office of Inspector General, CIA, *Report of Investigation: Improper Handling of Information by John M. Deutch,* February 18, 2000, page 27.

34. L. Britt Snider, July 26, 2002; *New York Times,* February 1, 2000, page 1; *Improper Handling of Classified Material by John M. Deutch,* Report of Investigation, Office of Inspector General, CIA, February 18, 2000, page 79.

35. CIA, Office of Inspector General, February 18, 2000.

CHAPTER 3.

36. George J. Tenet, May 15, 2003.

37. L. Britt Snider, July 26, 2002.

38. Lloyd Salvetti, January 7, 2003.

39. George J. Tenet, remarks at OSS Memorial Service, June 6, 2002.

40. Eloise Page, July 16 and 28, 2002.

41. Laurence R. Houston, June 29, 1990.

CHAPTER 4.

42. Wright, *Spy Catcher,* page 208.

43. Pamela Kessler, *Undercover Washington,* page 11.

44. Gates, *From the Shadows,* page 34.

45. Angus Thuermer, July 15, 2002.

46. Rolfe Kingsley, August 20, 2002.

47. Donald F. B. Jameson, October 25, 2002.

48. Richard F. Stolz, July 3, 2002.

49. Burton L. Gerber, April 24, 2002.

50. Oleg Kalugin, September 3, 2002 and January 28, 2003.

51. Kessler, *The Bureau,* page 212.

CHAPTER 5.

52. Richard Bissell, July 11, 1990.

53. Bissell, *Reflections of a Cold Warrior,* page 128; "Chronological Account of Handling of U-2 Incident," CIA, page 1.

54. John N. McMahon, October 8, 2002.

55. Eloise Page, July 28, 2002.

56. Arthur C. Lundahl, August 24, 1990.

57. Burrows, *Deep Black: Space Espionage and National Security,* Random House, 1986, page 219.

58. Arthur C. Lundahl, August 24, 1990.

59. Thaxter L. Goodell, *Studies in Intelligence: Directorate of Intelligence,* page 8.

60. National Photographic Interpretation Center, *Summary of Activity in Cuba: July 1, 1931–December 1968,* May 1969.

61. S. Eugene Poteat, August 17, 2002.

62. Richard J. Kerr, September 21, 2002.

63. R. Evans Hineman, August 14, 2001.

CHAPTER 6.

64. *Fifty Years Supporting Operations,* Office of Technical Service, August 2001, CIA. OTS was originally called the Technical Services Staff (1951–1960) and the Technical Services Division (1960–1973).

65. Herbert F. Saunders, September 10, 2002.

66. Robert Barron, September 10, 2002.

67. James Hirsch, September 10, 2002.

68. Richard J. Kerr, September 21, 2002.

69. Robert M. Gates, December 18, 1990.

70. Brugioni, *Eyeball to Eyeball,* page 146.

71. Ford, *Estimative Intelligence: The Purposes and Problems of National Intelligence Estimating,* pages 38 and 86.

72. Edward W. Proctor, September 5, 1990.

73. Johnson, *America's Secret Power,* page 85.

74. Stansfield Turner, December 27, 1990.

CHAPTER 7.

75. Angus Thuermer, July 15, 2002.

76. George J. Tenet, May 15, 2003.

77. Stansfield Turner, December 27, 1990.

78. Samuel Halpern, April 8, 2002.

79. AP, April 29, 2000.

CHAPTER 8.

80. Report of the CIA Inspector General, August 25, 1967, page 14.

81. Angus J. Thuermer, July 15, 2002. In virtually the only exception to the "no comment" rule, Thuermer in December 1972 denied a report by the weekly *Virginia Gazette* which quoted a former CIA "agent" as saying that the CIA trained assassins at Camp Peary near Williamsburg, Virginia, and that "mini-nuclear weapons" were tested there as well. The former CIA employee admitted he had been fired. Thuermer would not confirm that Camp Peary was a CIA training base.

82. CIA, Inspector General, August 25, 1967, page 4.

83. Helms, *A Look Over My Shoulder,* page 279.

84. Rolfe Kingsley, August 20, 2002.

85. L. Britt Snider, July 26, 2002 and February 2, 2003.

86. Richard F. Stolz, July 3, 2002.

87. E. Peter Earnest, October 9, 2002.

88. Charles A. Briggs, August 1, 2002.

89. Powers, *The Man Who Kept the Secrets,* page 10.

90. Powers, *The Man Who Kept the Secrets,* pages 303–305; Ranelagh, *The Agency: The Rise and Decline of the CIA,* pages 612–614.

91. Richard Helms, October 25, 1990.

CHAPTER 9.

92. William F. Donnelly, July 11, 2002.

93. James McCullough, May 5, 2002.

94. John A. Rizzo, October 24, 2002.

95. Peggy Donnelly, July 11, 2002.

96. *Final Report of the Independent Counsel for Iran-Contra Matters,* Lawrence E. Walsh, August 4, 1993, page 24.

97. Kessler, *Escape from the CIA,* page 11.

98. Kessler, *Escape from the CIA,* page 185.

99. Robert M. Gates, April 23, 2003.

CHAPTER 10.

100. *Washington Post,* October 12, 2001, page A31.

101. Albert "Bud" Wheelon, June 25, 2002.

102. Clarridge, *A Spy for All Seasons,* page 323.

103. William F. Donnelly, July 11, 2002.

104. Duane R. Clarridge, December 16, 2002.

105. William F. Donnelly, February 11, 2003.

106. Robert M. Gates, April 23, 2003.

107. Gates, *From the Shadows,* page 414.

108. L. Britt Snider, July 26, 2002.

CHAPTER 11.

109. James McCullough, May 6, 2002.

110. Richard F. Stolz, July 3, 2002.

111. Colin R. Thompson, April 2, 2002.

112. John C. Gannon, April 5, 2002.

CHAPTER 12.

113. Janine Brookner, July 18, 2002.

114. *Los Angeles Times Magazine,* July 21, 1996, page 10.

115. David Manners, April 3, 2002.

CHAPTER 13.

116. Edward J. Curran, March 13, 2002.

117. Burton L. Gerber, April 24, 2002.

118. Douglas F. Groat, March 1, 2003 and e-mail, March 4, 2003.

119. Edward J. Curran, January 18, 2003.

120. Douglas F. Groat letter to James W. Zirkle, July 18, 1997.

121. Frederick P. Hitz, August 26, 2001.

122. *Washington Post,* September 26, 1998, page A2.

CHAPTER 14.

123. William E. Colby, August 17, 1990.

124. William H. Webster, January 8, 2003.

125. John A. Turnicky, March 6, 2003.

126. Kessler, *Inside the CIA,* page 145.

127. Kessler, *Inside the CIA,* page 145; Alan C. Wade, August 22, 2002.

128. Robert M. "Bear" Bryant, January 30, 2003.

129. Bradley J. Garrett, August 21, 2002.

130. Bradley J. Garrett, January 23, 2003.

CHAPTER 15.

131. A.B. "Buzzy" Krongard, August 22, 2002.

132. Ruth David, February 28, 2003.

133. Joanne Isham, March 11, 2003.

CHAPTER 16.

134. Sammon, *Fighting Back,* page 107.

135. George J. Tenet, May 15, 2003.

136. Ibid.

137. Toni L. Hiley, March 12, 2003.

138. *Prologue,* National Archives, winter 1994, page 257. After retiring from

the CIA, Virginia Hall lived with her husband on a family farm in Maryland where she raised French poodles, tended her garden, and made French cheese. She died at the age of seventy-six and was buried at Druid Ridge Cemetery in Pikesville, Maryland.

139. Cofer Black, September 5, 2002.

140. Joan A. Dempsey, March 6, 2003.

141. John O. Brennan, August 22, 2002.

142. Stanley M. Moskowitz, December 6, 2002.

143. L. Britt Snider, July 26, 2002.

144. Kessler, *The Bureau,* pages 330 and 331.

CHAPTER 17.

145. Kessler, *Spy vs. Spy,* page 269.

146. Jami A. Miscik, August 13, 2002.

147. John A. Rizzo, October 24, 2002.

148. Cofer Black, September 5, 2003.

149. *Washington Post,* August 17, 1998, page A1, and September 1, 1998, page A18.

150. Gilman Louie, March 6 and March 12, 2003.

CHAPTER 18.

151. John E. McLaughlin, June 9, 2003.

152. Woodward, *Bush at War,* page 52, and Cofer Black, September 5, 2002.

153. Cofer Black, September 5, 2002.

154. S. Eugene Poteat, August 5, 2002.

155. *Parade,* August 18, 2002, page 6.

CHAPTER 19.

156. William Harlow and Mark Mansfield, August 13, 2002.

157. Rolfe Kingsley, April 21, 2003.

158. Robert A. Rebelo, September 25, 2002.

159. Martin C. Petersen, September 5, 2002.

160. Frans Bax, September 6, 2002.

161. Martin C. Petersen, September 6, 2002.

CHAPTER 20.

162. Jack Devine, June 13, 2002.

163. Eleanor Hill, May 1, 2003.

CHAPTER 21.

164. A. B. "Buzzy" Krongard, August 22, 2002.

165. Donald M. Kerr, August 13, 2002.

166. Anthony Lake, March 31, 2003.

167. Baer, *See No Evil,* page 203.

168. Baer, *See No Evil,* page 5.

169. Robert Baer e-mail, April 1, 2003.

170. Frank Anderson, March 27, 2003.

CHAPTER 22.

171. David Manners, April 24, 2003.

172. Michael Battles, April 10, 2003.

173. Robert S. Mueller III, December 20, 2002, and George J. Tenet, May 15, 2003.

174. Chris Eades, April 25, 2003.

175. The author's op-ed on the subject, "No to an American MI5," appeared in the *Washington Post,* January 5, 2003, page B7.

176. Charles E. Allen, September 5, 2002.

CHAPTER 23.

177. William H. Webster, January 8, 2003.

178. *Defense Intelligence Journal, July 2, 1998, page 33,* and Charles E. Allen, September 5, 2002.

179. Donald M. Kerr, August 13, 2002.

180. John Macartney, *Intelligencer,* Summer 2001, page 34.

181. Richard J. Kerr, May 3, 2003.

182. John C. Gannon, April 17, 2003.

CHAPTER 24.

183. James L. Pavitt, May 20, 2003.

184. Ibid.

185. John E. McLaughlin, June 9, 2003.
186. Ibid.

CHAPTER 25.

187. Steven Pressfield, *Gates of Fire,* Bantam Books, 1999, page 412.
188. George J. Tenet, May 15, 2003.
189. Rolfe Kingsley, April 13, 2003.

BIBLIOGRAPHY

Andrew, Christopher. *For the President's Eyes Only: Secret Intelligence and the American Presidency from Washington to Bush.* New York: HarperCollins, 1996.

Andrew, Christopher, and Oleg Gordievsky. *KGB: The Inside Story.* New York: HarperCollins, 1990.

Andrew, Christopher, and Vasili Mitrokhin. *The Sword and the Shield: The Mitrokhin Archive and the Secret History of the FBI.* New York: Basic Books, 1999.

Baer, Robert. *See No Evil: The True Story of a Ground Soldier in the CIA's War on Terrorism.* New York: Crown, 2002.

Bamford, James. *Body of Secrets: Anatomy of the Ultra-Secret National Security Agency.* New York: Doubleday, 2001.

Bearden, Milt, and James Risen. *The Main Enemy: The Inside Story of the CIA's Final Showdown with the KGB.* New York: Random House, 2003.

Beschloss, Michael R. *Mayday: Eisenhower, Khrushchev, and the U-2 Affair.* New York: Harper & Row, 1986.

Bittman, Ladislav. *The KGB and Soviet Disinformation: An Insider's View.* Pergamon-Brassey's, 1985.

Bower, Tom. *The Perfect English Spy: Sir Dick White and the Secret War, 1935–1990.* William Heinemann, Ltd., 1995.

Breckinridge, Scott D. *The CIA and the U.S. Intelligence System.* Westview Press, 1986.

Brown, Anthony Cave. *The Last Hero: Wild Bill Donovan.* New York: Vintage Books, 1984.

Brugioni, Dino A. *Eyeball to Eyeball: The Inside Story of the Cuban Missile Crisis.* New York: Random House, 1990.

Burrows, William E. *Deep Black: Space Espionage and National Security.* New York: Random House, 1986.

Central Intelligence Agency. Studies in Intelligence. *Directorate of Intelligence: Fifty Years of Informing Policy.* November 2002.

Chavchavadze, David. *Crowns and Trenchcoats: A Russian Prince in the CIA.* Atlantic International Publications, 1990.

Clarridge, Duane R. *A Spy for All Seasons.* New York: Scribner, 1997.

Clifford, Clark, with Richard Holbrooke. *Counsel to the President.* New York: Random House, 1991.

Cline, Ray S. *The CIA Under Reagan, Bush & Casey.* Acropolis Books, 1981.

Colby, William, and Peter Forbath. *Honorable Men: My Life in the CIA.* New York: Simon & Schuster, 1978.

Commission on CIA Activities within the United States (the Rockefeller Commission), Report to the President, U.S. Government Printing Office, 1976.

Corn, David. *Blond Ghost: Ted Shackley and the CIA's Crusades.* New York: Simon & Schuster, 1994.

Darling, Arthur B. *The Central Intelligence Agency: An Instrument of Government (to 1950).* Pennsylvania State University Press, 1990.

Dulles, Allen. *Great True Spy Stories.* Castle, 1968.

Earley, Pete. *Confessions of a Spy: the Real Story of Aldrich Ames.* New York: G. P. Putnam's Sons, 1997.

Emerson, Steven and Brian Duffy. *The Fall of Pan Am 103: Inside the Lockerbie Investigation.* New York: G. P. Putnam's Sons, 1990.

Ford, Harold P. *Estimative Intelligence: The Purposes and Problems of National Intelligence Estimating.* Defense Intelligence College, 1989.

Gates, Robert M. *From the Shadows: The Ultimate Insider's Story of Five*

Presidents and How They Won the Cold War. New York: Simon & Schuster, 1996.

Gertz, Bill. *Breakdown: How America's Intelligence Failures Led to September 11.* Chicago: Regnery, 2002.

Gilligan, Tom. *CIA Life: 10,000 Days with the Agency.* Foreign Intelligence Press, 1991.

Grose, Peter. *Gentleman Spy: The Life of Allen Dulles.* New York: Houghton Mifflin Co., 1994.

Helms, Richard M., and William Hood. *A Look Over My Shoulder: A Life in the Central Intelligence Agency.* New York: Random House, 2003.

Hood, William. *Mole.* New York: W. W. Norton, 1982.

Jeffreys-Jones, Rhodri. *American Espionage: From Secret Service to the CIA.* The Free Press, 1977.

———. *Cloak and Dollar: A History of American Secret Intelligence.* Hartford, Conn.: Yale University Press, 2002.

Johnson, Loch K. *America's Secret Power: The CIA in a Democratic Society.* Oxford University Press, 1989.

Kalugin, Oleg. *The First Directorate.* New York: St. Martin's Press, 1994.

Kessler, Pamela. *Undercover Washington: Touring the Sites Where Famous Spies Lived, Worked and Loved.* EPM Publications, 1992.

Kessler, Ronald. *The Bureau: The Secret History of the FBI.* New York: St. Martin's Press, 2002.

———. *Escape from the CIA: How the CIA Won and Lost the Most Important KGB Spy Ever to Defect to the U.S.* New York: Pocket Books, 1991.

———. *Inside the CIA: Revealing the Secrets of the World's Most Powerful Spy Agency.* New York: Pocket Books, 1992.

———. *Moscow Station: How the KGB Penetrated the American Embassy in Moscow.* New York: Scribner's, 1989.

———. *The Spy in the Russian Club: How Glenn Souther Stole America's Nuclear War Plans and Escaped to Moscow.* New York: Scribner's, 1990.

———. *Spy vs. Spy: Stalking Soviet Spies in America.* New York: Scribner's, 1988.

Mangold, Tom. *Cold Warrior: James Jesus Angleton.* New York: Simon & Schuster, 1991.

Marchetti, Victor and John D. Marks. *The CIA and the Cult of Intelligence*. New York: Knopf, 1974.

Marks, John. *The Search for the "Manchurian Candidate": The CIA and Mind Control*. New York: W. W. Norton & Co., 1979.

Melton, H. Keith. *The Ultimate Spy Book*. DK Publishing, 1996.

Mendez, Antonio J. *The Master of Disguise: My Secret Life in the CIA*. New York: William Morrow and Co., 1999.

Meyer, Cord. *Facing Reality: From World Federalism to the CIA*. University Press of America, 1980.

Miller, John, and Michael Stone, with Chris Mitchell. *Inside the 9/11 Plot: And Why the FBI and CIA Failed To Stop It*. Hyperion, 2002.

Miller, Judith, Stephen Engelberg, and William Broad. *Germs: Biological Weapons and America's Secret War*. New York: Simon & Schuster, 2001.

Moyar, Mark. *Phoenix and the Birds of Prey: The CIA's Secret Campaign to Destroy the Viet Cong*. Naval Institute Press, 1997.

Payne, Ronald, and Christopher Dobson. *Who's Who in Espionage*. New York: St. Martin's Press, 1984.

Peebles, Curtis. *Guardians: Strategic Reconnaissance Satellites*. San Francisco: Presidio Press, 1987.

Penkovsky, Oleg. *The Penkovsky Papers*. New York: Doubleday, 1965.

Persico, Joseph E. *Casey: The Lives and Secrets of William J. Casey*. New York: Viking, 1990.

Pillar, Paul R. *Terrorism and U.S. Foreign Policy*. Brookings Institution, 2001.

Polmar, Norman, and Thomas B. Allen. *Spy Book: The Encyclopedia of Espionage*. New York: Random House, 1998.

Powers, Thomas. *The Man Who Kept the Secrets: Richard Helms and the CIA*. New York: Knopf, 1987.

Prados, John. *President's Secret Wars: CIA and Pentagon Covert Operations from World War II through Iranscam*. New York: William Morrow, 1986.

————. *The Soviet Estimate: U.S. Intelligence Analysis and Soviet Strategic Forces*. Princeton, N.Y.: Princeton University Press, 1982.

Ranelagh, John. *The Agency: The Rise and Decline of the CIA*. Touchstone, 1987; originally published by Cambridge Publishing Ltd., 1986.

Richelson, Jeffrey T. *America's Secret Eyes in Space: The U.S. Keyhole Spy Satellite Program*. New York: Harper & Row, 1990.

————. *The Wizards of Langley: Inside the CIA's Directorate of Science and Technology.* Westview Press, 2001.

Rositzke, Harry. *The CIA's Secret Operations.* Reader's Digest Press, 1977.

Sammon, Bill. *Fighting Back: The War on Terrorism from Inside the Bush White House.* Chicago: Regnery, 2002.

Smith, Russell Jack. *The Unknown CIA: My Three Decades with the Agency.* Pergamon-Brassey's, 1989.

Sorley, Lewis. *The Central Intelligence Agency: An Overview.* Association of Former Intelligence Officers, 1990.

Thomas, Evan. *The Very Best Men: Four Who Dared—The Early Years of the CIA.* Touchstone, 1995.

Troy, Thomas F. *Donovan and the CIA.* University Publications of America, 1981.

Treverton, Gregory F. *Covert Action: The Limits of Intervention in the Postwar World.* Basic Books, 1987.

Turner, Stansfield. *Secrecy and Democracy: the CIA in Transition.* New York: Houghton Mifflin, 1985.

U.S. Congress, House Permanent Select Committee on Intelligence, Compilation of Intelligence Laws and Related Laws and Executive Orders of Interest to the National Intelligence Community, U.S. Government Printing Office, March 1987.

————. Senate Select Committee to Study Government Operations with Respect to Intelligence Activities (the Church Committee), Final Report, U.S. Government Printing Office, 1976.

Westerfield, H. Bradford, editor. *Inside the CIA's Secret World: Declassified Articles from the Agency's Internal Journal 1955–1992).* Yale University Press, 1995. Hartford, Conn.: Yale University Press, 1995.

Wise, David. *The Spy Who Got Away: The Inside Story of Edward Lee Howard, the CIA Agent Who Betrayed His Country's Secrets and Escaped to Moscow.* New York: Random House, 1988.

————. *Molehunt: The Secret Search for Traitors That Shattered the CIA.* New York: Random House, 1992.

Woodward, Bob. *Veil: The Secret Wars of the CIA 1981–1987.* New York: Simon & Schuster, 1987.

————. *Bush at War.* New York: Simon & Schuster, 2002.

Wright, Peter. *Spy Catcher: The Candid Autobiography of a Senior Intelligence Office.* New York: Viking, 1987.

Wyden, Peter. *Bay of Pigs: The Untold Story.* New York: Simon & Schuster, 1979.

INDEX